The Not-So-Empty Nest

The Not-So-Empty Nest

*How to live with your kids
after they've lived someplace else*

Phyllis Feuerstein
and Carol Roberts

Follett Publishing Company/Chicago

Designed by Sue L. Doman

Copyright © 1981 by Phyllis Feuerstein and Carol Roberts.
Cover design copyright © 1981 by Follett Publishing Company,
a division of Follett Corporation. All rights reserved. No portion
of this book may be used or reproduced in any manner
whatsoever without written permission from the publisher
except in the case of brief quotations embodied in critical
reviews and articles. Manufactured in the United States of America.

Library of Congress Cataloging in Publication Data

Feuerstein, Phyllis, 1930–
  The not-so-empty nest.

  1. Young adults—United States—Family relationships. 2. Housing—
United States. 3. Conflict of generations. 4. Young adults—
Housing—United States. 5. Parent and child—United States.
I. Roberts, Carol, 1942–   II. Title.
HQ799.7.F48   306.8'7   80-27046
ISBN 0-695-81441-9

First Printing

To Maita Simon, to whom we owe so much
(and who typed her own dedication).

Contents

Preface

When this book was almost finished, I overheard a conversation between two women who were browsing through display racks of greeting cards in a stationery shop. The younger woman chose a graduation card and confided, "My son's finished with college, and he's coming back home. I never expected him to." The older woman gave her a look I'd seen in the eyes of my friend Lila, who had given birth while I was still in the last week of my first pregnancy. The look said, "You don't know what's in store for you."

Aloud, the older woman said, "It's the trend. I don't have time to change sheets between one kid going and the next kid coming. It's happening to all of us." Hearing this, the shop owner burst out, "God forbid!"

I had heard similar snatches of dialogue in supermarkets, in movie theater lines, and wherever parents of young adults gathered. Whether it was across a bridge table or at a dinner party, at least one parent couldn't refrain from saying, "God forbid!" It was usually someone who had discovered pleasures in the empty nest.

No one I interviewed in eight states across the country turned down a child who needed the comforts of home, and only four sets of parents out of two hundred and fifty families who talked to me and my coauthor Carol Roberts took drastic measures to avoid housing a grown child. These parents either moved to a smaller

9

place or out of town. In one instance a thirty-year-old daughter followed them. She had spent seven years at home.

On our questionnaire and in interviews, young adults expressed feelings as mixed as their elders' about coming back. They found it hard to think of themselves as "someone's kid again" after living on their own. Only five families reported feeling completely content with the relationship resumed under one roof. The discontents weren't cramped for physical space. In these middle- and upper-middle-class homes the issue was breathing space. Each generation, in some way, felt suffocated.

I didn't have to use case histories pulled from office files. The information came "live" across restaurant tables, over the telephone, or in people's homes or mine. It came from parents and young adults in the throes of reunion or about to separate and from those who had just parted. They were trying to hammer out a loving relationship without banging each other's thumbs or their own. Some, so to speak, wore bandages on their fingers.

Because the information given was so personal, I sacrificed the use of any details that might identify the speakers. To avoid making our book as cumbersome as a telephone directory, I combined people into prototypes and composites, making an enormous effort to violate neither their privacy nor the integrity of our report. The situations are true, and the quotes (except for the omission of some four-letter words) came from the lips of real people.

In one way, this is a book of commiseration. Both age groups were willing to share their views and unload their feelings in the hopes of benefiting someone else. They were so candid about the problems common to a homecoming you may think they were peeking into your windows. They weren't. They opened their hearts, and we reported what we saw.

In a practical way, this is a book offering as much help as a reader cares to take to keep a homecoming from turning into a disastrous situation. Twenty-three professionals involved with family counseling, the education of young people, and financial management added their educated opinions to our perceptions. Since they, too, draw from personal experiences, they give you a plethora of lively opinions with no two exactly alike.

There is no *great* answer nor one *great* way to ensure a peaceful household, but writing this book with the help of my coauthor's objectivity answered a lot of questions I asked when my own child moved back home. I hope reading it will do the same for you.

Phyllis Feuerstein

Acknowledgments

We extend our appreciation to family who were as helpful as friends and to friends who were as helpful as family. They interviewed, proofread, gave us the benefit of their sharp observations, and provided leads and moral support: Sy Feuerstein, Jay Feuerstein, Amy Feuerstein, Edie Turovitz (who became a Feuerstein ten days after the book was completed), John Coopersmith, Joanne Greenwald, Maxene Kotin, Merritt Kotin, Gene Simon, Carol Heller, Ida Wilcher, Pat Bosco, Goldie Brounstein, Elizabeth Nicholson, and Joyce Sagerman.

We also appreciate the patience of staff members in the reference section of the Park Forest Library, the Skokie Library, Stanford University Library, College of DuPage Library, and the library at the University of California, Berkeley. And a special thanks to Dr. Rosalie Kirschner for the personal attention she gave our book.

Nor could we have done without the willing families who furnished the material for our book and the professionals who gave their expert opinions. We also thank friends and family, whom we haven't seen in months, for their patient understanding.

Phyllis Feuerstein
Carol Roberts

11

Part One

Tradition

Tradition is a guide and not a jailer.

Somerset Maugham

1

Way Back When— Children Lived at Home

A surefire way for a parent to terminate a conversation with his or her child of adult age is to start a sentence, "When I was your age . . ." The offspring, in childhood, may have listened wide-eyed to tales about "the olden days." But in adulthood, he or she has little patience for tales of times when parental authority went unquestioned and children stayed home until married. As a member of the "now generation," the adult child is more interested in the ways life should be lived today.

Let's face it. Parental disapproval lurks behind each reminiscence beginning, "When I was your age . . ." The conversation stoppers are invariably followed by, ". . . I was out working," ". . . I was in the army," or "When I was your age, the only pot I knew about was a kettle." The short phrase is a prelude to a lengthy sermon.

Listening to tales of parents' youth during the hard times of the thirties and the war years of the forties emphasizes the different world conditions in which each generation grew up. Children reared in the comparatively good times of the fifties can't help but feel inadequate hearing the odds their parents overcame. Reared in an economically stable home and by Dr. Benjamin Spock's book, *Baby and Child Care,* which advocates permissive behavior, they find it painful to relate to more stringent times.

Time lines between the two generations in this chapter are as distinct as B.C. and A.D. The parent was born Before the Crash and the child was born long After the Depression, close to the years following World War II.

In an association test sprung on parents and children interviewed for this book, *depression* to the older family member was a time for making do or doing without. To the younger family members, *depression* was the state they fell into when they flunked an exam or broke up with a girlfriend or boyfriend.

War years, in a similar test, resulted in similar polarized answers. To parents, World War II brought back memories of bond drives, V-mail letters to servicemen overseas, a dearth of dating opportunities for young girls, and a country united in spirit against the enemy. To young adults, the Vietnam War was associated with draft evasion, riots for peace, the killings at Kent State, and the young united in body against the government. Both generations were born on earth. But judging by their memories, each was reared on a different planet.

The division extends to options available to each generation during the crucial years of growing up. The children of the depression—now members of the middle or upper-middle class—had fewer career choices than their offspring.

In the thirties children expected to put personal ambitions aside to help their families survive. Rules for their behavior were firmly fastened to the work ethic and to the group effort. Social mores, coupled with the crash of 1929, left the children of the depression with as much control over their early lives as cargo thrown overboard from a sinking ship.

Tom, a fifty-five-year-old pharmacist, was the quintessential depression child who didn't have to seek troubles. Problems commonplace in those hard times awaited him on the doorstep. He recalled the impact of the depression hitting him when he was a ten-year-old growing up in a working-class neighborhood on the West Side of Philadelphia. It was 1935.

"That's the year my father killed himself," he remembered. "He had lost all his savings in the stock market crash of 1929. A year later, the factory where he worked shut down without notice to its employees. For a while he worked with a bootlegger, and then he helped my mother deliver homemade strudel to local bakeries. I'll never forget the day one fell off the window sill where it had been left to cool. We had to eat oatmeal for dinner the rest of the week.

"The worst time was after my father's death. The landlord evicted us because we had no rent money. Our belongings were put out into the street. Luckily, my father's brother and his wife took us in. They had a two-bedroom apartment, and we were seven people. I slept in the dining room and had to go to bed after everyone else did.

"Things eased up a little by the time I got to high school. My mother worked in a women's clothing store, and I earned pocket money delivering groceries and ushering in a movie house. But money wasn't loose enough for me to consider college. I had wanted to be a general practitioner like Dr. Christian.

"Instead, I took trade courses in high school so I could get a job after graduation. By that time the war had broken out. The thing to do was join the army. I did."

Tom sent home his monthly pay as a private and conformed to the military code. At the war's end, however, he was liberated from more than patriotic duty. Provisions of the G.I. bill gave him the opportunity to make important decisions for the first time in his life. He was eligible to go to college tuition-free and to receive a monthly stipend of fifty dollars until he finished school.

In no way would he return to live in his uncle's cramped quarters. He set aside his mustering-out pay of $300 for a furnished apartment, found a part-time job, and became a full-time student. His uncle talked him out of becoming a doctor for reasons Tom does not remember today. Tom listened. The habit of deference to an older person's judgment was hard to break.

As soon as he became a pharmacist and self-supporting, Tom took over the responsibility for his family. He moved his mother and sister out of his uncle's place into an apartment roomy enough for three. Even though he had been separated from them for several years, he followed society's unwritten law: Family members stayed together until each could make a home of his own.

Tom's struggles to determine his destiny were compounded by being fatherless and penniless. He was limited in his spending, but a boy reared by a working father was as limited in the way he could spend his time. Another unwritten law was: You don't cross the old man. He is bigger than you, and you are living in his house.

Stan, now a fifty-three-year-old food salesman, was the prototype of a depression child tied to a family business. His services were demanded in his father's butcher shop located in a Brooklyn neighborhood populated by German-Jewish immigrants. From the age of nine, he spent as many hours among haggling customers and sides of beef as he did at home or school. His time was worth money to his father. To keep one step ahead of bills, a small businessman needed the help of every family member.

"My older brother went to market with pop at four in the morning before going to school," Stan recalled. "Mom plucked chickens. My sister rang up sales. I was the delivery boy. If I didn't show up on time, pop came and dragged me out of the schoolyard where he knew I was playing handball with my friends.

"As I grew up, he literally pulled me off street corners or out of the drugstore where most of the guys hung around looking for girls. The way pop saw it, if you weren't learning, working, or praying, you were a bum. He closed the store on Friday nights and Saturday and made us go to shul with him. In his mind, if you didn't observe the Sabbath, you were a double bum. Besides, all his cronies would ask, 'Where's your son?'

"College was out of the question. Pop was of the school that believed a man should work for himself. I wanted to be an engineer. That meant I'd have to work for someone else. In *his* mind, anyway.

"No, he never paid me. When I needed money, I asked for it, and God help me if I took money from the register without asking."

By the time Stan graduated from high school, his brother and sister, considerably older than him, were married and out of the house and butcher shop. That was fine with pop. Marriage entitled a child to the privileges of adulthood, namely, striking out on his or her own.

Although Stan was expected to continue to live at home and work in the butcher shop, he enlisted in the Marine Corps. Underage at seventeen, he needed pop's signature. Pop had been ready to tell the draft board that Stan was needed more in the business than by the military. But the patriotic tempo of the times forced him to sign the enlistment papers.

During four years in the marines, Stan saw action on the islands of Guam, Saipan, and Okinawa, and was wounded twice. By comparison, military police duty in China during the last four months of the war seemed easy. Stan played with the idea of reenlisting. Instead, he followed written orders from pop to come home.

Decorated veteran or not, he was expected to move in with mom and pop, who now lived in a one-bedroom apartment, where Stan would have to sleep on a living-room cot. At 4:00 A.M. Stan's first morning home, pop awakened him to go to the market. Stan obeyed. As a sergeant in the marines, he had given orders. At home, pop outranked him.

If a son needed the model of a Machiavelli to outmaneuver parental authority, a daughter needed the determination of a Susan B. Anthony. When both reached physical maturity in the early 1940s, military service provided a young man with breathing space outside the family environment. A young woman who stayed at home was suffocated by restrictions designed to protect her chastity.

A daughter was expected to keep her hymen intact until her wedding night and to regard sex only as a way to propagate another generation. While waiting to assume the responsibility of "kinder, kochen, and kirche," she was permitted to consider jobs deemed appropriate for a female, preferably those where she could meet a potential husband in a safe setting. In weighing choices, intelligence and talent were low on the scale.

Adele, born in San Francisco in 1925, was talented enough to become a professional dancer and is an extreme case of the overprotection that stymied a young woman's career choice. Today, as the mother of three grown daughters whom she reared contrary to her own upbringing, she still tries to understand why she was submissive to her mother's will.

"I was very sheltered," Adele explained. "Mother expected me home from school each day at a certain hour and accompanied me to my dance lessons. I could have girls sleep over at my house but couldn't attend sleep-over parties at their houses.

"When my ballet coach said I was ready to make my debut and arranged a dance audition, she wouldn't let me go. She wanted me to stay home and learn, from her, the ways to be a good housewife.

"My father was passive. It took outside family members to convince my mother to let me go to business school—to have something to fall back on in case I never married. When I was ready to take a job, I had to work where another family member was employed. I guess that was her way of keeping an eye on me.

"I don't know why I allowed myself to be dominated. Maybe it was because I loved her, and I sensed she loved my brother better. Yes, he enjoyed more freedom."

Even when a girl was freely given an opportunity for higher education, parents set the priorities. A career came second; marriage came first.

Pearl, fifty-two and a caseworker for a Catholic agency in New York City, was barely touched by the money drought of the thirties. The only budget cut she remembered at home in suburban Yonkers was in the maid's hours. They were cut from daily to twice a week.

But her ambition to become a sociologist was blocked by her architect father. Social work was out of his frame of reference. Nor was she permitted to go to the out-of-state college that offered the courses she needed.

Pearl recalled, "My dad operated on the double standard. My older brother could go away to school. Not me. Although he didn't vocalize it, my father worried that I might lose my virginity before marriage. I was angry because he didn't trust me.

"I cried, stamped my feet, and thought of paying for my own education. But I didn't put my rebellious thoughts into action. I had no way of earning money, and none of my friends were going away. I began to suspect there was something wrong with me for wanting to leave home."

Pearl commuted for four years by subway to New York University in Manhattan, where she earned an undergraduate degree in the field her father chose—library science. Then she applied to graduate school. Her father was unimpressed with her ambitions. He worried that Pearl, at twenty-two, was still single.

The year was 1944, and most of the men in New York considered eligible by Pearl's father had been drafted. To satisfy his need to see her settled, he relaxed his restrictions on travel. Pearl could leave home to go to California, where her married brother knew "scads of eligible men" at the San Diego Naval Base.

Let loose for the first time in her life, Pearl went a little berserk in California—running around, drinking, and staying up all night. But she kept the covenant to keep her virginity. When she came close to losing it, she remembered, "A nice girl doesn't sleep with a man until they're married."

The trip served its purpose. Pearl was engaged to an English teacher by the time she returned home. She scotched her plans to go for a master's degree without conflict when her future husband contemplated earning a Ph.D. His career came first.

The script for her future was written the day she was born. Once married, she was to stay home, raise a family, and return to school or work, if she wished, after the youngest child was in high school. She did.

Ironically, a daughter who got out from under a parent's thumb by going away to college found herself ruled by the iron hand of a housemother. Dress codes, curfews, hours for meals, and restrictions against male guests were strictly enforced. The consequence of breaking the rules was a letter sent home or expulsion.

Frances, a home economics major at the University of Illinois in Champaign-Urbana from 1946 to 1950, recalled, "Sometimes I'd sneak out. Or I'd leave an outside dorm door open so my boyfriend could sneak in. But I was always afraid of getting caught. When I returned to live with my parents after graduation, there was no transition. I had never really been on my own."

Daughters who obeyed campus rules often acted out rebellions in other ways. Shirley, reared in an Orthodox Jewish home, would have preferred to attend a state school along with her Christian friends from her small Wisconsin town. Instead she was sent to Brandeis College in New York City to find a Jewish husband. Annoyed by her parents' obvious motives, the education major made it a point to write home that she ate bread on Passover (when leavening is forbidden) and didn't keep the fast day Yom Kippur.

"It really strained their finances to send me away to college," Shirley said in retrospect, "but I wished they had done it for me and not because they wanted a Jewish son-in-law."

Other college girls found they were unprepared to fend for themselves after finishing curriculums thrust upon them by parents. Helen, the youngest in a family line of matriarchs, was groomed to be a lady. 'A lady, she was repeatedly told, is interested in art and is fluent in foreign languages. She majored in French and German at Georgetown University in Washington, D.C. "All that prepared me for," she recalled with bitter humor, "was to help my date order knowledgeably in a gourmet restaurant."

Sons, by contrast, were encouraged to take courses leading to a profession, and parents, at great hardship to themselves, left legacies untouched to ensure an education for their sons. In more than one instance, the money wasn't there when needed if it had been deposited in one of the 3,604 banks that failed between 1930 and 1932.

A small business that survived the desperate years became a guaranteed legacy to a son willing to keep it going. Leonard, fifty-six, can't remember a time other than the war years when he hadn't worked in his father's men's clothing store. Today it carries women's apparel, too, and its corner location in an industrial town in California has been expanded to half the block. "But my son couldn't care less about the business," he laments. "The family tradition ends with me."

Leonard was twenty-three when he came home from World War II and like many of his friends went to work on his two main objectives: to marry Ethel, the girl he left behind, and to make it financially. When their son Tim was born, he acquired another goal: to give the child everything his heart would desire, including the right to a higher education and the freedom to make choices.

Parental duties were divided by what society deemed each sex could do best. More pressure was put on Ethel to be the perfect mother than on Leonard to be the perfect father. Although he was expected to sacrifice personal needs to provide for the family, he was less expected to participate as a parent on a day-to-day basis. The responsibilities of bringing up Tim were left to Ethel.

In the late forties, how-to-parent books encouraged a mother to relax the rigid rules by which she had been brought up in the late twenties and thirties. Dr. Spock, in particular, dismissed the fear of spoiling infants with instant gratification. It became all right to immediately pick up crying babies and to feed them on demand. Ethel eagerly complied. The new approach seemed more humane and satisfied her instincts. Who can endure the sounds of a squalling infant for long?

But behaviorists didn't take Ethel completely off the hook. They replaced the fear of spoiling Tim with the fear of inhibiting his development by repression. A how-to-parent book might well have carried the warning "This child-care expert has determined that civilizing a youngster before he's ready may be dangerous to his mental health." Two of the more popular admonitions were to delay putting him on the potty and to avoid strict punishment of out-of-bounds behavior. Ethel slavishly followed the advice given between book covers as carefully as she followed a recipe.

There were no older family members close by to challenge either her cooking or her child-rearing methods. By the time Tim was three, she and Leonard had moved to a suburb thirty miles from home base. Living in a bedroom community alongside other young mothers equally immersed in how-to-parent books, Ethel created an anomaly in the fifties. She molded an idol-smasher during a decade known for its conformity.

Tim, as soon as he could talk, talked back—the terrible twos would last until he was thirty. He made all his own decisions, based on inexperience, and he was given implicit permission to follow his impulses; consequences for his actions were never clearly defined. Prior to his generation, a child was brought up to represent the values of a culture. Not Tim. Living among the emblems of the fifties—the gray flannel suit, the organization man, and tracts of look-alike houses—Tim received a license to satisfy his whims.

Nor was he given time to develop inner motivation. Ethel encouraged Tim to join the Cub Scouts, the Little League, and park district programs in addition to taking music and swimming lessons and attending Sunday school. While Leonard was busy accumulating to provide Tim with a secure financial future and she was chauffeuring Tim to his activities, neither had an inkling that their well-meaning efforts would backfire. As a member of the subculture in the late sixties and early seventies, Tim would feel free to put aside traditional notions of morality and to question the importance of family ties. He had been raised to do his own thing. And he did.

2

But Mom, Times Have Changed

The author of Ecclesiastes, in about 250 B.C., wrote, "There is nothing new under the sun." But the biblical observation never stopped a child from arguing, "Things are different now, mom." When college kids, however, made that point during the sixties, for a change they were right. The country faced problems in the sixties ignored in the fifties.

In the sixties, the authority of the family, school, and government was continually challenged with demonstrations and civil disobedience. The amount of discussion and analysis of political, social, and economic problems was unprecedented.

The decade of dissent opened in 1960 with a sit-in on the steps of San Francisco's City Hall by two hundred students from the University of California at Berkeley. They were protesting the subpoena by the House Committee on Un-American Activities of several local teachers and a Berkeley sophomore, all suspected of left-wing activity. In addition, students across the nation joined the fray for black civil rights. Front-page photos showed white students standing hand in hand with blacks in opposition to the color barrier. The decade closed with a dramatic antiwar protest, Vietnam Moratorium Day, drawing the support of hundreds of thousands of diverse people across the country.

The handwriting on college walls was no longer graffiti. Young people, through the generosity of their parents, had more money, leisure, and opportunity than ever before to examine the quality of life—and found it wanting. They had no yardstick of bad to measure the claim of "You've never had it so good." In the thirties young people spent their energy desperately walking the streets looking for work. In the sixties young people used their energy to post flyers on campus bulletin boards to rally support for a timely cause, one usually considered radical by the older generation.

Nevertheless, the folks sent the college-age kids to school to fulfill the folks' expectations. Dad hoped his son would graduate Phi Beta Kappa or, at least, with enough knowledge to enter the family business. Mom hoped her daughter would marry someone else's Phi Beta Kappa son or one entering a prosperous family business. What girl wasn't half-seriously told, "It's as easy to fall in love with a rich man as a poor man."

Daughters left for school carrying suitcases filled with cashmere sweaters, matching pleated skirts, and dresses with name-brand labels. A son's trunk was stuffed with prep-school clothes, sharply creased trousers, and sport jackets. Parents never anticipated less than a conventional education from a school requiring a student to dress up for dinner.

Over the breakfast table parents read about flower children washing their clothes, while still wearing them, in a Boston Commons pond. Rumors flew. The kid down the street had fled to Canada to avoid the draft. A niece smoked marijuana. And mom and dad had seen the nephew who grew his hair as long as the niece's. But, not their kid. Not yet.

The view from the picture window was old-fashioned grass. Parents were too far removed from campus to see the conformity of the fifties being replaced by the coercion of the sixties. Kids would be faced with either joining the fight against "the enemy" or being considered "the enemy." Forced to choose sides, they would identify in dress, at least, with the dissidents. At Thanksgiving break both sexes would turn in their straight clothes and shop for jeans, sandals, and love beads. The son would sport an army jacket, and the daughter would hunt for a moth-eaten fur coat at a resale shop.

Bruce, who is now thirty-two and wears three-piece suits, explained, "In the sixties, you were either for or against. To survive at school, you were forced to choose sides. Remember, people were dying in large numbers in Vietnam."

The kid waiting to receive a draft notice to fight in what was probably the most unpopular war in our nation's history would leave the ranks of the silent majority and possibly the country. By 1968, ten thousand Americans eligible for the draft had emigrated to Canada. Others sought deferments from draft boards for medical, psychiatric, or religious reasons, or they joined the reserves. Bruce received a deferment as a conscientious objector for "other than religious reasons." He didn't have to pay the penalty of imprisonment. As he put it, "I lucked out. My draft board had filled its quota."

All this time and energy channeled into protest left little time and energy to devote to studies. The way the kids saw it, that didn't matter. They had become disillusioned with the quality of a classroom education.

American colleges and universities would show the effects of a student enrollment spiraling upward. In 1946, enrollment stood at 1.6 million. By 1960, it had doubled in size to 3.2 million and was inching its way upward to stand at 6.6 million in 1968. This meant that one out of every three persons of college age, between eighteen and twenty-four, would be attending a college or university in the late sixties.

To parents, this would be a statistic to celebrate. They had made it and were helping their children to make it. To educators, the numbers spelled trouble, and to the students, anonymity.

In terms of educational needs, there was a shortage of professors and classrooms for the massive student body. The kid became a number on a computer card and was herded into lecture halls with two hundred to two thousand other students. He or she attended seminars led by a teaching assistant whose undergraduate diploma had just been printed. No wonder the sixties generation later claimed they had learned more from rap sessions with friends than from formal classes with faculty. The subjects discussed—sex, politics, and the new morality—weren't listed in the curriculum. In essence, parents were paying for a street education, one they had received free hanging around street corners.

Parents also were paying another price for their hard-won financial security. It wasn't enough that dad had worked retail-store hours or had been sent on business trips or taken night courses to further his career. Nor did mom's contribution count. How many barrels of household goods had she unpacked in a strange city when dad was forced to accept a job transfer? How many emergencies did she cope with single-handedly while he was away? The new cost was, therefore, unexpected. It was the kids' contempt for their parents' prosperity.

Kids weren't going to kowtow to customers or management or cut their hair to gain employment. They were going to serve humanity, not be cogs in a technocratic machine.

Their dilemma was whom to serve. Children who had chosen their breakfast cereals at age two, their television programs at age four, and their own clothes before they entered kindergarten were indecisive about choosing careers. They took a lot of courses ending in -ology and turned to their friends for guidance. Two out of three intended to join VISTA or the Peace Corps. Three out of ten expected to make lifetime careers in social work. By the time the kids reached their senior year, they had changed their majors more often than they had changed their jeans.

Who was buying them this respite from responsibility? Who else? Their parents. Dr. Theodore Roszak, a member of the history department of California State College at Hayward, explained, "The middle class could afford to prolong the ease and drifting of children. They let the young take all the 'Mickey Mouse' courses which had the corrupting effect of leaving them unprepared for the real world."

It seemed immaterial to the kids that they had disavowed materialism. They were more than willing, on money from home, to earn as many degrees as on a thermometer or run around the world to get their heads together. "I felt it was coming to me," said Jeffrey, now thirty-five, who has two undergraduate degrees, two unfinished theses in different master's programs, and no regular source of income. "My folks had paid for my older brothers' educations and stays in Europe. Why not me?"

An objective observer might ask, "Why them?" Why should parents continue to feed children old enough to feed themselves. Roszak contends, "Historically, parents become acquisitors to benefit their children. Cutting them off would have been abnormal."

A segment of the sixties generation was less reluctant than their parents to break a historical precedent—living at home until they married. They moved out of their parents' homes earlier than previous generations.

The marked difference between the two generations is the way each was reared to think. The parents were taught to think in terms of "us." The children were reared to think in terms of "me." Dad had sacrificed family life to be a good provider. Mom laid aside personal ambitions to be the "perfect" mother. To them the earth revolved around the son or daughter. During the depression, the children were never allowed to forget they were part of a family unit. In more affluent times, they were encouraged to be individuals.

Consider some of the self-gratifying reasons former college students gave for breaking home ties. Minnesota-born Sandra, a zoologist, preferred the climate she discovered at the University of Arizona in Tucson. Jack, an unemployed teacher, grew dissatisfied working for his father's market research company. Jeff, one of the "gentle people" into pottery, resented his father's hawkish views on Vietnam. Susie, an art major, was annoyed by the way her parents treated her hippie boyfriend. Jenny saw no reason why she couldn't have an overnight male guest.

Each headed for the greener grass on the other side of the fence. Zoologist Sandra took a salesclerk job and a furnished room to remain in Arizona. Teacher Jack joined a cult whose members proselytized on the streets and at airports while waiting for the Kingdom of God to be established. Gentle Jeff went to live with drug-addicted radicals, burned his draft card, and then fled to Canada. Susie moved into the house her hippie boyfriend shared with three other school dropouts. Sexy Jenny cohabited with one man after another. Dr. Roszak comments, "Even though the young are told they are grown-up, they have no taste for responsibility. The 1960s were the first time in history there was a flight from something rather than to somewhere."

Other members of the sixties generation presented stronger cases for striking out on their own. Neil, the son of a schoolteacher in rural Iowa who was as poor as the people he taught, is an example of the minority who were expected to cut loose at the age of legal majority.

"In our home," he recalled matter-of-factly, "the kids left immediately after high school on the premise you are supposed to live your own life. My older brothers went into military service, went to school, or got married. I left home intending to make the money we never had.

"If I had wanted to stay, I could have. But I knew my parents felt that, after eighteen, it's time for people to find their own way. I was sad at parting with my family. But I knew I could go back if I ever fell on my face."

He didn't even though he changed goals and direction. Financed by student loans and scholarships, Neil started out in the school of commerce intending to work with numbers. Through endless discussions on campus with liberal arts students, he sought a higher meaning to life than overcoming an impoverished background. Neil directed the idealism exemplified by his schoolteacher father and reinforced in the climate of college to become a special education teacher. Today, he works with autistic children and has a modicum of financial security and a plentitude of emotional satisfaction.

Independence was stressed in Ellen's home, too, by action rather than words, but never to the extent that she was expected to leave before she was married. Ellen cut loose the year her father was transferred out of state. After spending the summer between her freshman and sophomore years at the new address, she found the Pennsylvania State campus more attractive. Home's warm, loving atmosphere didn't compensate for a lack of friends and few activities. In the next three years, she went home only on holidays.

"I got flak about it from my parents," she recalled. "They were hurt that plays and movies at student prices and impromptu get-togethers were more important to me than living with them.

"They tended to be overprotective when I was younger. But my mother was an independent lady. She had to be—moving so many times while I was growing up. I made her my model. Besides, she had moved away from her mother. Why shouldn't I?"

In still other instances, young people weren't fleeing from their parents. They were fleeing from their hometowns. From afar, a familiar neighborhood was inviting. Close up, after a year at school, the warts were magnified. Rachel, in particular, found suburban life inane after living in the midst of campus activism.

The daughter of a minister in a Charleston, South Carolina, suburb, she selected Mt. Holyoke College in South Hadley, Massachusetts, as the place to take courses in political science. Her parents approved the choice. The women's college of fourteen hundred students was reputed to be such a bastion of the status quo that "autumn leaves dropped in the same place each year."

But the leaves went flying in all directions the fall of 1969. By midyear more than sixty-five predominantly white colleges had introduced one form or another of black studies. Not Mt. Holyoke. When Rachel arrived in September, black students went on strike demanding these courses plus buses to take them to black mixers. Rachel was ambivalent about taking sides. Although she sympathized with the students' desire to know black history, she thought the demands for special transportation unreasonable.

Little practical advice was offered by her folks when she called to say the school was on strike. "Why aren't you in class?" they wanted to know. They did not realize that Mt. Holyoke was so small that a student was forced to respect picket lines outside the school or become an enemy of the people. She stayed away from classes and began her education outside of books. Later she said, "The campus, not the classroom, provided 99 percent of my education."

By the end of her freshman year, Rachel was in the thick of campus politics. She had demonstrated in marches asking to release political prisoners in the United States, to impeach President Nixon and Vice-President Agnew, and to end the war in Vietnam. The day she came home on summer break, events conspired to show her hometown in its least flattering light.

"I had just jumped out of a friend's van dressed in farmer's jeans to see ladies wearing white gloves traipsing across our lawn," Rachel recalled. "There was a house walk going on sponsored by a garden club. Two houses on display were on either side of my house.

"After a year of grappling with political issues and fighting for social change, the placid scene seemed unreal. Didn't people have anything better to do than spend time looking at what someone else owned? I was so disgusted I turned on the sprinkler so they couldn't use our lawn as a pass-through."

Having no other plans for the summer, she stayed home. To appease her conscience for "laying back while the world was in turmoil," she tried to organize a social action committee at her father's church. People, she found, were more interested in going to the country club than coming to hear the speeches she wrote. The following semester, Rachel made arrangements to live on campus throughout the school year and later transferred to a college with a more radical image. These days, she is living in a midsized Midwestern city working for a state representative. "I always taught Rachel to think for herself, to stick to her guns. I'm almost sorry I did," her mother said.

A change in family structure can be as unnerving as seeing a hometown in a different light. An unexpected divorce between parents shattered the illusions of a percentage of college students who had intended to return home in the sixties. Willingness to see the world change didn't include the personal world. David, now twenty-eight and in a Ph.D. program at the University of California in Berkeley, considers himself an authority on the grown child of divorce. He found plenty of company at Berkeley.

"The occasion of my going to school was the occasion of my

parents' divorce," he recalled. "I never had an inkling they weren't getting along. And I had been so proud of our open relationship.

"Away at school, I had fantasies about bringing them back together. Reality struck when I came home to New Rochelle, New York, for Christmas. I had to spend my time divided between my parents. I preferred staying with my mother in the house where I grew up, where our dog was. But I wouldn't tell that to my father. Rather than tear myself apart, I've stayed on the West Coast and let my parents visit me."

The death of the more supportive parent also can shorten the time grown-up children consider their parents' house "home." Marian and her father had always been at odds. Nevertheless, she continued to come home at each school break, hoping things would be different. They worsened. The opinionated man showed continuous disapproval of Marian's vegetarian diet, her concern about the environment, and the budding of her feminist mentality. Marian tried to ignore the sniping for her mother's sake. "The year mom died," she said, "I stopped coming home. There was no longer a buffer between me and my dad."

Another excuse for leaving the home of a single parent was role reversal. A bereaved or deserted father or mother could begin to lean on a child for emotional support and advice. The father became the son, and the son, the father. David, the Ph.D. candidate, had felt uncomfortable in that role. Cathy, a college dropout now working as a waitress, claimed she had not received enough parenting to become a parent to her mother. "I knew there was a stage other than childhood," she said, "but the rules for being an adult weren't clear in the sixties or early seventies. Adulthood wasn't an issue then."

The byword *independence* gave the members of the sixties generation a nebulous concept of what it means to be a grown-up. Their perception, learned in childhood, was that the adult gives and the child takes. Another perception was taking control over one's "space." At school, students could keep their rooms as neat or as sloppy as they liked. Trash baskets could be empty or overflow with debris. Kids could nap at will or stay up all night. They weren't subject to censure except perhaps from finicky roommates. Combining both perceptions, they took their own apartments and let their parents pay the rent.

Without looking beyond immediate gratification, they didn't realize they were prolonging childhood. But adulthood cannot be staved off forever. The suspect age of thirty would be waiting, and the clock of world events would be running. As pseudochildren, they would leave themselves open to the depths of childhood grief and yet be too big to sit on someone's lap for comfort. The aging members of the sixties generation would find themselves in a "Catch-22." Because something is new doesn't mean it's better. The kids would learn this hard lesson in the next decade.

3

Back to Square One

In school, we learn the law of gravity—what goes up must come down. In life, we learn a graver lesson—Newton's law can apply to hope. But to no generation more than the youth of the sixties did the collective hopes rise so high or fall so low. By the early seventies, the prospect of recreating the world in their image became a pie in the sky that fell and splattered.

The Vietnam War raged on. Racial tensions continued. The subculture spawned the drug culture. Youth's candidate for president in 1968, Eugene McCarthy, dropped out of sight. Young people relied upon the Beatles to sing of peace and love so they could listen to hope spinning off a plastic disc. In 1970, the Beatles disbanded.

How deep was the disillusionment? The higher the ideals, the further they fell. Student Karleton Armstrong was dedicated to stopping the Vietnam War—so much so that in the predawn of an August day in 1970 he helped bomb Sterling Hall, the Army-Math Research Center at the University of Wisconsin–Madison.

By contrast, other war protests achieved momentum by accident even at the University of Wisconsin, the prototype of a politically active campus. Mike, a law student who arrived there in 1970, described the making of a demonstration: "Someone would organize a rally on the library mall. Passersby would join. The crowd would march through student housing shouting, 'Join us, join us.' And the kids would join without knowing why. We got a kick out of seeing ourselves on television. And we really went nuts when our school made the Cronkite show."

Mike's interest in the Vietnam War fell between the overzealous and the superficial. Vietnam was not a personal issue. Poor eyesight exempted him from military service. None of his friends or family was serving overseas. But for the first time since participating in high school pep club and managing a sports team, Mike found a cause he really cared about. A political naïf, he knew something was wrong about this war, and something was right about stopping it. As to the violence and civil disobedience accompanying the demonstrations, Mike rationalized, "The police are inciting the students as much as purpose and happenstance."

In retrospect, Mike wondered how much he and his classmates really accomplished. Still another thought, he said, nags at him: "Some people claim the students prolonged the Vietnam War because we created a backlash."

Although time moves forward, times can move backward. By the early seventies, the fervor of the sixties was reverting to the apathy of the fifties. Amy, Mike's wife-to-be, arrived at the University of Wisconsin in 1973. It was the tail end of the era of campus demonstrations, a time when streaking was more exciting than protesting. Seeking a meaning to life, she became involved in what was left of campus politics. Karleton Armstrong was tried that year for the antiwar bombing of Sterling Hall, which killed a professor. She demonstrated on Armstrong's behalf. He was convicted and sent to prison.

Determined to get involved, Amy was stirred when the school threatened to close its Afro-American Center. A strike was called, and she ran to the cafeteria to rally support. The scene at the lunch tables disgusted her. "The room was full of blacks who couldn't care less," Amy recalled. "I decided not to strike."

To Amy's surprise, the decision was approved by the sixties activist who had been her model. Gerry, Amy's older sister, was a fervent advocate of campus causes from 1965 to 1969. Gay rights, women's rights, Students for a Democratic Society, Fair Play for Cuba— Gerry demonstrated for all of them. But the highlight of her student years was hearing McCarthy, her idol, speak on campus in 1968. Gerry recalled bumping into him in an airport later, and all she could think to say was "What happened?"

Within this family of Madison alumni, Gerry's husband typified the student who had lent a hand to the present yet kept an eye to the future. Caught up in the movement, Bob, an engineering major, was cautious about identifying with the radicals. As early as 1964, he told a friend, "I don't think they'll get anywhere by throwing bricks at cops or calling them pigs."

He looked, however, for a way to promote the values he had selected from the barrage of philosophies on campus that dovetailed with those he had learned at home: Be kind and hate things, not people. The field of psychology, not engineering, seemed to be the answer. In his sophomore year he switched his major and his residence. Bob moved out of the fraternity house occupied by engineering students to room with three -ology students in an old frame house on Mifflin Street, the hangout for campus radicals.

By his senior year, however, the street began to attract nonstudents who were into hard drugs and openly hostile to any form of authority. As Bob put it, "Mifflin Street became a dangerous place to live. The counterculture and hard hats confronted each other daily. At night fires were set, the streets had to be cleared, and helicopters hovered looking for signs of trouble. It was time again to move on."

His roommates considered joining a back-to-the-soil group on a working farm outside of Madison. They were ready for a simple life. Bob discouraged them. Raised in a rural area, he knew how hard farm work could be. Instead, they moved to a less-troubled block on Mifflin Street.

In 1968, as graduates, they discovered that undergraduate -ology degrees had prepared them for nothing. The anthropologist took a graduate course. The sociologist drove a taxi. And the ecologist worked outdoors—as a member of a construction crew.

Bob's venture into the field of psychology was frustrating. He learned that about 40 percent of all psychologists worked at colleges and universities. Their second largest employer was the government. In both places Bob's humane instincts were throttled by red tape. And the pay was poor.

Bob's demonstrations of protest had not been statements against materialism. He had merely set aside a childhood dream of becoming a millionaire for a set of ideals. The prospect of spending his life within a bureaucracy seemed ludicrous. To channel his values into a system that could promote change, he chose another course—law. As Bob put it, "The changes we fought for in the sixties had broader parameters than the war. We wanted to change the automatic assumption that government is infallible. But government can't be changed by college students. The cause has to be carried by middle-class adults. As a lawyer I could get there."

Today, Bob, an attorney, is director of an organization geared to protect children's rights by introducing new legislation. His self-description is "I am not a child saver. I take other cases when I'm jammed for money. But, generally, I have a sense of being in a struggle involving human values."

Bob was lucky if luck is purposely avoiding open manhole covers on a street marked Under Construction. The foresight put him steps ahead of his contemporaries. In a December 24, 1979, *U.S. News & World Report* article, "Old-Fashioned Values Are Coming Back," Norman Podhoretz wrote: "In the counterculture of the 1960s and early 1970s, there was a tendency to question traditional notions about families and the importance of work. There was also a lot of emphasis on self-gratification. Now people are beginning to realize this whole tendency is not the road to happiness but the road to misery, loneliness, depression."

Years before the Podhoretz article was written, overaged college students pursuing self-gratifying studies had a prescience of walking the wrong road. This was particularly felt if they had chosen poverty to foil the plot to "program" them into the "system." Supporters of this position were defaulting. They were sending wedding invitations, Seidman and Son business cards, and news of friends studying accounting. It was even rumored then that the notorious radical Jerry Rubin was becoming a member of the establishment.

The sense of solidarity with other students was dissipating. A new type of freshmen walked the campus, ones who wanted to sever purse strings but not apron strings. These freshmen were apathetic to the issues of the early seventies that called for a halt to nuclear power, pollution, and rising tuition. None of these causes inspired their full attention or received front-page coverage by the media. No wonder overage students in their torn jeans and worn theories began to feel like anachronisms. To add injury to insult, the usual weekly check from home barely covered rising expenses of room and board. A new fact of life, inflation, was touching their lives. Where once they had joked, "At least the checks are tax-free," they began to wonder whether they would have enough to eat.

In the sixties they had become vegetarians in principle. In the seventies vegetarianism was also their beef against the high price of meat. Occasionally, they would scrounge a meal from an enterprising neighbor across the hall who shoplifted to make money from home meet his or her needs. Scrounging and stealing were symptoms of a new pain—the fact that they weren't self-supporting was lowering their self-esteem.

Without companions in arms to fill their free time, the overage students were forced to take stock of their surroundings. Their walk-up apartments were a mess. Paint was peeling. The faucets dripped. The sinks were rust stained. As they cleared chipped plates from wobbly tables, the hems of their jeans touched roaches. These conditions were in sharp contrast to the well-maintained houses where they had been reared. Tim, who had gone the full route described above, said, "I realized I was fooling myself by living like this to show my folks I didn't have to be like them. I was taking their money to pay for this dump."

Initially, Tim had sought control of his space. Now he wanted to take control of his life. A language major proficient in French, he looked for a full-time job to use his education. He refused the one solid offer he received. He didn't want to be a waiter in a French restaurant the rest of his life. He dialed a rarely used number and asked, "Can I come home?"

The college dropouts were counterparts to the overage students. They, too, awakened in the early seventies to discover that drifting from one interest to another bred loneliness and self-contempt. Growing up, they observed that career demands on their fathers did not bring happiness nor had money been a cure-all for deficiencies in family life. These observations had pushed them away from their parents' notions of work and family. The dropouts discovered that a lack of career and a lack of money were not the answer to finding happiness. It was time, as they pushed thirty, to deal with making a living and to look outside of themselves for fulfillment. Their typical solution: drop out of dropping out.

In *Liberal Parents, Radical Children* (New York: Coward, McCann & Geoghegan, Inc., 1975), author Midge Decter addressed this attribute of the sixties generation: "You are more than usually incapable of facing, tolerating, or withstanding difficulties of any kind. From the time of your earliest childhood you have stood in a relation to the world that can only be characterized as a refusal to be tested." This weakness, Decter contended, led to "in American history, at least, unprecedented voluntary mobility."

Dan, whose gesture of dissent was thumbing his nose at his parents' emphasis on education, recalled the dropout years as "excruciatingly lonely." The rewards of privacy and autonomy paled before the shortcoming of "being alone and loose in the world." His pervading feeling was "No one gives a damn about me." On the practical side, the higher cost of filling his stomach and his gas tank obsessed him with exactly what he wanted to avoid—money. He turned nostalgic, remembering childhood as a time when substantial meals were ordinary events and a financial crisis led to an increase in his allowance. Home never looked so good as in retrospect.

After two years of erratic communication with his folks, Dan appeared on the doorstep of their bi-level carrying a battered suitcase in his hand and his pride in his pocket.

Meanwhile, at other homes, moms and dads of kids approaching college age no longer talked about the counterculture at the breakfast table. The worry words were *recession* and *inflation.* Newton's law didn't apply to prices in the 1970s. They were going up without a sign of coming down. The disturbing 5.5 percent inflation of 1970 was looking good in 1974, the year the figure more than doubled. The invisible tax ended one of their illusions, and they agreed grudgingly with the dissenters they had despised. The government could not do everything. It was fallible and had limits.

Not that inflation was taking the bread off mom and dad's table. Dad, in his fifties, was well established in a business or profession. True, he felt the pinch of tight money when his customers, clients, or patients became slow payers. There were paper losses in his stock portfolio, and the minimum wage for employees had risen to two dollars per hour. He used money set aside for a rainy day to tide him over. Mom worked to fill time, to pay for extras, and to make a token gesture to involvement in the women's movement. The high school senior living at home worked part-time to earn spending money and sometimes to save toward his or her higher education. Despite the downturn of business and the upturn of prices, in 1974 part-time jobs were easier to find than in the sixties. By then, one-third of the nation's retail business came from the seventeen thousand shopping centers sprawling over suburbia. According to available figures, of the 2.8 million retail salespeople, 60 percent were women. Job opportunities in sales were better than ever for a mom with a pleasant personality. Job opportunities were more plentiful for teenagers, too.

Jeans and T-shirts were no longer the exclusive dress of the dissidents. Teenagers of all types flocked to buy the comfortable clothes, and storeowners hired young people to sell them. If a teenager didn't find employment in one of these youth boutiques in the shopping mall where mom worked, he or she could find work at one of the one hundred forty thousand fast-food franchises spreading like catsup across the country. Transportation posed no problem. Where once the symbol of prosperity had been a chicken in every pot, now it was two cars in every garage.

Two groups of people were less sanguine about their financial futures. The first was the generation who had lived through the depression of the thirties. After the debacle, the government gave them a level of economic security through the enactment of programs to protect their savings and to provide for their retirement. With years of hard work and prudent spending behind them, they believed they had earned the right to a prosperous life. Inflation, however, infringed upon this right by eroding the value of their savings and Social Security checks.

A second group of people remained untouched by inflation, but not out of choice. They were the young people of the seventies, descending upon the marketplace at a rate of two million each year. The majority of them, armed with substantial skills, had been lead to believe they could aspire to the "good life" by preparing for a career and then working hard in their chosen fields. But the rising unemployment induced by the recession gave them an unexpected message: "We don't need you. No jobs available." They felt betrayed.

Back at the ranch house and the high rise, mom and dad hatched plans for a new life after the nest was completely empty. Dad seemed less excited about the prospect than mom. While the kids were growing up, he had been too busy to watch them develop or to look toward them for companionship. But these days he had a modicum of free time and thought he would rather spend it on his grown children than on the golf course.

Mom felt a degree of sadness at the impending parting with her children. But the overwhelming emotion she felt too embarrassed to admit was relief. She had "done time" as feeder, chauffeur, nurse, psychologist, and all-round nurturer, and she was ready for phase two of her adult life—to return to the twosome of marriage and to pick up the personal ambitions dropped for parenthood. As one mother put it, "If I had worked for one company all these years, I would have been ready to receive a gold watch."

She saw nothing on the horizon to defer the couple's plans. Son Bill was a college senior. Daughter Sue was a sophomore. Jeffrey, the youngest, would leave for a state university in the fall. Business news in 1975 lulled money worries. Inflation had dropped from 12 percent to 7 percent. Sure, free road maps, for the trips they planned, now cost fifty cents each, and postage on letters requesting travel brochures had risen to thirteen cents. But there was no question that once the kids finished school, all three of the offspring would strike out on their own. Living under separate roofs, a worry in the sixties, was a standard expectation by the midseventies. They were surprised when an older friend's child ensconced himself at home to work on a graduate degree. To them, he was the exception, not the rule.

Mom and dad could not anticipate that the events in the first half of the seventies would boomerang to bring the children back in the second half. Before the OPEC oil embargo in 1973, a barrel of crude oil cost $2.90. By 1979, it would bring $40 on the spot market, and prices would be pumped up accordingly at service stations. The condominium boom of 1973 would seem like a soft noise in comparison to the thunder of 1977-79, when condominium conversions tripled. Inflation, abating in 1975 to 7 percent, would rise steadily and reach 13.9 percent in 1979. The tax bite would become a gouge.

Young people trying to act out the sixties definition of independence would be hard-pressed to live under a roof separate from their family. If an apartment turned condominium, they would be forced out. The resulting scarcity would make a new apartment at least 10 percent dearer to rent. As popular demand for a fuel-saving auto increased, so did the purchase price, the cost of maintenance, and the insurance rate. The kid's pleasure vehicle would become a dependent. Taxes on a modest starting-out salary, $8,500 to $12,000 a year, would lower spendable income by 12.5 percent at least. Looking up and down the decade, the cost of living in the United States rose 98 percent. And while prices heated, the government asked businesses for voluntary freezes on wages. There have been no indications of a respite. What is going up only shows signs of rising higher. And economists believe that in the eighties the problem to focus on is inflation, which will be with us for a long time.

What parental prosperity could not reverse in the sixties and early seventies—grown children's flight from family—the high cost of living turned around in the midseventies. The birds who flew from the nest flocked home in droves large enough to be noticed. Ostensibly, they were heading to a well-stocked sanctuary in an economic storm. This reason was unacceptable to peers who appraised personal independence by how little someone needed parents in his or her life. Actually, home-ing pigeons hid other reasons under their wings. These were as complex as the reasons that drove them out in the first place, giving each home-ing pigeon a different tale to tell.

Part Two

Home-ing Pigeons

Home is the place where, when you have to go there, they have to take you in.

Robert Frost

4

I Only Came Home Because . . .

Home-ing pigeons is a tag for grown children who resume living with their parents after a separation. Like their avian counterparts, they have the ability to find home base from any distance. In terms of miles, human home-ing pigeons come back from places as close as local colleges and state universities and as far away as France, Israel, and Vietnam. But unlike the birds, they travel an additional distance on the way back—one measured in emotion, not miles. While the feathered homing pigeons are doing what they were intended to do, human home-ing pigeons are driven home by circumstance. Or so they say.

As early as a child can remember, all the answers to precocious requests began with "When you grow up." "When you grow up . . . you'll get a two-wheeler . . . you'll ride without training wheels . . . you'll cross the street by yourself." Each answer rang as a promise of privileges to come. Later, there was a subtle change in the phrase. "When you grow up" became "When you're old enough." "When you're old enough . . . you'll watch the late show . . . you'll learn how to drive . . . you'll see an R-rated movie." The variation on the theme contained a sour note. Before there seemed to be a choice in the process of growing up. Hadn't the folks been told by the child to take off the training wheels? Now the child felt subject to a mysterious authority. Each new privilege would require permission.

47

Although the kids would not admit it to friends or family under penalty of death, being a kid was still all right with them. At thirteen or fourteen they were in the permission slip stage, needing parental OK to do something extraordinary outside the home or school. Several high school freshmen interviewed said they really wanted "to be young for a while." They might talk about the pleasures and privileges of becoming grown-ups, but they didn't want the duties. "I don't want the responsibilities that go along with being a grown-up like cooking, shopping, and paying the bills," one freshmen said. This ambivalence, as noted in Daniel Levinson's *The Seasons of a Man's Life* (New York: Alfred Knopf, Inc., 1978), could last until they were thirty-two.

By age seventeen, they were tired of hearing promises and asking for permission. Eager to be their own persons, they listened for votes of confidence in their ability to act grown-up. They got a mixed message. The new refrain was "Soon you'll be ready." "Soon you'll be ready ... to leave the house ... to go to college ... to learn what life's all about." To their ears it sounded like, "Kid, if you were bread, you'd only be half-baked." Again, someone else would tell them when they were "done." The message came around high school graduation time. Suddenly they were grown-up, old enough, ready, and done in the eyes of their parents, peers, and society to cut loose, let go, and break away.

It didn't matter that they might be uncomfortable about cutting ties (at home they had their place) or worried about making new friends (in high school they had the same group of friends for four years) or uncertain about making decisions (their folks and friends made them in committee or issued orders). They were arbitrarily ejected from the nest and expected to fly even though their self-confidence was in the pinfeather stage—just breaking through the skin.

College counselors, on a regular basis, hear students express uncertainties about the direction they have taken. "There are exceptions," said Dr. Joyce Nolen, an associate professor on the student development staff at William Rainey Harper College, Palatine, Illinois. "But often a kid leaves home without a real sense of identity. How can he feel like his own person when he has relied on external forces such as peer, parental, and societal pressures to make his decisions for him? He hasn't learned to trust himself."

In the bird world, some parents stand a distance from the nest dangling a bit of food to encourage the fledglings to try their wings.

No one forces them to fly until they are ready to take the bait. In the people world, home-ing pigeons' self-distrust is often amplified by opinionated adults who show little faith in their judgment to stay home until their flying muscles are developed. Danny, who preferred working with his hands to learning from a book, recalled the fight he put up to keep from going away to college in 1973.

"I told my folks college isn't for everyone. I asked for a semester off to figure out what I wanted to do. They said, 'Try physical therapy.' I asked if I could work as a hospital volunteer to see whether I would like it. No! I had to go away. There were no ifs, ands, or buts. I thought, 'I'll go, but you'll be sorry.'

"My first year, I didn't try my hardest. I didn't want to be there. The school was far from home in a small Midwestern town. There was nothing to do except watch the corn grow.

"My second year was worse. My new roommate had a car and liked to party, and I would rather do something other than study. I got put on probation, and my dad said I'd have to pay for the next semester. He made me work in his hardware store that summer. I couldn't cross him. He had always been there when I needed him. He might not be if I refused.

"It turned out better than I thought. I liked selling tools and hearing how people fixed things. But my father fired me and made me go back. I flunked out my third year and had to come home. Strangely, home isn't like I remembered it. I had a lot of freedom at school. Here, I feel like I'm serving a prison sentence. As punishment for failing, I got a lot of chores laid on me. My mother bitches and screams at me every chance she gets. My father won't rehire me. He said, 'Make it the hard way.'

"Last week I got a job at a service station and a student loan to go to vocational school. I'm going to get good grades and a job and this time leave home because it's something I want to do."

Danny gives plausible reasons to adults or peers who ask, "How come you're home?"—implying he is too old to be a home-ing pigeon. Acknowledging "the school was too cornball" or "too hard," depending on whom he answers, is easier to admit than "I came home because I was afraid of losing my place in the family." Asked if he would have felt more secure leaving if his parents hadn't insisted he go, Danny said, "Yes, I wouldn't have felt as if I was being pushed out with no say in the matter."

His statement lends itself to another comparison between home-ing pigeons and their avian counterparts. Young pigeons or squabs survive their early days through forced feeding. Pigeon's milk produced by both parents is pumped down each bird's throat until each one is ready for solid food. Young people survive their early years in a slightly different fashion. Their parents feed them their own parental values and expectations to promote their emotional growth. But it becomes another matter when they are too old to have the values and expectations shoved down their throats.

In social situations, a home-ing pigeon can be hatched from a pervasive sense of loneliness. The truism "You can feel more lonely in a crowd than when you sit alone" needs the amendment "But it's more painful to sit alone if you think you should be out with the crowd." Student counselor Dr. Nolen has observed, "A kid doesn't rely on his instincts. He grew up with television, and what he sees on the tube exerts a pressure to live up to impossible ideals. He usually runs with a pack and measures himself by what someone else is doing. This easily leads to a feeling of alienation in the outside world because, as I said before, he doesn't know enough to trust himself."

The young person who feels "I never measure up" sees himself or herself out of step in a large group yet conspicuous in a smaller group and reacts with alarm when thrust into a new situation. Mark, an aspiring artist from a small town in Nebraska, felt like an oddball among a student body of forty thousand in a major city. It seemed to him they were always ready to socialize while he preferred to paint or talk to someone about art.

At the same time, he could not bear to be considered different and was continually caught in a conflict between what he wanted to do and what he thought he should do.

At a college of five thousand students in his junior and senior years, Mark's habits were more open to scrutiny. Any comment about his tendency to be a loner reinforced his self-image of a misfit. He painted less, socialized more, and compared himself to the Roman god Janus, who is usually shown with two faces looking in opposite directions. When finished with school, Mark faced one direction—Nebraska. Home was his port in a storm even when it wasn't raining.

But his grandparents gave him an unexpected graduation gift—a free summer to wander France alone. Mark panicked. His French was only so-so. He would get lost. As an American he would stick out like a sore thumb. The opportunity, however, to visit world-famous museums and see original works of art led him to agree to an adjustment in plans. He would go as a student, not as a back-packer. His grandparents enrolled him in the University of Grenoble to give him a home base and the company of people who shared a mutual interest. Mark recalled the experience: "I was in for a lonely time. Most students were transients, here one day, gone the next. There was no one to fill in my free time. It's funny. When I had the chance to live art twenty-four hours a day, I didn't want to. So I started to roam by myself and for a while it was marvelous.

"I found out how other people live and how much the French know about their history. I wasn't as well versed in mine. I discovered what it's like to live in a minor country after growing up in a major country. I got a whole new perspective on someone else's outlook.

"I'd never been sure my thinking was right, and I learned a person doesn't have to be right or wrong. There are many ways a person can think—and it's OK. That was a great relief."

Frequent visits to museums were less reassuring. Seeing originals of his favorite impressionists within touching distance made Mark feel uneasy about his talent. "I knew my work would never be half as good as what was done already," he said, and put away his brushes and easel as tools to earn a living.

He came home without knowing what to do. Cut loose from school, he was cut loose from structured time. He considered obtaining a marketable skill at a local college until he met students who claimed they were unhappy enrolled in a graduate program. They felt they had been forced into a career rather than pursuing one they wanted. Mark's instinct to reconsider going into a field he didn't care about was a healthy one. A Terman-Sears study of life gratifications among gifted people, as reported in *Pychology Today* (February 1980), shows that a feeling of choosing one's career, not drifting into it, is an important part of job satisfaction. Unfortunately, Mark, the perennial self-doubter, didn't follow his instincts.

He took marketing courses and drifted into his father's grainery business. Working with his dad supplies an admirable answer for living at home. "My dad needs someone to depend on in his business," Mark says. "It would be foolish to get my own place when we leave for work and come home together."

Is Mark happy? His reply indicates why he really stays at home. "I'm not lonely anymore," he said, evading the real question. "My parents accept me as I am."

Social workers in family counseling situations tend to give pathological reasons to explain why adult-age children resume living with their parents. A prevailing opinion is that "the child never separated emotionally from his family." The theory implies they are lagging behind in normal development. How much? Human maturation cannot be measured like the wingspread of a bird. One social worker said, "Leave-taking is painful for everyone, but the degree of pain can be gauged in terms of a pimple versus acne. The emotional dependence becomes acne when it interferes with functioning and becomes an impediment to living."

Few home-ing pigeons are aware of the separation-individuation theory expounded by professionals. They just sense that home is a place to fill up emotionally when something in the outside world leaves them with an empty feeling. Nor do they want to face the lacking element. They do know, however, that society is contemptuous of laggards. Invariably they conclude "I came home because . . ." with a prosaic reason unless pressed to be more honest.

Ed, a Vietnam veteran with a chemical engineering degree, returned to his parents' house after receiving his discharge because "I had no place else to go." After a couple of months, he found a job and took his own apartment. Less than a year later, he had the job but had given up the apartment. "The neighborhood was dangerous," said Ed, who had seen action in the casualty-ridden Tet offensive. Upon further questioning, he admitted, "I missed my folks. Remember, I had been a number at a four-year college and another number during three years of service. It was good to be someone's son for as long as they'd let me."

Another type of home-ing pigeon sheds the family plumage while he or she is away. These home-ing pigeons find an ephemeral sense of "me" by affecting habits they know are unacceptable to their parents. Social workers describe this means as "separating in an artificial way." Missy, who entered the University of Illinois as a communications major in 1974, adopted the sloppy dress and wild hairdo of a hippie although the posture was going out of vogue. "My statement to my mother," Missy said, "was 'We're of different generations. Dressing nice and going to the hairdresser may be important to you, not to me.' "

Like others in her clique, Missy planned to extend the separation by going abroad. Her destination was a pen pal's home in Iceland. Instead, after graduation in December 1978, she lived at home. "I scotched my plans to go to Iceland when I realized I would be there in its dark season," she said. "Without other plans for the immediate future, I had to come home."

What was her real reason for returning? Prior to graduation Missy learned her folks intended to retire in Arizona in late spring. She wanted to spend "just a little time" in the house where she grew up. "I realized the true.'me' was lurking somewhere in the family," she said. "I had a job and couldn't go with them, so when they left, I moved in with my grandma. It was good to belong to someone who has known me for a long time."

Sharon, a teacher who followed through with travel plans, came to a similar conclusion but experienced it in another way. She took off for Israel a week after college graduation to find personal fulfillment. In the homeland of her religious ancestors she expected to find the "real meaning of life." But there was nothing there to provide a satisfactory answer, not even after a second and third trip back to work on a kibbutz and to attend an Israeli university. Finally, she came home for good because she felt disoriented from all the shuttling back and forth. Or so she told anyone who asked.

Actually, Sharon came home looking for stability. She said, "Most of my relatives still live near my folks. It's nice to be able to drop in on them. They know me from day one. And it's good to spend a long stretch of time with my parents. As I get to know the family again, I also get to know me."

As a young person gains a sense of self, it would seem natural for a sense of "feeling good" to follow. Perhaps so good that a person in his twenties would feel a modicum of happiness with the choices he or she has made. Yet, an interview in *U.S. News & World Report* (December 24, 1979) with Angus Campbell, the director of the study "The Happiest Americans—Who They Are," showed this segment of the population ranks themselves low in happiness. Seventy-one percent reported "not feeling very happy." Doesn't this statistic seem incongruous of a generation of young people who have had the advantages of education and travel and the opportunity to keep looking for themselves longer than any other generation?

Campbell, a professor of psychology and sociology at the University of Michigan in Ann Arbor, lays the sense of unhappiness at the feet of the "do your own thing" trend. "Doing your own thing has a lot of hazards," he said, "because it creates very uncertain situations. The decisions aren't laid down for you by precedent or expectation, and you face problems you don't understand very well because you haven't any experience with them. This uncertainty, I suspect, has created a lot of stress and tension among young people."

Clearly, young people looked for precedents when they came

home. What they considered forced feeding when they left is now succor. But they have to save face. How can they admit they want to reconsider the values and expectations they once took lightly or rebelled against? In terms of masking their feelings, no one can deny they are masters of cover-up.

Andy, an honors student, dropped out of college to drive a bus and live in his own apartment. As soon as the novelty wore off, he came home saying, "It was lonely out there." His real motive? "I knew my folks would push me to go back to school. Hadn't they told me often enough that driving a bus was marginal use of my intelligence?" Larry, a lackadaisical student, left a prestigious college a thousand miles from home to enroll in a commuter college. He told his folks, "The kids there are all snobs." His real reason? "My folks used to make me study, and I want them to keep me on the right track." Bride-to-be Gale completed her senior year in college at a local school to be near her boyfriend. Actually, she wanted her parents to reassure her that getting married was the right thing to do.

"Saying I'm coming home because I got a job down the street or going to a school nearby is a rational rationalization," said Dr. Nolen. "A parent can't say, 'Well, that isn't so.' But underneath, these kids have emotional needs that are being met at home."

Returning to the analogy between the feathered homing pigeons and the human home-ing pigeons, each has a means of camouflage. The coloring of its feathers blends a bird into its surroundings. The coloring of an excuse for coming home fits the young person into adult society. There, the likeness ends. Nature provides the bird with camouflage to hide from an enemy. The human devises the camouflage to hide from himself.

This is not to say our home-ing pigeons are not driven home by circumstance. Along with the unfulfilled, the undecided, and the single come the married, the divorced, the widowed, the sick, and the needy. Underlying the practical excuse they give is an impetus few have the courage to voice. "Look, mom. I'm big enough, I'm old enough, I'm ready—and it scares the hell out of me!"

5

Who's Knocking at the Door Urgently?

A general assumption accepted without proof for more than 2,300 years is that a straight line is the shortest distance between two points. This basic postulate of Euclidean geometry was intended for application to physical matters. Those with a sociological bent, however, can apply it to human matters. Is the straight line the shortest distance from childhood to adulthood?

Parents answering this question in interviews were divided on the criteria for adulthood. A majority agreed that adulthood constitutes completing an education, maintaining an apartment of one's own, and holding a job. These accomplishments are major signs of self-sufficiency according to the consensus. Other parents added another requirement. They maintained, "Children are not full adults until they start families of their own. They are kids until they are willing and able to assume responsibility for the welfare of other human beings."

For the sake of argument, the two contentions have been combined to draw a hypothetical straight line to becoming a complete adult. It begins at point A—getting a place of one's own—and leads to point F—starting a new family. At prescribed points along the way, the budding adults acquire an education, a career, a source of income, and a mate. Parents of grown children who have been the route contend this is the shortest and the surest way to go from dependence to independence.

It is easier, however, to follow a straight line in a geometry book than in life. Life can throw a curve to catapult the young person back on his or her parents' doorstep.

"It's natural for someone in crisis to gravitate towards his earliest source of comfort," said Carol Olson, acting director of social services for the Family Service and Mental Health Center of South Cook County, Illinois. "The pattern is established in childhood. Parents are the lap, the broad shoulder, and the welcoming arms."

Who pounds the door most frantically? Sometimes the panicked caller is the child the parent least expects, the one who walked the straight line as carefully poised as a tightrope walker. Anna, a goal-oriented young woman, took all the proper steps in perfect order. She graduated from the University of New Mexico and found a job and an apartment in Albuquerque. After a two-year art career, she married a young man whose adventurous spirit augmented her more cautious attitude. At thirty, she was the doting mother of two babies still in diapers. They both were napping the day she was knocked off the line. Her husband was reported missing in a plane crash. "They searched for his body for two weeks," the soft-spoken widow said. "The uncertainty almost killed me."

Anna remembered little else after his "death by accident" was confirmed. Her mother's memories were vivid, however. "Anna bore up after the funeral. She refused to come home to California with us. But two weeks later she was knocking on our door, too depressed to function. She slept most of the time, ate a lot, didn't pick up after herself, and ignored the boys. We didn't pressure her to resume functioning or ever think of asking her to leave.

"We just worried and waited for the depression to go away. It took six months, and Anna became the independent soul I remembered. She insisted upon maintaining her former home. Her latest letters mention a job, a housekeeper, and a man."

As Anna's parents see it, walking the straight line is no guarantee against accident. They do believe that having a direction and the discipline to follow it helps a person cope with crisis. It's easier to get back on the track if you have walked it before. "We considered Anna an adult before she became a mother," her mother said. "Having the children gave her another incentive to go on."

Divorce is another type of death, especially if it is asked for "out of the blue" as it was in Sara's case. There were no mold breakers in

Sara's family. She was expected to walk the prescribed line to independence, and she fulfilled all of her parents' expectations except for giving them a grandchild. By age twenty-five, she had a master's degree in business, a statistician's job with a prestigious corporation, and a husband who was as self-assured as she was anxious. "I'd always been told it's a jungle out there, a cold cruel world. So I armed myself to the teeth by doing all the right things the right way," she said.

She felt impervious to the traumas befalling less-directed friends until the night her husband made it clear he didn't love her anymore. He wanted another woman. Although Sara was enamored by statistics, the rising divorce rate in the United States did not alleviate the agony of rejection. In the ensuing months, the "good girl" who had been a virgin on her wedding night became promiscuous, accepting overtures from friend, stranger, or someone else's husband anywhere, anytime, or anyplace. "I felt compelled to prove I was a woman a man would want," she said.

The night she climbed into the backseat of a car with a pickup from a singles bar was the night she fled home. To sleepy-eyed, astonished parents, Sara had the presence of mind to say, "I lost my key. I'm locked out of my apartment." Later in the week, she broke her lease and moved into the room she had occupied as a girl. "I told my folks, 'I need home. That's all I know. I need home.' They asked no questions and let me stay.

"As time passed, I realized why I came home. I had needed to spend time in a familiar place. I had come back to the place I had learned self-restraint. At home I would be able to check my impulses until all the inner turmoil died. And I didn't consider myself less of an adult for running home. It was a temporary stay."

Olson observed that "the promiscuous divorcee or anyone driven to excess who returns home is asking, 'Parents, control me. I can't control myself.' "

There are kids who fight any form of parental control. Parents say "Night." These kids will say "Day." Show them a direct route. They'll take side streets. Give them step-by-step instruction in a craft. They'll see the raw material, envision the end result, and hear nothing in between. Reared with a fast-food mentality, they look for a quicker way than the straight line to become regarded as grown-up. Without apparent reason, they leap from youth beds into marriage beds without any preparation for supporting themselves—often exchanging one dependent situation for another.

Lori, at eighteen, eloped with a twenty-four-year-old man disapproved of by her mother and stepfather. He was in arrears as a potential wage earner. No education or vocational skill. No history of holding a job. "I didn't care," Lori, a former cheerleader, said. "I worked in a bakery; we could always eat."

Less than a year later, Lori was pregnant and alarmingly aware of her husband's shortcomings as a provider. She worked until she could barely fit behind the counter, then ran home asking for financial help.

"I didn't want anything for me," Lori recalled. "I was worried how we'd take care of the baby. All my stepfather said was 'I'm not going to support someone else's brat,' and my mother didn't argue when I said I'd have to give my baby up for adoption. There was nothing else to do. I gave up my baby and my husband and came back home.

"It hasn't been easy. I don't want to be here. My mom and stepfather don't want me here. I work at the bakery during the day and take a night course at college. They ask me where I'm going and with whom. They treat me like a kid. What do I have to do to prove I'm grown-up?"

Olson pointed out that there is a common denominator among children who rush into early marriages. "An early marriage," she said, "is a kid's response to a family problem. He can't put his finger on it or resolve it. He just knows he wants to leave and takes the quickest way to shortening childhood—rushing into marriage."

John, at eighteen, had considered himself the family problem. "My mother didn't think much of me," he said. "She kept calling me lazy because when I was nine I refused to collect money for the newspapers I delivered. All I ever heard was 'You'll never amount to anything.' But I showed her I could take care of myself—for four years anyway."

The day after high school graduation John married his childhood sweetheart, intending to support her with a job in an Indiana steel mill and with savings squirreled away through two summer working periods. Until he was twenty, he provided the basic necessities for his wife and looked forward to the baby on the way. A steel strike threw him off the track.

Before it was settled, John got sick. Conditions in the mill had aggravated latent respiratory problems. Worried about his pregnant wife, who was expecting "any day," John broke a precedent. He finally allowed his mother to visit him. "I had kept her away because I knew she'd call our place a dump," he said. "And I didn't want any more put-downs. But what else could I do when things piled up but ask for help, and she insisted on coming here."

John correctly gauged his mother's reactions. "His home was a hovel," the fastidious woman said. "The stairs were broken. Drafts came through the doors and windows. No wonder he always caught cold.

"His father agreed that we'd help on one condition. The family had to come home with us. I blamed myself for the way he lived. Somewhere I missed the boat to motivate him. I hoped to get another chance."

Olson is pessimistic about second chances at parenting: "If you miss the first, there's nothing you can do about it. It's the child's, not the parent's task to grow up."

It was hard for John to resume the role of child after being a head of a household. He sidestepped renewed attempts at mothering. As soon as the baby was born and his health was restored, he found a job in a distant city and, without giving notice to his mother, moved his family out. "I left some unpaid bills," he admitted, "but I'm going to pay back my folks as soon as we get on our feet. I'd rather live in a dump than where I'm constantly criticized."

Several family counselors pointed out that frequently parents have not given a child permission to grow up. One family counselor said, "A way to help him mature is to allow mistakes without chastising, without making him feel guilty, yet letting him accept the consequences of the mistakes. It's a hell of a job to bring up a kid and starts way back when, not when he's twenty years old."

At the least, these four prototypes of home-ing pigeons in crisis had stepped on the hypothetical line leading to full adulthood. Tina, a voluptuous sixteen-year-old, skipped the starting line prior to reaching legal age and while still living under her parents' roof. Between the ages of sixteen and nineteen, she became pregnant, moved in with her boyfriend, had the baby, and played house for a year. She laid the blame on her mother. "Mom had been an army lieutenant," Tina said. "At home she laid down hard-and-fast rules I had to obey. Either she didn't know much about the boy-girl thing, or else she just didn't talk about sex to me. So whose fault was it I got pregnant?"

Tina was not asked to come home, nor did she knock on the door when she returned. She almost kicked it in demanding to be let in. Her first act within the house was to hand the sodden-bottomed baby to her mother to rear. "Mom said she knew more about raising kids than me, so I let her prove it and went out to work."

When home, Tina treats her child more like a baby brother than a son and even balks at minding him. According to Olson, her reaction is typical of the adolescent who is not ready to be a mother. "The baby she brought home has nothing to do with the attachment to the man who fathered it," Olson said. "Mothers who are kids themselves have an ambivalent tie to their own mothers. In essence they are saying, 'You didn't give me what I wanted when I needed it, and here is the result.' "

Underage mothers aren't the only ones who, in a roundabout or direct way, tell parents "You owe me something." Jeff, twenty-eight and divorced, brought two preschool boys along when he moved back home, fully expecting his mother to mind them while he was working. Dora, a twenty-nine-year-old divorcée, put her eight-year-old into her mother's hands, saying, "The only time you'll have to watch him is after school." Libby came home directly from the hospital, bringing a newborn. She intended to pursue a career while her mother minded the infant. "She never refused me anything," Libby said, "and my husband and I were in the midst of a trial separation."

Olson has found that working children who bring home a child for mom to raise are responding to the "anything for you, darling" attitude they grew up with. Olson believes, "These kids have been overly gratified. They never mastered the anxiety syndrome. The underlying attitude is 'Mom always relieved my frustrations, so let her.' "

As shown by this overview of children catapulted home by extraordinary circumstances, neither a career nor marriage nor parenthood nor having one's own place creates a complete adult. The intangible element on the straight line that makes it the shortest distance between the points of dependence and independence is a sense of responsibility, at the least, for one's self and, at the most, to others, not necessarily to a child.

Bruce, now thirty, went off to college in Washington, D.C., from his parents' home in St. Louis, his mind filled with specific goals. He planned to become a lawyer, set up a practice, and eventually marry and have children. Returning home was not on the agenda. Having worked and contributed to the family coffer throughout high school, he could not imagine any situation he would not be able to handle alone. Like most children, he did not foresee life throwing a curve to his parents. From his vantage point, they sat as securely at the point of self-sufficiency as two crows on a telephone wire.

The blow came at step three on the straight line to independence. Bruce had just begun to work for a congressman when his father, at age sixty-eight, suffered a fatal heart attack. "I knew I had to go back home," Bruce said. "If dad was alive, I would have stayed here. With him gone, mom was all alone."

In addition to finding a job locally, Bruce set for himself the chores of cutting the lawn and doing home repairs. He worried about his mom selling the house if he did not maintain it. He said, "After all those years of living in her own home, I couldn't see her living in a strange apartment. All her friends and neighbors live nearby, and she's familiar with the shopping."

At first, he was teased for living at home by friends who had their own place. Bruce, however, found it easy to defend his position. "Too many people in this country forget older people," Bruce said. "I think you have to be a stronger person to be with family. There's nothing wrong about loving mom. I was taken care of. Now it's my turn to care."

There were adjustments to be made upon coming home after four years, but Bruce worked them out well enough to stay for six years. Before he married, he and his wife chose a condominium seven miles away to enable the successful lawyer to continue to do his mom's chores and visit her easily in his spare time. "I came home a grown-up," Bruce said, "and that carries responsibility. If the time comes and mom is unable to live alone, there'll be no problem taking her into my house."

Children who come home voluntarily to help a parent in crisis generally have an easier time than children forced home by crisis. There is a different mix of elements involved. "They have fewer expectations," Olson said, "and a sense that it was up to them to be there." Peggy Papp, codirector of the Brief Therapy Project at the Ackerman Institute of Family Therapy, was quoted in *Mademoiselle* magazine ("How to Cut Loose Without Cutting the Cord," December 1979) as saying, "Maturity arrives 'when children can see parents as human beings and relate to them as one adult to another.' "

Scott, now thirty-six, backs both statements. He came home twice, each time during a different stage of his development. A precocious youngster, he spent a year at a state university between the ages of sixteen and seventeen. He was not ready to leave home and made childish demands on his family when he returned. The second time, he was gone for seven years, having spent five years earning graduate and postgraduate degrees in engineering and two years as a soldier in Vietnam. The impetus to return was an emotionally and physically disabled father. "The burden of his care was on my mom while I was gone. She was no youngster, and I wanted to be there giving emotional support. I worked all day and sometimes had to go out of town, but she always knew I was on call."

Eleven years passed before Scott moved out to take an apartment of his own. One of the reasons he gave for leaving was "I wanted my mother to have the freedom to travel and move around after dad died. She had spent a lot of years taking care of him, and I didn't want her to be tied down by me."

In most cases, the benefits to the rescuing child are intangible. The greatest reward is intrinsic, feeling good about helping out, and, unless martyrdom is involved, the child considers such actions a privilege of adulthood rather than a sacrifice. Sometimes a return to a parent in crisis is tangibly beneficial to both parent and child. Leslie had accepted a low-paying job as a research assistant to an anthropologist and was concerned about the ability to pay for an apartment of her own on the stipend. Having spent the last few years abroad on digs, she knew no one, offhand, she could ask to be her roommate. A frantic phone call from her mother solved the dilemma. "My dad was having an affair with another woman and planning to move out," Leslie recalled. "I might have moved in anyway. Now there was no question about going home."

Leslie was a calming influence on her mother and eased the distraught woman's worry about finances. Between the two, they managed to maintain the family home and share grocery expenses and a car. As Leslie's earning power increased, she took the lion's share of the expenses. "I don't resent it," she said. "I feel I'm helping out my mom."

On occasion, Leslie considers moving out. But when she hears what her mother plans to do when she leaves, she gets too scared to go. "She plans to take in roomers," Leslie said. "My mom has a lot of idiosyncrasies, and I don't think anyone outside the family would stay for long. She's also naive about business matters and could easily be cheated." There is no question that after three years Leslie would like her own place. As she sees it, however, leaving her mother hinges on money. Leslie now earns enough to be self-sufficient but not enough to support two households. Leslie said, "There are pluses living at home. It's a steady environment. Mom is always home before me. The neighborhood is familiar. The house is familiar. I know there will be food ready to eat. And I don't have to deal with lonely feelings.

"If there was a man out there I was really interested in, maybe I'd find a way to take care of mom other than living at home. Truthfully, I'd rather go on living with a mother I know than a man I'm not sure of."

While none of these three home-ing pigeons with St. Bernard instincts had gone from point A, leaving the family home, to point F, starting a family of their own, they can still be considered adults by the third criterion—a willingness to assume responsibility for other human beings. Although thrown from the straight line by a family crisis, they landed with their feet on the ground, a sure way to eventually walk the remainder of the distance.

An answer to "What is the shortest distance between two points?" can be assumed in geometry. In life there is no pat answer because there are no pat people. It is good to have some form of road map and equally important to know what to do when life throws a curve. Some young people step off of their own volition to assess where they are going. They take time off from what psychologists call the tactics of separation and come home without a fanciful excuse and before a crisis hurls them at the front door.

6

I'm Only Staying
Until . . .

Shakespeare was not clairvoyant when he penned, "All the world's a stage. /And all the men and women merely players: /They have their exits and their entrances; /And one man in his time plays many parts. . . ." Had the Bard seen into the late twentieth century, he would have included intermission in his analogy between life and the theater. Starting in the decade of the seventies, when the young adult population increased more than 31 percent, adult-age children, in larger numbers have walked offstage between acts of growing up.

The term generally used by social scientists for this respite from performance is *psychosocial moratorium,* a term coined by Erik Erikson, a leading figure in the field of psychoanalysis and human development. Its description, published in the *Youth Transition to Adulthood: Report of the Panel on Youth of the President's Science Advisory Committee* (Chicago: The University of Chicago Press, 1974), is equally clinical: "A period before the assumption of adult tasks during which the person has time to work out his sexual and vocational identities and a coherent philosophy of life."

Home-ing pigeons between high points of growing up are more blunt if less couth. They define the psychosocial moratorium as "time we use to get our shit together."

Onlookers match the bluntness, calling kids who come home for

65

parental support freeloaders, moochers, and cop-outs. And here the analogy between theater and life continues.

A playgoer is seldom concerned with the way actors spend time out. It's what performers do up front that counts. To the ticket-holder who has spent money, the twenty-minute break is time to grab a smoke, buck a washroom line, or argue about the merits of the play. If a playgoer thinks at all about the actors during intermission, the certainty is "they're resting or boozing."

Meanwhile, backstage the players are preparing for the second act and sometimes for another play. Unseen by the audience, they change costumes, repair makeup, or simply mop up the sweat induced by footlights. If none of these is required, they use the pause to memorize lines for the next production. Some have been known to swig courage from a whisky bottle to face a blasé audience.

In some ways, young adults at home between college and a career, a bachelor's degree and a master's program, one job and another, or engagement and marriage emulate the actors in the dressing room. They assess character and costume changes, damages to their makeup, and general readiness to go on stage.

There is, however, one major difference between actors committed to roles and young adults in limbo. The home-ing pigeons write intermission into the script as time to switch roles, try out a scene, audition for a new play, or rewrite a love story. Compounding all these issues of commitment are money worries. Few home-ing pigeons are willing to "enter laughing" into adulthood without equity behind them, and they go home to find an angel.

Some critics without a full house give this breed of home-ing pigeon a bad review, sight unseen. "Where is that sense of self?" they ask, "Or of personal accomplishment?" These critics usually have been reared in less affluent families, and refuse to accept avoidance of hardship as a reason for coming home. They see it as a slough-off looking for a handout, and, as one said, "In reality this kind of kid finds it more comfortable to lean on parents than to fend for himself."

During interviews, fifty home-ing pigeons rebutted the accusation. The common defense was "How can you expect us to live on our own? Students can't save money." More specifically, one young man retorted, "I only had about five dollars to my name when I graduated. No joke. It seemed logical to go home." Another explained, "I had no job and therefore no income to pay for rent and food." A young woman asked, "Did you expect me to go to an office in jeans? I needed a whole new wardrobe."

Others were in debt for bank loans that helped pay for an undergraduate degree or a trip abroad to supplement their education. Those who had saved some money from summer or student jobs wanted to hold on to it until they got married. In conjunction with each reason for coming home was a time limit set for their stay. "I'm staying home until . . . I find a job . . . I fatten my bank account . . . I finish grad school . . . I get married." Another line was "I'm staying home until I can afford a home like my parents."

How did these players spend intermission? Kurt shuttled from typewriter to print shop to post office to mail résumés each day. Then he warmed the bench in front of a television set or ran to the mailbox looking for replies. Bill phoned banks to arrange interviews and read biographies of successful men to help him face the interviewers. Gale apprenticed herself, without pay, to a well-known chef to gain restaurant experience. Still others took part-time jobs using hobby or educational skills. A former high school tennis star gave lessons at a club. A drama major solicited customers by telephone for an aluminum siding company. An art student taught drawing in a continuing education class for adults. These were each walk-on parts until the right job came along.

Tammy took an intermission encore because she found the first one so successful. "I had wanted to be a writer ever since first grade," she recalled. "I thought it would be a snap. Away at school, I discovered that a journalism course didn't exempt me from math and science. After almost flunking them, I came home in my sophomore year to take them at a junior college and stayed home until I got decent grades.

"The second time, I came home with a journalism degree and no job. In between job hunting, I put my name into a temporary placement service and worked periodically as a secretary and file clerk. It was the pits, but I needed to get some money together to buy a car. I knew I'd need one as a reporter."

There's the rub. Tammy now has a full-time reporter's job and three years of car payments ahead of her. She had intended to stay home just until she started working. The period, however, has been extended. She said she would like to get the car paid for before she moves out.

By contrast, Derek did not have a lifelong ambition. After finishing a business course at a Lutheran college in Iowa, the personable young man received several job offers. "All the companies promised money and success," he said, "but it wasn't enough to turn me on." It seemed natural to go home until he discovered his real calling.

The field he is interested in seems to be mental health and by living at home he is able to try out a low-paying job at a center for disturbed children. To augment the not-for-profit salary, he took a second job part-time as a youth director for a religious organization. The combined pay, however, does not equip him to live on his own resources and still accumulate money.

Derek explained, "I work a lot of hours and use home as a landing pad. It would be a shame to spend $300 a month on a place to sleep. Besides, the mental health field might not be for me. Why get saddled with a lease? I'll stay home until I know what I want to be."

Derek, like others whose minds boggle at apartment rents, had considered sharing one with a roommate. But the consensus is there are too many risks involved. A roommate is unreliable compared to a stable home. He or she could get fired, transferred, or married. "And where would I be?" is the predominant question among young adults concerned with financial security. Also, young people admit it is easier to deal with a new job or a new course of study without the additional responsibilities of cleaning, cooking, and shopping and the myriad of mundane matters taken over by a mother. One young woman who has taken a full-time job but who is still job hunting admitted, "My mom serves as my secretary. She takes my phone calls and types up my résumés."

To the professional observer, it seems that these kids have been struck by stage fright. "For one reason or another they have a fear of going out into the world under their own steam," according to Chicago psychotherapist Dr. Sandra Kahn. "In some cases, it is because a generation of parents, in an attempt to give kids everything they didn't have, overprotected them financially and indulged them emotionally.

"Generally, these kids can't tolerate frustration. Mommy and daddy have always been ready to rush to the rescue instead of letting a kid work it out on his own."

As often happens, an exception can lend insight to a rule. George, twenty-one, had dreamed of becoming a veterinarian as long as he could remember. In his stalwart household this was fine as long as he paid for his education. George accepted the challenge and worked part-time throughout high school. "But," the lanky young man admitted, "the money kept slipping through my fingers. There was always something more important to spend it on at the moment.

"All I had left when I graduated was about $400 and a bright idea. I flew to my grandparents' home on the West Coast to establish residency to take advantage of California's low tuition. But was I ever homesick! I couldn't wait out the year. Besides, I wasn't terribly welcome after a stray dog I adopted ripped up my grandmother's garden."

Back home, his folks cosigned a loan to help George go to hairdressing school. Why hairdressing? According to George, it was a fast way to start a career and save money toward veterinarian school. Again, although established as a hairdresser, money slipped through his fingers. He complained, "I have no expenses at home, yet I don't know where it goes." His solution? "I'll have to hang around until I repay the loan and get some money together for school."

George's shortcoming seems to be a common one among young people. "Their ignorance of financial realities is abysmal," said Dee Dee Ahern, founder of money management workshops. "Parents keep money matters more secretive than sex, and kids have no reality to budget from and no understanding of how to reach financial goals."

The overspender has a counterpart in the hoarder. Edie taught herself to budget from the day she received her first allowance and considers herself financially savvy. "I read the financial pages, *Fortune* magazine, and always watch for sales," the bespectacled young woman said. "I even thought of becoming an economist, but I couldn't handle the math."

Directly out of college, she accepted a job paying enough to keep up an apartment. Edie chose two furnished rooms located within walking distance of her office and close to public transportation in case of bad weather to preclude the need for a car. Food, clothing, and personal expenses were carefully budgeted. Yet, the economic independence lasted only eighteen months.

"When I visited my folks, I couldn't help comparing their comfortable home with my junky furniture. I'd come back to my old building with its leaky pipes and falling plaster and think, 'Edie, you really ought to buy a house of your own.'

"A quick calculation showed I could save a bundle of money living at home even with paying room and board. My parents agreed. I didn't get flak from my friends. They were living at home for financial reasons, too. It was my folks' friends who gave me a hard time with their innuendos that I was scrounging from my retired parents. I only planned to stay until I saved up a down payment."

Three years have passed. Edie was promoted twice on her job, receiving commensurate salary increases, and her bank account is a hefty $30,000 or more. She has looked into buying a house and is now afraid to assume the responsibility. The down payment would wipe out her savings, and the monthly charges would be four times more than the sum she pays her parents. "Maybe I'll use some of the money to improve my chances of getting a better job by going back to school," she said. "In the meantime, I'll stay home until something or someone out there gives me a reason to move out."

A good percentage of home-ing pigeons are doing what Edie contemplates. They use intermission to gain stronger marketable skills by adding a master's degree, taking credits toward a teaching certificate, or taking courses in a related field. To move ahead in the social sciences, additional education is almost mandatory. Some young people combine part-time jobs with school. Others add part-time schooling to full-time jobs. They claim that living at home, free from demanding financial responsibilities and housekeeping chores, keeps them single-minded at the task of retooling. One law student said, "It's easier to study at home than on campus. There are fewer distractions."

Generally, these types of home-ing pigeons set a definite time to leave. They are only staying until they find the job that pays at least $20,000 a year at the entry level. Occasionally, this takes longer than they think.

Home-ing pigeons of the category who live up to their avowed reentrance are the ones who have set a wedding date, put a deposit on the wedding hall, sent out invitations, and reserved the services of a member of the clergy. The groom is usually candid about coming home to save money to get married. If possible, he would like to set up house without using family rejects for furniture. This desire is laid directly at the feet of his parents. One groom put it this way: "We who grew up in affluent homes were taught to appreciate good quality things. We've always heard, 'Nothing but the best for you, darling.' If we're the wool set earning a polyester income, we come home to save up for the best."

A bride also gives lip service to mercenary intents. She's ostensibly home to accumulate a nest egg for her own nest. If parents scratch the surface of these gold-plated brides- and grooms-to-be, they see another reason they came home. They want to spend time with their parents before giving up their childhood.

This is easy to believe. Sometimes, it does not look as if a prospective bride and groom are saving for their future. Budget items include flying lessons, ski weekends, and the accumulation of assets such as gold jewelry. Yet, Lenny managed to save $6,000 during his eighteen-month engagement; Laura, $4,000 in eight months; and Betsy, in two years, an undisclosed amount considered adequate enough to furnish an apartment. Feeling financially and emotionally secure, the to-be-marrieds rarely extend their stays unless intermission gives them a different perspective on the mate they have chosen.

Jenny, a sparkling twenty-four-year-old, broke her engagement after she returned to doting parents. "I realized he was super critical," she said. "Picky, picky. I'll stay here until I meet someone who makes me feel special."

The psychosocial moratorium is applauded by social workers on the basis that it is good for a kid to take time off from the tactics of separation when he or she uses the time constructively. "If the kid is not depressed or passive, something wonderful is going on inside of him," said social worker Carol Olson. "In a normal case, he will use the time to further his own development, and you can see a change in a year or so. There's a clarity of purpose and movement as he becomes his own person on his own terms."

Here's another rub. Unseen by adult-age children parents, too, have been in the midst of scene and costume changes. Some of the changes have been subtle enough to go unnoticed when the kids were home for short visits. Others may have been dramatic but did not affect the kids while they lived on their own. An intermission with family is different from an intermission of actors in a dressing room. The kids often leave the stage just when their parents are answering their own curtain calls. The kids can find themselves taking time out with a cast of characters different from what they expect.

Part Three

The Old Folks at Home

The ideal mother, like the ideal marriage, is a fiction.

Milton R. Sapirstein

7

Surprise! Mommy Is Daddy's Girl

It may seem coincidental that the only vowel in the word *child* is *I.* Yet, at certain stages of human development the only *I* seems appropriate. It corresponds with a pubescent state of mind. At puberty the "I-me" syndrome is particularly evident. The child finds so much to be fascinated by in the mirror.

During this period of rapid physical growth, the bathroom mirror seemed to reflect daily changes. Boys grew taller, broader, and hairier as nature sent them adult equipment. Away from the mirror, girls aroused new feelings. They had grown taller, hippier, curvier, and they knew it. They, too, had stood before bathroom mirrors. If, for a moment, they forgot about their advancement toward physical and sexual maturity, the comments of perceptive adults served as reminders. Each can be summed up in the cliché, "You look so grown-up, I hardly recognize you."

Once the young people had all the adult equipment, they worried about what to do with it. The male, now man-size, was expected to tackle "man-sized" tasks as was his female counterpart. Sent to college for their own good, they were goaded to learn and graded on performance. Linked to a social group for their own good, they were rated on looks and personality. Generally, they were "fives" who strived to be "tens." The pressure to appear successful continued on

75

short visits home. Parents assured them, "We'd love you even if you were a dummy," and then judged their progress (or lack of progress) in the classroom and on the dating scene. Feeling the eyes of the world upon them, the male began to believe the earth revolved around the son and the female believed she was the sun.

Continually self-conscious, they rarely perceived changes in others unless these changes affected them. While they were away at school, parents, in particular, remained fixed the way they were last seen. Moms were not quite immobilized in their minds like Whistler's portrait of his mother seated in a chair. Nor were dads congealed in time looking like Robert Young playing "Father Knows Best." But the grown kids retained mental pictures showing their parents in a way it seemed good to perceive them.

"These are frozen perceptions," said Dr. Robert Mark, an assistant professor in the School of Medicine at Northwestern University and the coordinator of Consultation and Community Services of the Center for Family Studies, Chicago. "They stem from childhood and probably got stuck at the beginning of the adolescent rebellion.

"The kid away at school, in particular, needs to see parents unchanged to affirm the rate of his own growth, to reassure himself he is becoming an adult or individual. By seeing his parents as static, he can confirm how far along he has come."

In other words, parents are a landmark from which grown children can measure the distance they have covered. If the landmark moves, they lose their marker. In instances rare enough to be mentioned, parents continue to match the frozen perceptions begun in children's adolescence. Avis's physical description of her mom and dad was Mutt and Jeff. "He's so tall, and she's so short," said the literal-minded daughter. "I saw myself as middle-size, and that didn't change. I stayed the same height at college as when I left home." But Avis grew in a way that softened another epithet for her folks—the advice givers.

In high school, parents were rarely the topic of conversation. Therefore, Avis had no way of comparing other parents to hers. When mom and dad advised her "for her own good," she would become upset, and what rankled the most was they were always right. "But at college," Avis said, "I realized some parents couldn't care less about their kids. They pushed them to study harder, to get better grades. My close friend was on the verge of a nervous breakdown, and her folks wouldn't get off her back. Seeing how other children were treated made me appreciate my folks more."

In reverse, Dody altered her anger toward mom while away at school by amplifying the positive aspects of the woman's character and allowing the negatives to fade away. Years of complying with mom's habits had engraved the image of an "excellent, organized homemaker." In retrospect, Dody appreciated the sense of order characterizing the household and "forgot mom had made every day seem the same. I didn't want to admit that her regimented attitude used to make me mad. That would imply I wanted her to change, and then how would I know if I had become more flexible?"

Most commonly, grown children would rather accept their own need to grow than contemplate transformation in their parents. Dody preferred to adapt to a situation rather than see a loving parent deviate from a familiar role. "The kid away from home maintains an image of mom and dad relative to the way they treated him," Dr. Mark said. "In a family system there's a tendency to create a lot of habits over a period of years. Sometimes a kid can feel displaced or abandoned if he thinks a parent is going through her own change."

Chances are mom, more than dad, was making changes while the kid was away, especially if the child was the last child to go. Without live-in children, the erstwhile family circle was open to new ideas. Alone with dad, mom has been known to redirect her energies to restoring romance to a marriage. Kids are not the only ones with frozen perceptions. Mom's self-image may have gotten stuck at young, attractive wife with outside interests. Most often, she takes it off ice by streamlining her figure, updating her hairdo, revamping her wardrobe, or working part-time. Without a child's immediate needs to satisfy, the emphasis no longer has to be on her child. She can choose to spend time and money to satisfy herself.

The perception of mom that Gerry, a daddy's girl, took away to college was "a plump lady with wispy hair who wore baggy slacks and sweaters. Her hands were always at the end of a broom, a spatula, or a frying-pan handle. If I picture mom outside the house, she is carrying bags of groceries from the car. She is a comfortable kind of mother, more interested in how her daughters look than how she does."

In the interval: Gerry's mom became a part-time receptionist at a beauty shop and realized there were other ways to live. "I had never worked during our marriage," Pat said. "I enjoyed playing wife. I cooked and baked and entertained before the girls came along. When they arrived, I cooked and baked and shopped for them.

Somewhere along the line, I became more mother than wife.

"Who had time to look in the mirror with three growing daughters around? If I did, I was convinced I looked the same as I did before my small bones got hidden under fat. Not until the girls left did I think about the way my husband might be seeing me. And I decided to do something about it—fast."

The result: A petite woman with a pixielike hairdo, who, if she happens to be at home, will let Gerry in. In addition to working, Pat goes along on her husband's business trips when her job permits. They spend weekends away with other couples without worrying about leaving a child at home. "The only schedule I work around is my husband's business hours," Pat said. "Our relationship is back to where it was before we had kids."

Had Gerry noticed her mom's metamorphosis on short visits home? "Just enough to borrow my clothes and look put out when my husband refers to me as 'gorgeous,'" Pat remembered.

Other children take away a more exciting image of mom by picking out a specific action and convincing themselves it is general behavior. The frozen perception of drama student Van was of "a glamorous hausfrau who served dinner by candlelight even when she was due on stage at a local theater that night."

"I don't know where he got that idea," Van's mom said. "I may have done it once or twice for his birthday but never as a regular routine." True, she kept a self-made promise to sit down to dinner with Van every night regardless of her acting schedule. "Van was such a domestic soul, I enjoyed catering to him," Linda said. "Besides, he was our only child."

In the interval: She and his dad overhauled their way of life. She gave up acting. He gave up his sales territory. In a joint decision, they sold the house "too big for two" and sank the profits into an art gallery committed to shopping mall hours. "We work nights and weekends," Linda said, "but we're both kind of arty and love working together."

The result: Cooking is something Van's mom did when he came home to visit. Alerted to his arrival, she prepared meals ahead of time and kept them frozen until his homecoming. "But on a regular basis, this would drive me nuts," she said.

Housekeeping habits are also subject to change when the last child leaves home. The sense of urgency to fight dust or keep up the laundry sometimes leaves with the child. Eleanor's perception of her mom: "Amazing! She could work full-time as a buyer and keep up a household routine. She gave us a real sense of security. It was like living with a human calendar. If she was washing, it was Tuesday. If we ate meatloaf, it was Thursday, and if she had gone shopping, it was Saturday."

In the interval: Eleanor's mom became more flexible, no longer driven by guilt to prove a working mother can be as satisfactory as a stay-at-home mother. Routine flew out the window. In fact, Carolyn once came to the point of writing *dust!* on a gritty buffet as a reminder to clean it.

The result: Carolyn has no desire to turn back the clock. Evenings, she steps out with her husband to dinner or to a show. Or she spends them propped up in bed reading if that suits her. When Eleanor makes brief visits home, she keeps a modicum of routine. "But darned if I'll go back to it full-time," she said.

Along with an image of mom, grown children usually take away a definite picture of home. Lolita saw her house as "a great one to grow up in." The frozen perception was that "mom was an easygoing housekeeper who preferred working outside the home to cleaning. She never said, 'Take your feet off the couch' or 'Wipe them on the mat.' We had the run of the place. Who worried about having friends in? Mom didn't notice if we got something dirty or broke it."

In the interval: The financial situation in Lolita's home changed. "My husband began to make a mint," her mom Geraldine said, "and he made me stop working. It had something to do with his tax bracket and my earnings going to Uncle Sam."

The result: All of Geraldine's energies were poured into the house. She was a late-blooming domestic engineer. Each room was completely redecorated, and for an outside diversion, she enrolled in a gourmet cooking class. "I'm having a ball," she said. "Our social life expanded because I'm always having people over to show off the place and my cooking. The kids? They're so busy running in and out when they stay over you'd think it was the same sloppy house. I grit my teeth when they leave things around. I thought one would faint when I said, 'Wipe those fingerprints off the refrigerator.' "

In terms of an earthquake, these changes might score one on the Richter scale. But to the kid who has left one type of parent or home and comes back for an extended stay to other kinds, the score could be six—a real shaker. "A kid doesn't understand why these changes had to be made," Dr. Mark said. "He wants the parent or household recast into the old mold, and he tries to draw the family into the old pattern."

Upon occasion, the change may not be visible like a "before" and "after" mom or a refurbished house. It may be intrinsic. Judd's dad mellowed. His son's frozen perception was of "a real macho man who ruled mom with an iron hand. She couldn't make a date with friends without asking him first."

In the interval: When Jeff, the last of four children, left, his mom felt useless. "Like I was floating in space without knowing where to land," Florence said. Without a by-your-leave, she applied for a job in a furniture store and got it.

The result: Jeff's dad gave her "hell" for six months. "It was a blow to my ego. It took away from my image as a provider, and my pals gave me a lot of flak about having a working wife," he explained. "Then I realized she had done right. She wasn't turning into a nag like a lot of other women with nothing to do. We get along great now. I even let her visit an out-of-town girlfriend without me."

The marriage seems to be flourishing under the new terms. It is likely Jeff will be able to weather the sight of his dad helping in the kitchen or taking his mom to a ballet, acts he fought against while Jeff was growing up. It is another matter for a grown child to come home to warring parents if his perception of their relationship has been tight-knit. The picture Billy took away to school was that "they were so considerate of each other. Dad would call if he was coming home late, and if he didn't, mom would worry. She would wait up for him and tell us to leave them alone together. Sure, they'd argue, but dad was always making a pass at her in front of us kids."

In the interval: A problem kept hidden from the children came out into the open. Billy's dad, an episodic drinker, shortened the time between sprees and was admitted to an alcoholic treatment center to dry out. Billy's younger brothers and sister living at home saw their father black out and smelled his sour breath. Away at school, Billy could only intellectualize the symptoms.

The result: Billy's mom, pushed beyond her endurance, issued an ultimatum to her husband when he came out. "One more binge, and we'll leave you," she recalled saying. Humiliated because his wife did not keep the secret from the kids, Billy's dad began to snipe at her. She snipes back. The younger kids look forward to leaving home.

Divorce also hovers in Chuck's home. His impression of home was of "such a close family, people envied us." He toned down his mother's pigheadedness to "a strong will" and his father's sarcasm to "a biting wit." The overall picture was an affluent version of television's "The Waltons."

In the interval: The two high school children left at home think they ought to be wearing referee shirts and avoiding their parents' company. In private, they refer to the battling pair as the Bicker Brothers. Invariably, they are asked to take sides.

The result: Chuck's dad has made it clear he is only staying until the younger children leave for college. Chuck's mom fights bouts of depression. "It's been a volatile marriage," she said. "But this is a hell of a stage of life to think about going it alone." Away at school, Chuck dismisses his brothers' description of the relationship as an exaggeration.

Even if home-ing pigeons will reenter families in which the status quo of routine, residence, and marriage have been maintained, they will be dealing with other forms of change. Human evolution cannot be held back. Mom may let her gray hair grow out from under the dye and sometimes "talk old" to be reassured she is still considered young. Dad may give up singles tennis because it is too tiring, and the old family pet may have to be put to sleep. A younger sibling will have gone through puberty and looked in the bathroom mirror, too.

The perception of his little sister kept by Bob throughout four years of college was "the little kid who idolized me. Before I left, I gave her a sweatshirt stamped *12* on her twelfth birthday. I always think of her biking alongside me as I jog."

In the interval: Now a fully developed young woman, Bob's little sister is self-conscious about sprinting from down the block to hug Bob as she used to do. Worries about getting into college, finding a summer job, and being asked to the homecoming dance absorb her time and thoughts.

The result: She is no longer the "lovable little puppy" content to trail after a big brother—unless he belongs to some other sister.

Catalysts for other forms of change in the people who will let in the home-ing pigeon are shifts in career, values, or opinions based on disappointment. Lynn's father was a gung ho organization man when she left home. She came back to someone struggling with a small business. Ted left a clergyman father and returned to a real estate salesman railing against organized religion. Diane said good-bye to a divorced mother with strict sexual standards and said hello to a swinging divorcée. Adjusting gradually to these changes on a day-to-day basis while living at home would have been difficult. But finding a radical change can be difficult to handle. Parents and child are both in a critical state.

Frozen perceptions may be a comfortable way for grown children to take their families and home to the outside world. Unfortunately, these perceptions leave children open to disappointment if the *I* in *child* has blinded them to seeing the development of others. In the sixties the kids told their folks, "Times have changed" when they moved out. Now it's the kids' turn to hear that line when they move back in.

8

Roll Call—Mom Answers "Absent"

By the time grown children resume living at home, they and their parents are moving in different directions. While one sees adolescence passing, the other sees obsolescence approaching. To the child, time seems infinite. To the parent, time seems short.

Generally, mom is the hardest hit by a sense of mortality. All the wrong people seem to be getting younger. Storeclerks are her children's age, and candidates for public office run in jogging suits. Whatever happened, she wonders, to the motherly saleswoman who fitted her first bra or presidents like Franklin Delano Roosevelt who projected a fatherly image. Mom does not want to dwell on it. Were they really old at the time, or was she just younger then?

A critical look in the mirror offers no consolation. Mom's face is losing the battle against gravity. One mom described herself this way: "If I was a car, they'd recall me." The most disturbing sight to contemplate, however, is signs of old age in her parents. They are the shield between mom and the inevitable.

"I always perceived my mother as a vibrant working woman," said Mary, fifty-three, "but since she retired five years ago and moved into a senior citizens' building, I see a drastic change. I want her back as she was."

Mary's children want her back as she once was, too. They refuse to admit she has crossed the middle line of life. In particular, they fight her spoken need to manage a smaller house. Five sons and two daughters use the portals of the twelve-room house as a revolving door while switching jobs and apartments. The question they ask among themselves is "Where will we go if she sells the house?" Mary's reply is to keep it. "There'd be no place for the kids to come back to if I took an apartment," she said.

Each has come home at different times and sometimes they've arrived together. In exasperation, Mary has threatened to change the lock on the front door. One day, she hired a locksmith to replace a broken knob. Her son, arriving at two in the morning, was astounded. His house key did not fit. Half-seriously he said, "I knew she was going to lock us out eventually, but I couldn't believe she went ahead and did it."

A new house key is a minor change compared to the change in Mary since she realized her own mother was growing old. Once Mary was a full-time homemaker. These days, she runs out to do as she pleases. "The kids are old enough to fend for themselves," she said. "Keeping busy is my salvation."

In addition to taking a morning job as a teacher's aide, Mary spends two afternoons a week as a docent in the reptile house of Brookfield Zoo near Chicago. Two more afternoons are spent at the Lighthouse, where she works with blind, retarded people. An avid Chicago Cubs fan, she watches them train every spring in Scottsdale, Arizona. Recently, she took off to Africa to see the animals she admires in their natural habitat. "I've made my time pretty much my own," she said. "My husband doesn't mind. It's better than getting hung up on a towel problem. The five boys now living at home use three a day. That adds up to a lot of laundry by the end of the week."

The value of time, now considered finite, has become doubly precious. After twenty-seven years of keeping track of seven children, Mary has reversed roles. When her sons inquire, "Where were you?" or "When will you be back?" Mary answers, "That's my business." It is her way of saying, according to clinical psychologist Dr. Rosalie Kirschner, "Don't ever forget I'm a person."

How do Mary's children react? The one who most recently graduated from college said, "It's not a home anymore. It's a frat house with an absentee housemother."

In other large families, mom still has younger children at home and finds it harder to relinquish her role as caretaker. "My life hasn't changed since the older ones went to college" is the typical comment. "I have three more at home." In still other families, grown children are expected to return if they have finished their education and are single. "I wouldn't know how to cook for less than five children," said Italian-speaking Rosa through her son Lenny, who acted as translator. "They got to come back. We are Italian. Very old world. Very old-fashioned.

"There are no problems. They save money. It costs them nothing to live here. Yes, ma'am, I take care of the laundry. I prepare the food. I make two dinners, sometimes more. Kids work different hours. How else they going to eat?"

Home seems the same to Lenny except that one sister is married, but she is there every Sunday for dinner. He considers the setup "a good deal." He has already saved about $12,000 to get married. Although he has an accounting degree, he entered his father's florist business when he realized he was never going to be a great accountant. His mother, he said, reared him to be practical. "To do what's best for him," Rosa said after he repeated his words in Italian. "Me, I'm happy. Soon I have the grandchildren."

Looking forward to grandchildren is a way of looking forward to immortality, states Dr. Kirschner. In another sense, keeping to the old pattern does a lot of good for the child according to Marijean Suelzle, an assistant professor in the department of sociology at Northwestern University, Evanston, Illinois. "Why move out on your own and be independent and lonely when you have a family situation to walk into?" she asked. "For the parents, it's a way of providing a dowry for a young person."

Greek-born Helena, reared in the old tradition, used to feel that a child should come back home. Now she believes the homecoming depends on whether the child returns as a family member or as a freeloader. The way her neighbor lives arouses Helena's envy. "She never cooks," said Helena, who has lived in Detroit for the past twenty-eight years. "In the morning I see her going out with friends. At dinnertime, she steps out with her husband. In my house, every night the dinner must be ready, prepared from soup to dessert, and all my kids like this or don't like that."

Within a three-month period two grown kids rejoined the family composed of four children and two adults: a daughter saving for a trip to Spain and a son who gave up his apartment to become coowner of an airplane. Day in and day out Helena seems to be picking up possessions they drop around the house, doing laundry to the extent of ironing jeans at their request, shopping for special food and rushing home to have dinner ready for one at four thirty, the others at five thirty, and for her husband at seven. "They won't even carry up the laundry basket," she said. "They just take the clothes they need and leave the basket standing there. Enough is enough. I don't need the money, but I'm going to take a job."

Lurking beneath the resentment, according to Dr. Kirschner, is the question, "What has there been for me all these years?" Bitterness builds up in a parent who never asks anything back for the outlay of energy to children. "But that's what life's all about," Dr. Kirschner said. "Family members should pitch in to alleviate each other's burdens not add to them." If not, a mother may finally say, "I'll use the time I have left for me," and, by making herself absent, give the kids the message, "I find it difficult to make time for you." Sometimes the resentment is verbalized, and she asks, "What am I? Your maid and laundress?" Dr. Kirschner's advice is "Don't wait until the kid initiates the idea to help. Ask for it."

If mom is jarred by the thought of her own mortality, she is terrified of being a widow. As the nest empties, dad becomes her focal point. She watches his diet, encourages him to exercise, and reads enough articles on the subject of hypertension and cholesterol to talk like an authority. The grown child who has left is likely to return to meals lower in salt, fat, and calories. A weight-conscious child might appreciate them, but not a hearty eater whose perception of home includes a refrigerator packed with fattening goodies. "My biggest problem with Sara was eating habits," a mother said. "She's a tiny girl weighing ninety-five pounds who wants more than three meals a day. She was always looking for a snack after the ten o'clock news. After getting my husband's weight down, I didn't appreciate Sara encouraging him to eat more. We went up to our room at nine o'clock so he wouldn't be tempted."

A more weighty problem is picking up the pieces of a broken marriage after the grown children have left. A mom who has given twenty years or more to rearing a family can be gripped with fear if she thinks it has all been thrown away on children.

Sometimes different views on child rearing hurt the marital relationship. In Tamara and Ivan's marriage, she was the lenient parent, and he was the strict one. "He had a sledgehammer approach," said the forty-three-year-old woman who had been a bride at seventeen and a mother at eighteen. "At the slightest sign of misbehavior he would start slugging even when the three kids were teenagers. Behind his back I'd comfort the kids and side with them. By the time they left home, Ivan and I had grown apart."

In fact, during their twenty-second year of marriage, Tamara took Ellen, their high schooler, with her and left Ivan for three months. It was common knowledge in the small town that twice a week during that period she cleaned his house, brought over his groceries, and went to bed with him. "We never stopped loving each other," Tamara said. "I think he was jealous of my love for the kids."

When Ellen left, Tamara and Ivan went to a marriage counselor and through concerted effort worked out their problems. "It was easier to do when we were alone," she said. Two years later, Ellen returned home to live after a fire destroyed all her belongings. By then Tamara and Ivan had grown as close as two burrs on a thistle. "In a way, it was wonderful to see," Ellen said. "You could feel they had gotten things together. They didn't have to work to be nice to each other. But their closeness made me feel like an intruder.

"It's the way you feel around newlyweds. They were demonstrative, and you knew they would rather be alone. I was very uncomfortable. They never said I was in their way. But I felt I had lost a mother."

Ellen's solution? She took a nursing job with hours opposite to those her father worked. She does not come in contact with her parents when they are together except for lunch on Sunday. Even though she was reared in the house she lives in, she cannot call it home. "I feel like a guest. When I left, I felt like a daughter," she said.

Like other couples who revive a faltering marriage when the children leave, Tamara and Ivan innocently shut out Ellen from the family unit. But if there is anything left of any marriage when a husband and wife live alone, there is a tendency to focus most of their attention upon each other. Numerous women have described the initial time after the children leave as "a honeymoon when sex became spontaneous again," or as "going back to how we felt when we were first married." What Ellen sensed was a renewed sexual interest between her parents. "The fact that you become closer and give each other emotional support increases the physical activity," Dr. Kirschner said. "Alone, you renew the habit of sitting next to one another and indulging in playfulness. With no one around you don't have to wait to have sex until late at night when you're tired. It can be anywhere in the house at any time. The only drawback is maybe your back can't take it."

In some rocky marriages, however, the absence of children magnifies, to a discontented mom, how far apart she has grown from her husband. Variables keeping a couple from moving toward one another can include serious money or health problems or irreconcilable personality differences.

Naomi, at age fifty-two, feels burdened by all three. She said, with a trace of bitterness in her voice, "I feel life is passing me by. I've worked since day one of my marriage, and I'll probably work as long as I live. I don't think I'll ever feel comfortable about money. Every time we take a step ahead, we get kicked in the teeth. We have some security. A four-family house. But it's not worth much.

"We never go on vacation. I get a paid vacation, but I take it at home—alone. My husband likes to sit and watch TV. He'll only spend money on necessities. Never on a birthday card. A present? You're kidding. For our anniversary, he fixed the dryer.

"We're working people. But I'd like to live better, like going someplace. We can afford a movie. You know, I don't look forward to spending the weekend with him."

Compounding the sense of life passing her by is her fear of cancer. Thus far, Naomi has been "lucky." Tumors removed from her breast have been benign. But worry has taken a toll on her looks. A neighbor pointed out, "She's gained a lot of weight. Food is her solace. Not that she doesn't keep herself well groomed. She just doesn't look the same."

Before Elliott, her only son, came home from military service, which enabled him to go to college free, Naomi had tried to reconnect to her husband. The result was he was willing to help in the house but not to step out of it unless to go to work or to shop. With Elliott back home, her emotional burdens have been somewhat lifted. She confides her problems to her son and enjoys his thoughtfulness. "I laugh a lot with my son," Naomi said. "And he teases me by saying I'm his girl. His relationship with his father? That man would rather watch 'Loveboat' than talk to him or me."

From Elliott's point of view, he has come home to a person in need. "She's not the feisty mom I remember leaving two years ago," the sensitive young man said. "She caters to my dad instead of hollering to get a rise out of him. Our apartment looks nicer. But mom looks bad."

In a way Naomi, like other unfulfilled wives, is behaving as if she was a widow or divorcée by relying on a grown child to satisfy needs unmet by a spouse. "In a sense it's selfish," said Dr. Kirschner, "to ask a child to assume responsibility for emotional support that should be given by a mate. A woman in this situation needs the child more than he needs her."

Martha, a widow, had tried to do without her daughter Eileen's support when her husband suffered a fatal heart attack two years ago. Eileen, her oldest child, who had been living in Colorado, returned home for the funeral and offered to stay. "She had been ready to break away before her father died," Martha said, "and I told her not to come home for me. Then, I also had a teenage son and my mother living at home. I felt I could manage."

As sometimes happens, death struck again that year. Martha's mother died, and Eileen came home without being asked. Martha recalled that Eileen had been a big help and very supportive. At the same time, Eileen was more affected by the double deaths than Martha realized. "She took over my mother's room and began to have nightmares. Little by little, we redecorated and the bad dreams started to subside."

Having gone through the worst, Martha has come to terms with her sense of mortality and has begun "to live." Supporting herself and her teenage son, now in college, is a necessity, and she "lucked out" into a field she enjoys—interior decorating. The work keeps her busy days, several nights a week, and sometimes on weekends. She and Eileen see each other on the run. "I came home to a widow," Eileen said, "and when I get married this June, I'll be leaving a career girl. We're not so much mother and daughter as we are friends."

Unlike some of the dramatic changes mom undergoes when she asks herself, "If not now, when?" dad's changes are usually less noticeable as he pursues his "last chance." To begin with, a child is accustomed to seeing dad leave for work and does not expect him to provide personal care. But occasionally, there is a change in dad's personality as he makes a last attempt to hold on to youth. He may wear his shirt unbuttoned to the navel to show off a hairy chest. Or he may exhibit new-found business success by buying a car priced the same as a house once cost. If he is single, he may start to talk to a son like a fellow swinger. But generally the most noticeable new trait in a married dad is a new sense of possessiveness toward his wife. "It was good to have my bride back" was the consensus of husbands who were pleased to be done with the child-rearing years so they could enjoy a wife's full attention.

Often dad is the agent who turns mom into an absentee mother. In some cases, he brings her into his business, and they get into the habit of going directly from work to a restaurant for dinner. They may start the day by eating breakfast out and at midday grab a sandwich alone or together. At home, the refrigerator becomes a storehouse for dad's cigars and mom's moisturizer.

Should dad's work entail travel, he sees no reason to leave a nonworking wife alone in an empty house. Taking her along pleases him, too. "Staying at a posh place by yourself loses its glamour fast," a corporate executive said. "When you come down to it, any motel room is a lonely room to return to in the evening." In other instances, dad includes mom at business dinners or asks her to make dinner for out-of-town customers. By the time a grown child comes home, dad has become accustomed to having mom at his side whether he is away from home or there.

Dad's new attitude becomes evident particularly if it interferes with a home-ing pigeon's expectations of mom. "My son expects physical care," an optometrist said, "and that puts additional demands on my wife. After thirty-two years of marriage, she's entitled to do less laundry, cooking, and cleaning." A lawyer forbade his wife to clean his daughter's room and insists the young woman help with the dishes on the grounds that "it isn't fair for a parent to be burdened." In the same vein, a retired pharmacist complained that his son insisted upon substantial meals in place of the light ones usually served. "There's no reason for him to make extra work for my wife," he said.

While a home-ing pigeon expects home life to be unchanged from the way it was when he or she was growing up, dad wants to keep it the way it has become since the children left. But as mom well knows as she turns the corner of her child-oriented years, few things remain static. Not even the looks of the physical household. As family members grow older, the roost changes, too.

9

Someone's Sleeping in My Bed

"I'm in" is a victory cry. It connotes admission and signifies acceptance. In terms of grown children, "I'm in" means they have met the criteria of a college, an honor society, a team, or the person they have been dying to date. A psychic bonus underlies the elation. "Getting in" gives them a sense of belonging. Where do you go? Who do you see? What do you do? Inclusion in units larger than themselves helps provide the answers.

Belonging gives the rookie adult a fixed location, an opportunity for recognition, and an outlet for input. A sense of self-importance ties up the package of admission and belonging. Who can resist taking a short ego trip on the thought, "They want me. They need me."

Similar dynamics are at work in the family system. But there is less elation. Having been an integral part of a family, the grown child takes home for granted. How can it change? How can being the oldest, the middle, or the youngest offspring change? Sleeping quarters have been either the large, middle-size, or small bedroom, and were always modified by a name. Every one had a particular chair at the dinner table. Closets are filled with childhood scrapbooks, diplomas, and trophies. Away from home, the child may stake claims on other places and on other people. Yet home, the child is sure, awaits, the clock hands set at the hour and minute of the rite of leaving. The privileges of a position in the family are inviolate, the home-ing pigeon thinks.

Odds are, time has tampered with home. Remember the story of *Goldilocks and the Three Bears* and what happened when the bears stepped out? Goldilocks ate the baby bear's porridge, broke his chair, and was asleep in his bed when he returned. And baby bear had been gone only a short time. Imagine what can happen while grown children are living elsewhere.

There is no question about a parent having the right to alter living quarters. "But it is not necessary to make changes you know will upset a child who is expected home," said Phyllis Warren, who uses reality therapy in marriage and family counseling. "As a family member, he has the right of input. He is no different than the rest of us who resist change when it threatens our sense of order."

Sameness resembles security in varying degrees for different people. There is the tyke who objects when someone sits in his place or when someone other than his father sits in daddy's place. A sleeper invariably has his "side of the bed," and a moviegoer knows where he "likes to sit." Even in an exercise class composed of grown women, each one has "her spot" and feels outrage when it is taken.

Home-ing pigeons are particularly sensitive to any change at home that affects their status. "Home is the base of stability," said clinical psychologist Dr. Eugene Southwell. "When a kid returns, he wants to see the things he grew up with." "If not," according to Lawrence Berson, ACSW, executive director of Family Services Association of DuPage County, Illinois, "he feels a sense of betrayal. It's hard for a youngster in a nuclear family to realize he is no longer the center of his parents' universe. If his room is no longer his room, he smarts under the question, 'How can they do this to me?' "

The consensus of other counselors is that "if he is not consulted about major changes, at least advise him of them before he comes home." Otherwise, the grown child can rightfully feel, "I'm not an important part of my family anymore. I've been depreciated." In other words, prepare the grown child for Goldilocks to prevent the feeling of being shut out when a home-ing pigeon finds someone else sleeping in a childhood bed.

"The consequence for parents is an argumentative youngster. At his age, he is too sophisticated to ask, 'Why haven't you preserved my way of life?' Instead, he fights back in other ways. He withdraws, exhibits aloofness, or criticizes anything the parents say or do," Berson said.

Margaret, a twenty-four-year-old speech therapist, was speechless when she returned to Sunnyvale, California, to spend the year before her marriage at home. Throughout a two-year sojourn in San Diego, she had kept her parents up-to-date on her career and social life. Margaret assumed they had been as forthright in their news about home. "I love my parents," Margaret said. "They taught me well enough to enable me to go out on my own and make it. I wanted to be with them before I took the irrevocable step of setting up a new household. I could hardly wait to move back into my old room among my old things and be a daughter again for a while."

Surprise! A Swedish exchange student had been given Margaret's domain. Margaret was asked if she would mind using the living-room couch as a bed until the student left in three months. "I certainly did mind," Margaret said. "A stranger was in my room. An outsider was more important than me, and I was totally unprepared for her presence."

In the same way, Bud's feeling of importance was diminished upon his return. He had no inkling his parents volunteered his empty room for use by runaways in need of temporary shelter. "I came home," Bud said, "and there was this kid on my turf. A family member, yes. A stranger, no."

Behind her folks' back, Margaret found another home for the Swedish student. "My folks were furious," she recalled. "They said I dislodged her. What about me? I was dislodged, too." Bud, while his family was out, moved the runaway's possessions into the room he had been allocated. "My mom sided with the kid, who didn't want to be moved out," Bud said. "Well, I didn't want to be moved either." In retrospect, Bud and Margaret were ashamed of their preemptive behavior. Yet both were sure they would not have "had a fit" if they had been consulted, notified, or forewarned about strangers in their rooms.

Bud said, "I felt as if I had been written off." Margaret admitted she reacted to feeling hurt. She said, "If I had been given time to think about it, I might have taken the girl's presence as a compliment. With me gone, maybe my parents needed another kid around."

In a comparable situation, Dale, a twenty-four-year-old accountant, was amenable to the use of her room by a three-year-old niece waiting to become a big sister. But she was appalled that the little girl had been given her Barbie dolls as playthings and ruined them. "I never expected to play with them again, but a Barbie doll is a collectible today. Do you know what one's worth?" said investment-minded Dale. "Besides, they were mine to give away, not mom's. She couldn't understand why I raised such a fuss." Another collector, Joseph, had expected a younger brother to move into his room while he was gone. A natural sequence of seniority had been established in the household. But Joseph did not expect his coin collection to be pilfered. Someone, who remained silent, had used the old coins as money. "I left them for safekeeping. Everyone knew that," Joseph said. "I felt violated, like you do when someone steals something out of your school locker or swipes your hubcaps." Joseph posted a red-and-white sign on his new room, KEEP OUT. THIS MEANS YOU.

Family counselors believe these problems can be prevented. "Before a youngster comes home, or during a visit back, ask him to go through his belongings to decide what he wants to keep or give away," Berson said. "Pack them in cartons marked with his name. Make it clear, however, that what he doesn't select will be subject to your judgment. Also give him your reason for the request. Usually, it's because the remaining family can use the room taken up by his accumulations."

In some families, there is an open understanding that living space will be reshuffled when a child leaves. Under those circumstances, home-ing pigeons may find a new room an inconvenience rather than a catastrophe. Jimmy described his situation in these words: "In our house there is no tenure on bedrooms." The room vacant when he came home to practice-teach was definitely feminine in decor. "I'm putting up with the flowery pink wallpaper and frilly curtains," Jimmy said. "But I keep my friends out of there." Jimmy had no strong sense of turf. He claimed, "I could have slept in a sleeping bag as long as I was home." His friend, Bob, however, has a rigid nature. He came back to his original room redecorated and refurnished as a sign of welcome. Bob's reaction? Distress. "I'd lived with the old furniture since I was a kid," said the computer science major. "And I was used to the old arrangement. I had been able to reach out in the dark and know what I would find. The new stuff took getting used to. I wish my parents had asked me before they went ahead."

Intellectually, he knows that a room is a petty reason for creating friction. Yet Bob couldn't help acting childish when its configuration had been changed without his permission. "He was real nasty about it," his mother said, "just like when he was twelve and we traded in a smaller bike for a bigger one as a surprise. I didn't think we did anything wrong that time either." Dr. Southwell pointed out that there is a lot of regression when a kid comes home. "The best of them go back to old patterns and habits, and problems are sometimes precipitated when they find changes."

Communication is a simple way of forestalling friction, according to Berson. If the youngster is far away, talk over the changes by phone. If he lives close enough, have him come home and discuss it face-to-face. "He'll find all kinds of changes when he comes back to stay," Berson said. "Handling them in increments, instead of all at once, will reduce his outrage."

Sometimes, the grown child most shaken by a new look is the youngster who never felt like number one at home. Aaron was the quiet member of a boisterous Chicago family who kept in touch while he worked in Oregon as a forest ranger. Each letter from the Midwest was a recital of family activities. "I should have felt good. But I didn't," Aaron said. "I felt left out. I was the pea out of the pod."

A project impelling him to go home was the remodeling of the old frame house Aaron had grown up in. Some of the work had been contracted out. The major portion was being done by family members. He had to find out if they had kept a place for him.

The transformation shook up Aaron. Walls had been taken down to turn two bedrooms into a rec room. The dining room had been enlarged, and the attic had been finished to serve as a bedroom for two brothers who wanted to bunk together. He was given a former utility room off the kitchen and what he called the cold shoulder. "Everyone talked about what they had done or what happened when they were doing it. I felt excluded." Formerly a neat and considerate person, Aaron stopped hanging up his clothes and left the bathrooms a mess to the extent of leaving a dirty tub. Each became a cause for family arguments. "The bathroom is sometimes abused to provide an excuse for a fight by people who don't like one another," Phyllis Warren commented. "Leaving it dirty is an open declaration of warfare. It would be a good idea for a family with this problem to sit down together to find out the real reason for the behavior."

Occasionally, children who felt perfectly at home before they left begin to think "I don't fit in" when they return. Sometimes, this has more to do with pitching in than fitting in. Janie, twenty-four, had been excused from household chores while growing up because of a rigorous schedule of dance lessons, rehearsals, and performances. The entire family had supported her emotionally and physically. But when she returned from seeking fame and fortune in New York, everyone was busy leading his or her own life. Meals were eaten on the run, and the washer and dryer were in use all hours of the day and night to accommodate a sudden need for particular items of clothing by working parents and children. "And I shared a bedroom instead of having one of my own," said Janie, who had expected a Prodigal Son welcome with creature comforts supplied. "Home just wasn't home anymore."

On the other hand, her sister Mona fit right back into the family. "Mona pitched right in whenever she had time available," the mother of the two girls said. "We'd come home to find dinner made or the laundry done. And she was a listening ear to Janie, who continually complained that things had changed. I brought up both these kids and can't understand why they're as different as night and day."

Dr. Southwell contends that if a parent-child relationship could be measured, he is sure its tone would be the same throughout a child's life. "I'm certain," he said, "it would be found that the demands of parent and child don't change. Whatever problems existed before a kid left will be resurrected when the kid comes back. After a separation, the behavior is more noticeable."

The basic reason given by parents of grown children for making changes is "We assumed he wouldn't come back." For example, Lana, her husband, and two daughters moved from a five-bedroom house to a three-bedroom house when the two older girls, Betty and Jo, got married. But within a year, Betty returned as a divorcée. Attempts to share a room with one sister and then the other sister failed. "I felt like a displaced person," Betty said. Lana felt terrible. She had not expected Betty to come home. "We fixed up a corner in the rec room furnished with some of the items she brought home. They weren't the greatest accommodations, and we had to curtail the use of the remaining half. But it made no sense to move again," the guilt-ridden mother said.

Betty's father didn't feel he owed his daughter a "damned thing" and berated Lana for her misgivings about having moved. His attitude was that "there is just so much you can do for your child at the expense of yourself."

Another father took a different position. He asked his wife to reconsider turning a spare room into a sewing room "just in case a kid comes back." The compromise was to give the room a dual purpose. Mom furnished it as a sewing room and added an armchair that converted into a bed.

Still other parents, if not forewarned, were at least forearmed. Lucy made it clear to the children living at home that the girls would double up should their brother come back. Countless parents who move to smaller quarters have mentally allocated and physically provided living space for children whom they assumed would return for a short stay. By these means, they tried to ward off the children's feelings of being shut out and their own feelings of being put out.

The adjustments to make room for unexpected home-ing pigeons are often borne by children who never left home. The privacy enjoyed by Selma was disrupted when she had to share her room with her sister. James was coerced to surrender his bigger room to accommodate the belongings his brother brought back. John had to move his darkroom out of a spare bedroom when his sister moved in. A family room used for practice by Frank's rock group became off limits when a brother studying for the bar exam came home. In each instance, home-ing pigeons saw changes. If they thought about it, however, their return also made changes.

There is no question that each child has a different view of home. Some go to college and never return for an extensive stay. Others come home every weekend while they are enrolled at school. For these children, familiar people and a familiar neighborhood are strong pulls. "To them, loving relationships are nourishment," Phyllis Warren said. "Home is sort of a filling station."

But neighborhoods change, too. Cornfields are replaced by shopping centers. Apartment complexes spring up. A two-lane highway becomes a four-lane highway. "Everything smacks of instability," said associate professor Dr. Joyce Nolen. "And the kid had a sense of uncertainty about coming home to begin with. As an adult he thinks he's failed because he doesn't have his own apartment and possibly neither a degree nor a job."

Any uncertainty home-ing pigeons feel about their future is easily aggravated by the appearance of a world moving forward while they seem to be standing still—or worse, people moving forward while they have gone back to square one. Jonathan saw himself in the same position as a beloved grandmother who began rooming with the family while he was away—and he took his frustrations out on her. He related in status to grandma, whom he saw as a dependent. "At first, he closed himself into his room when they were home alone," his mother said. "Now he faces her and aggravates her. I think to deliberately make someone else unhappy, you have to be unhappy yourself. His biggest complaint is no privacy when she's around. What about my privacy with both of them here?"

In the light of home-ing pigeons' reactions to the changes they find at home and the changes they precipitate, the welcome mat, initially out, may be pulled in. Parents are people, not paragons, and they, too, react when they feel their way of life is threatened.

Part Four

Is the Welcome Mat Really Out?

Blessed is he who expects nothing, for he shall never be disappointed.

Alexander Pope

10

Come In—But Remember You're Grown-up Now

When Harriet was a mother of preteens, she wanted to run away from home. She couldn't. Monday was laundry day, and the kids needed clean underwear. Tuesday was taken, too. Den 3 of Cub Scout Pack 54 depended upon her to lead them. Wednesday she drove the school band car pool. Thursday was impossible. One child had an oboe lesson; two others, piano lessons. The weekend was no better. Who would chaperon her daughters' slumber party or take her son to the orthodontist? She dared not leave on Sunday. The kids, given a choice, would abstain from church or religious school. "Besides, I loved my kids," the businessman's wife said. "But I had reached the end of my rope scheduling my days around their needs. I wanted to do something for me."

Social scientists, through the media, assured Harriet that her time would come. In 1979, when Harriet's last child left home, they were still encouraging. As noted in *Dynamic Years* ("Personal Notebook," March–April 1980), two independent studies reported by *Psychology Today* concluded that the best years of a woman's life may be shifting from her twenties and thirties to the years past forty—years her mother had dreaded because the nest would be empty. *Dynamic Years* (a magazine which Harriet's mother read) also noted the results of two decades of study done at the University of Michigan Institute for Social Research. Director Angus Campbell was quoted as saying: "One of the most satisfying times of life is the later period—ages 45, and up—when the children have grown up and left home and the parents are still married and living together." Happily married Harriet agreed and was ready to harvest the thought these and other studies had planted in her head, "When my kids are grown-up, I'll be free."

Harriet helped out at her husband's record store, took continuing education courses in music, saw friends, and didn't feel pressed for time. But "grown-up" is a variable, and her pipe dream of life after forty went up in smoke when her oldest son came back. He looked like a man but had the expectations of a child. "A baby sees himself as the center of the universe," said psychotherapist Dr. Sandra Kahn. "He can't understand that a toy pushed behind the table isn't gone because he can't see it. Later, he learns other concepts and understands that the table is blocking his view.

"But one perception lingers as long as he thinks of himself as a child. It makes no difference that he has been gone for a couple of years. When he comes home to mom, he sees himself as the center of home."

Where did Harriet's man-child put the fortyish woman who, while he was away, had been happier with less—less cooking, less laundry, and less arguing? Back in the same old bind, seething with contradictory feelings about his demands. "I love my son," Harriet said, "but he's a big boy now and should assume responsibility for himself.

"Am I obligated to cook every night for a twenty-four-year-old who eats at 4:00 P.M. because he has a night job?" she asked, preparing his dinner. "Or to do the laundry of a kid who did his own at school?" she grumbled, picking up his sweaty workout clothes to throw into the washing machine. Her husband lent a practiced ear to her complaints and answered with the same question he asked years ago when she drove their son to places he could have reached by bike: "Is this trip necessary?"

Like other mothers who believe in noise abatement, Harriet's answer was yes. "I can't take his accusation that I don't care for him," she said. "My son equates waiting on him with loving him. To keep a modicum of peace, I do what he expects."

The art of manipulation, other mothers suspect, is a course homeing pigeons take in secret. One way or another, mothers are put on the defensive to do their children's chores and to refrain from asking for help with their own tasks. "My two girls who came home don't lift a finger except to manicure a nail," said Celia, who had more time to spend with her husband and less housework while her daughters were away. "They claim they don't help because I wouldn't like the job they do anyway."

Sometimes the home-ing pigeons are solicitous. If Celia is cleaning up what one messed up, the other will invariably say, "Don't mom, it'll only get dirty again," or "Mom, you look tired."

Celia takes the blame for her progeny's behavior: "It's my fault. These were my beautiful girls who were going to grow up to become everything I was not. I catered to them, supported their interests, told them how wonderful they were. If they took a false step in a dance class, I never mentioned it. So why shouldn't they walk around the house like privileged people?"

Taking the blame relieves a mother from dealing with home-ing pigeons as young adults. They're still her children, the ones she had to protect from physical and emotional harm. Internally, she believes she fulfilled her role. Didn't she keep medicines and cleaning supplies out of their reach and teach them how to cross the street? Didn't she praise their virtues and downplay their faults? What more could she have done? The answer, perhaps, is less.

"If we don't cut through our need to protect, we can damage the child," said Dr. Kahn. "There was an attempt by this generation to make the kid feel positive about himself. This was all right as long as it was done with honest reinforcement. But it's harmful to tell a kid, for instance, that he looks like an Adonis when he actually has the shape of a blimp. At any age, deal with him so he can see what he really is."

Still other moms take self-centered kids off the hook by blaming their behavior on heredity. He's stingy like Uncle John. She's vain like Aunt Helen. The mother of a kid of average intelligence who couldn't hold a job and relied on her for money said, "You can't expect an Einstein if you're not. Genes and chromosomes are important to keep in mind. My son is smarter than me, but heredity plays a big part in what happens to a kid. I had an uncle who couldn't earn a living until he was thirty-five."

Another common lament of mothers is, "I've been too good. That's why my kids expect so much from me." Irene, a good-natured soul, continued to tie her sons' shoelaces long after they'd learned to tie their own. She picked up after them, hung up their clothes, and dashed to school to bring a homework assignment they'd left at home. In time, she ran their errands and typed their themes. "I always felt their time was more important than mine," she said. "They were young and had so much to accomplish."

Were they asked to reciprocate? "I asked nothing for myself," Irene said. "I just wanted them to be achievers and do well in school." Irene had been taught to give without expecting anything back but had passed the lesson down in reverse to her sons.

"If you give to a child without asking in return, you bring him up with unrealistic expectations," said reality therapist Phyllis Warren. "You have a right to expect something back. Respect, at least. You have to be firm about a child's obligations even when he comes home as a young adult. It's not fair to treat him well and let him dump on you."

Irene sees her boys in a new light since they came home. She said they use her as a "welcome mat to wipe their feet on." They treat advice as interference and requests for help as infringements on their time. The eye-opener was their refusal to carry up the laundry from the basement or to take the garbage pails down the driveway when she was recuperating from surgery. "All I wanted," she said, "was to be treated like a mother. Shown consideration. My dog is treated better than me. I was too good, I think, and it's too late to change my ways. I made my bed and have to sleep in it."

At the same time, she has become hostile. "They're not kids anymore. I ask myself, 'What are they doing home?' They come and go like boarders. I've told them, 'Get out,' and they're quiet for a day or two because they have no money to leave. I'm torn apart trying to make them act their age and being afraid they'll go hungry."

Most parents know that home is low on the list of places where grown children want to live after they have been away. In our questionnaire sent in 1979 to fifty recent graduates, they were asked, "Why do you live at home?" Each could have been accused of cribbing. The answers were variations of "My economic situation brought me home."

The young adult–parent relationship often supports the old saw, "No news is good news." "The only times my sons called me when they were living away from home was to cry on my shoulder," Josie said. "When I didn't hear from them, I knew everything was all right."

A mother is somehow able to bear the long-distance indifference. It is preferable to being treated as the villain when the children come home. "I'm the bad guy," said Josie, who relies on a sense of humor to get through trying days with her two home-ing pigeons. "My twenty-year-old sleeps until ten thirty every morning and takes part-time jobs when he needs money. He expects me to tiptoe around the house like a ballerina. Otherwise, I'm accused of waking him on purpose.

"The twenty-four-year-old with two degrees finds more reasons to refuse a job than I have hairs on my head. He's mad at me because I refused to let my husband buy him a $10,000 Jeep to use as a snowplow to earn pocket money. To make it pay off, we'd have to live at the North Pole, and I'm not sure igloos have driveways."

Josie's flippant remarks cover real worries about her boys. "It's not the money we spend on them that bothers me," she said in a more serious vein. "I worry about their future. They're boys, not girls, and have to earn a living. All I can do is stand by and watch them waste their time. They say 'Bug off' when I give advice."

Worry also stalks the mother of a kid with more drive whose expectation of the marketplace seems unrealistic. She sympathizes with the kid's need to make "big bucks." Mother knows it's a competitive world out there and prices are crazy. But she would like to see the kid willing to start out at a pay level lower than she expects and eventually earn a higher salary by proving herself. "It burns up my daughter when I say she wants too much to begin with and doesn't qualify for the high pay she asks," an outspoken mother said. "She claims I'm jealous of the options now open to women. If she was living on her own, she couldn't be that fussy."

At the root of mom's frustration is a sense of helplessness. When the kids were small, she was able to rescue, advise, or comfort them. Now, all they want is a place to park and change for the meter until they get into gear. Other forms of help are vociferously rejected. "A kid doesn't listen to parents anymore," said Lucy, who is thwarted in any attempt to help her son. "He says he knows more than me. Then he makes a boo-boo and runs home for mom to make it all better."

Lucy recalled the night Barry, her older son, appeared unexpectedly at the door. He had been living with a girl he hoped to marry, one Lucy called unstable. "He fell into my arms crying, 'Why did she leave me?' I was heartbroken to see him so crushed. I took him in. There was nothing else I could do.

"Any observation I made enraged him. If I said, 'Good riddance,' he was furious. If I found something about her to praise, he asked, 'Whose side are you on?' If I told him to broaden his social life, he told me to get lost. Finally, I just stood by and let him work it out. My role was to shut up and put up with his moods until they passed."

Family counselors are familiar with Lucy's conflict. "In dealing with a grown child, you're damned if you do and damned if you don't when he comes home," one counselor said. "A little kid fights for control. A young adult fights for power. He doesn't want to hear answers. He wants to give them."

Florence's son Alan brought his bride Lois home after the honeymoon to save on room and board while they looked for jobs. Soon it became clear they considered the house "mom's" when there were chores to be done, and "theirs" when they had company or were home at night. "My husband and I felt like intruders," Florence said. "At night they either tied up the phone or locked themselves in their room. Once, when they had friends over, they asked us to leave." Why did Florence stand for such rude behavior? "What could I say?" she asked. "We were the bad guys without saying anything."

She feels she learned a lesson. She will never let another child come home to live. "Kids feel guilty about dependency," she said, "and cover it by being mean as hell."

To escape the tension in the house, a mother may once more consider running away from home. But she's out of luck again. This time she doesn't have to drive a kid anywhere. A car with a college sticker, however, is blocking her exit from the driveway.

For example, Edith, once referred to as "My Mother, the Car," now describes her driveway as looking like a used car lot. Two home-ing pigeons added their wheels to the two-car family composed of six drivers. The traffic jam gives her mixed feelings. On the one hand, she has to jockey cars (sometimes theirs and their friends') just to run out to the store. On the other hand, she gave up her title due to the extra sets of wheels available to the younger kids. "But it's a can't-win situation," Edith said. "This frees me up except when the kids take both sets of keys and leave a car parked behind me. Then, despite all the means of transportation at hand, I'm stuck at home again."

Sandy, whose daughter hitchhiked around Europe after she was graduated from college, would settle for an overcrowded driveway. Her home-ing pigeon is phobic about getting behind a steering wheel. At seven each weekday morning, Sandy transports the young woman to work and at five each weekday afternoon picks her up.

On the weekends, Sandy and her husband coordinate their errands with the ones their daughter wants to run. Frequently they leave a party early to bring her home. "I thought my chauffeuring days were over when she went away," Sandy said. "Now things are back to where they were."

Della, who never had an envious bone in her body before her son and daughter returned, sees her car as a symbol of being a non-person. Before the two home-ing pigeons owned cars, they took Della's without a "May I, mom?" "But I can't take theirs," she said. "Their attitude reeks of what's mine is theirs, and what's theirs is theirs." She has begun to envy her sister Susan who keeps complete control over her car despite the presence of a grown child. Della interprets the control as keeping an upper hand on her life. To Della, her kids' cars block more than the driveway. They block the freedom of movement she enjoyed while they were gone.

Della's sister Susan refrains from saying, "I told you so." Susan contended that she always tried to give a child lots of love and attention but also demanded respect. When her home-ing pigeon was about three years old, the little girl spilled a bottle of expensive perfume she had been warned not to touch. "I put her across the bed and spanked her," Susan said. "Then I explained to her, 'What's mine is mine and what's thine is thine.' " Even today, the daughter asks before borrowing. "I don't have any complaints about her," Susan said, "and I think I would ask her to move out if I did."

Some mothers get out of the driveway and escape the tension by taking a job. Beverly's daughter had her teenage rebellion at age twenty-one. Although it was the posthippie era, she went barefoot, cut down the values of the home, and was having a sexual affair. "I went back to teaching to avoid facing her," Beverly said, "and was delighted when she left to bum around South America. I was tired of rescuing her even though I tried not to get involved."

The next time Beverly's daughter came home, she was a Jesus freak. "We're Jewish," Beverly said, "but took her in. It didn't occur to me not to. You don't throw out a kid without resources, and hers were zero." The tolerant mother's outside interests let her go through a trying period without being too affected by her daughter's actions. "When I became self-involved," Beverly said, "I wasn't as controlled by her behavior. I have my own values. I feel good about myself, so I wasn't bent out of shape. When she left again, it was like taking off a tight pair of shoes."

But taking a job, in some instances, is just another cause for arguing. Diane, who had worked part-time when her daughter left, took a full-time job when the former airline stewardess returned home. The young woman had decided to go to a commuter college, expected motherly attention, and took her mother's absence from home as a personal affront. "Actually I took the job to help pay for her education," Diane said, "but she can't understand that."

Each way mom turns can be the wrong way when grown children come home expecting to be treated as if they were still the center of her life. A feminist daughter, in fact, before she left might have been indoctrinating mom to ask herself, "Why do I always get stuck with the laundry?" Then she comes home and wants her laundry done.

"If parents and children are alert, which is not usually the case," said clinical psychologist Dr. Eugene Southwell, "they should be able to talk out any problems they encounter after they live together."

A consensus from moms with irascible home-ing pigeons is that after a certain age, kids should leave home. The disadvantage to them is a prolonged childhood. The disadvantage to mom is prolonged motherhood at a time she is ready to direct her energies elsewhere.

A consensus from moms with amenable home-ing pigeons is that parents have obligations to children. Their homecoming doesn't have to be a detour to a career or a roadblock to the second honeymoon. These moms believe that family members can make changes to accommodate one another's needs and that having grown children at home can be a nice experience. These parents found, however, that each must be willing to find satisfaction without making the other person miserable. The ease or difficulty of the reunion depends in part on the prior relationship and each person's place in the family when the kid came home.

11

We're Glad to Have You—But Why Now?

Timing, they say, is everything.

When mom cradles the telephone and relays to dad, "We're expecting again," he has a right to think, "It's inconceivable." Mom's in menopause, and he has paused from the role of prime provider to three children. His pen no longer runs dry writing checks to pediatricians, to summer camps, and for high school field trips—to Spain and other distant places. Except for courses he and mom may take, he's free from paying college tuition. The last major expense looming on the postparenting agenda may be his daughter's June wedding.

Expecting again? At their age? What a pregnant thought. He and mom are growing short of the pep, the patience, and the years needed to rear an infant to adulthood. If it was in nature's plan to make an older couple parents again, mom would still be ovulating. "You're kidding," he says. "Not exactly," mom replies.

In the case of Harold and Beth, they were expecting—due date, next week—Frank, a six-foot, one-hundred-ninety-pound son. The twenty-five-year-old had called collect to announce, "I'm coming home to find myself." Harold, weary of the cliché, curbed an impulse to ask mom, "Doesn't he have something more interesting to look for?"

But he had to admit Frank's homecoming had positive aspects.

Harold had just lost a trusted employee in his wholesale house. Assuming Frank had sown his wild oats—and spent all his money—in California, he might be willing to come into the business. Harold pictured the sign: Lang and Son, Party Suppliers.

On a fatherly level, Harold had been vaguely unhappy since his last offspring packed up and took off two years ago. He missed the controversial conversations at the dinner table and the impromptu parties initiated by Frank's outgoing, albeit self-centered, personality. The aspect Harold hadn't missed was the bills Frank ran up indulging himself. "When I was twenty-three, I was feeding him," Harold recalled telling a friend, "and when he was twenty-three, I was still feeding him."

Yet Harold was optimistic. Employed in the family business, Frank might become money-conscious.

To prepare for Frank's return, Beth aired out the back bedroom, beefed up the grocery list, bought extra bath towels, and braced herself. She hadn't missed his habit of monopolizing dinner conversations or overrunning the house with friends. "I don't have the tolerance for noise I had when I was twenty-five," she said. "I wouldn't mind if it was my quieter son coming home."

Also, Beth was president-elect of the church women's society and would be expected to open her house to the membership. Each morning, she could just see herself setting in order what Frank and his friends had thrown askew. What was timely for Harold was untimely for Beth. The difference in attitudes underscores a point made by studies of the empty-nest blues. Until now, few researchers have polled dads about their feelings. They assumed the exodus of the last child would have its greatest effect on mom. Not always, concluded a systematic survey done at Arizona State University. As suggested to *Psychology Today* ("Newsline," October 1979) by the study's main author Robert Lewis, "The number of dispirited postparental fathers could be multiplying at the same time it appears that fewer mothers are experiencing crises with the launching of their children."

An article in *Dynamic Years* ("Personal Notebook," January-February 1980) makes the same point: " 'Often the father never had a lot of time for the kids in previous years,' explains Lillian Rubin of San Francisco's Institute of Scientific Analysis. 'He didn't share as much as the mother in their development and, suddenly, they're gone.' ... Her obvious conclusion: Men should better balance family and career commitments."

Frank fulfilled his mother's apprehensions. Even though he had a private entrance to the back bedroom, he used the house as if it was his own apartment. "He's the kind of kid who gets started when I'm ready to go to bed," Beth said. "About ten thirty each night his friends come over, in one door and out another."

At that hour, Harold was dead to the world. Keeping work hours of 6:00 A.M. to 6:00 P.M. six days a week put him asleep before the 10:00 news was aired on television. "He sleeps well at night," Beth said. "I don't. I'm too used to tuning in to the children." After Frank ignored numerous requests to show consideration, Beth wore earplugs at bedtime to shut out the noise. "I needed my sleep to be able to deal with my new church office," she said. "It was a rotten time for Frank to come home."

Mental health director Lawrence Berson doesn't believe there is a good or bad time for grown children to move back in with parents. He sees friction as a relationship problem rather than a matter of timing. "If the kid who comes home is a pain in the ass, there is no good time," he said. "If he walks in as a friend, there is no bad time.

"A parent has to know whom he or she expects and set up a livable arrangement. If the problem is a disruption of household routine, the agreement should be based on the territorial imperative.

"You say, 'This is your part of the house, and I have no say over it; this is my part of the house that you'll have no say over; and this is our part of the house, where we'll both feel comfortable.'

"Presumably, if a parent and child sit down beforehand and talk like a guest and a host about house rules, and if they both establish certain priorities, no time will be a bad time for a kid to come home."

Similar foresight can be helpful in the father and son's business connection. Around the time Beth bought earplugs, Harold began to toss and turn in his sleep. The resentment he didn't express during the day toward Frank's work attitude disturbed his rest at night. His complaints were that Frank was rarely on time, he called Harold a workaholic, he called the tasks given him menial things, and he made it clear he hadn't expected to start at the bottom in a company his father owned. "And he's become money-conscious," Harold said. "He thinks he's entitled to more pay."

Had Frank been an unrelated employee, Harold would have given him walking papers. But the loyal father hasn't the heart to throw out his own flesh and blood. "The job keeps him living at home, and I keep hoping he'll learn from me how to do a real day's work," Harold explained.

Harold was like a tree that volunteered the wood for the handle of the ax that eventually cut it down. According to Beth, he never spelled out Frank's work hours. One day he'd tell Frank to sleep late in the morning. The next day he'd ask Frank to leave for work with him. To lure Frank into the business, he built up the importance of the job. "Harold should have insisted Frank work doubly hard to prove he wasn't hired just because he was the boss's son," Beth declared.

Berson challenged the use of a double standard in hiring an offspring. "Preferential treatment, good or bad, for the boss's son can undermine the youngster. Making him work twice as hard as another employee places a burden on him. Pampering is equally harmful. The offspring will develop wild ideas of who he is. He'll think he's being groomed for 'big things' and will demand more pay."

The point is, Berson continued, that "when a child leaves home, it's a rite of passage. The familial relationship changes the moment he steps out on his own. Father and son are still related but as persons A and B, not person AB. The son is now an independent human being."

For a father "to try to recreate the symbiotic parent-child relationship is instant death to the relationship. He has to view his adult child differently than he did the baby boy or girl," Berson said.

A reception similar to Harold's was given to Felix by his father when he came home. The older man had been ready to wind down his career but was disheartened at the thought of selling a thirty-year-old electrical products company to strangers. "I was thrilled when Felix agreed to let me groom him to take over," the exuberant man said. "If I had my way, all my kids would live at home and work with me—instead of living far away."

Using golf terms to describe their personalities, the father was a driver, and Felix, a putter. Prior to working together, they had been at odds about Felix's reticence to take a long shot by going where the money was—in sales. "I was more comfortable working with plans than with people," said Felix, an electrical engineer. "I thought that's where dad would put me when I went in with him." Instead Felix was given the duties of an outside man, the position his father wanted to relinquish. Within six months, Felix became discouraged. "Dad would slap me on the back and say, 'You're doing fine.' I damned well knew I wasn't."

Soon, Felix quit the electrical supply company and found a job elsewhere. His father was genuinely puzzled. "I can't understand what happened. This would have been his business when I retired.

His life would have been a lot easier if he had stayed with me."

There doesn't have to be a problem between a father and son of different temperaments. A driver father and a putter son could be a good combination if the son is put into a job that suits his quiet nature. In the same way that parents take stock of the youngster who will live with them, a father should appraise his son as a potential employee when he takes him into the business. "He should evaluate his assets and liabilities and find a position to suit the kid," Berson contended. "Just to hire him because he is related creates a touchy situation. One possible outcome will be a disappointed father and a son who feels guilty getting paid for work he doesn't do well. And there goes the relationship."

On other occasions, a youngster in transition comes home to an oldster in transition in a related career field. The situation can unify the two men or drive a wedge between them, depending on how they handle the parallel circumstances. For example, William, Sr., a high school teacher, breathed a sigh of relief when student loans made it possible for Bill, Jr., to leave for law school.

He recalled, "I thought I was through supporting a child. We had invested so much time and money into our three kids. We put $1,000 into one daughter's teeth and $1,500 into another daughter's teeth. Bill's applications to about fifteen law schools cost us $10 to $20 each. We had never eaten high on the hog, and that semester, we ate even lower."

All along, the teacher had been preparing for a career change by taking night classes. As soon as Bill left, he gave up tenure to study full-time to become a divorce counselor. By the time Bill, Jr., got his law degree, William, Sr., had his Ph.D.

In a sense, he related to his son. Both were starting out—he at fifty-three and Bill at twenty-four. They had been one another's fans. The former teacher described his son as "an awfully nice kid." Bill said that his father was someone he could count on. But the rapport evaporated when Bill came home to "buy time" (in his father's words) to find a high-salaried job. After a firm, specializing in divorce cases, hired him, Bill bought more time at home to accumulate assets.

"I feel I'm being used," said William who is struggling to establish a practice in a related field. "I want him to succeed and to make good financial decisions, but I don't want to take care of him. He puts me under pressure living at home. I worry whether his work is going well and if he's doing his job properly. He becomes offended when I express my fatherly concern."

Bill is aware his father is anxious for him to leave and can't understand why. He sees himself as an aid, not as a burden, to the household. He pitches in to cook and clean and is solely responsible for the outside maintenance of the property. He even offered to share household expenses and was turned down. He brings home extra groceries and buys gifts for his parents they wouldn't buy for themselves.

"Yet, my father treats me like a kid who needs to be reminded to do his homework, and in the next breath implies I should be living on my own." Bill is disappointed. He thought he and his father would draw closer doing similar work.

The problem can be assessed as a misplaced Oedipus complex. Freud based it on sex, but it's applicable to a father, who in a way, feels threatened by a son. He sees himself as an older person challenged by a younger person. He may say he doesn't want to invest any more time and money in the kid. But that's a cover-up of his real worry. With both on the starting line, a father may be afraid the son will outrace him.

Neither father nor son, to get along, should be asked to give up the work he wants to do. Berson's advice in such a situation is to "talk about the issues with a professional. Husbands and wives go into therapy to clear up relationship problems. Why shouldn't a father and son? There's no room to modify behavior in this situation because father and son are working with feelings. But there is room for understanding."

On the flip side of the coin, Denny, a freshly minted accountant, moved back home during a trying period for his father. The older man had been phased out of his job with an accounting firm the week before Denny was employed by one of the Big Eight. "I was really depressed," Denny's father said. "It was an unexpected blow."

Father and son were reserved males who rarely engaged in small talk. Prior to living together again, the mother had been the dominant talker. Now she finds it difficult to get a word in edgewise. "They talk business at every opportunity, and one thing leads to another. Soon they're shooting the breeze about sports, politics, my cooking. Everything. I've never seen them so close."

Denny admitted he doesn't always agree with his father's business advice or judgment on who'll win a game or an election, but he listens to them. His father is careful to avoid coming on too strong as a mentor. He feels, "Denny's a man now, and I respect his abilities."

At this end of the father-son spectrum, the older man knows he's a seasoned accountant. He's been in the field a long time and assumes he has earned his son's respect. "They have a good relationship because neither considers the other a challenge," Berson said.

Denny's worst moment, however, was when he took his father along to the bank to cosign a car loan—and the bank wouldn't accept the signature of a man who was unemployed. "I felt terrible to have placed him in that humiliating position," Denny said. "I expected him to lash out at me. Instead, he said, 'Let's have breakfast out. My treat. That's the least I can do for you.' I remember answering, 'You've done plenty,' and we let the whole thing pass."

Seeing a father as a vulnerable human being can arouse disdain or compassion, depending upon the character of the son. An understanding child can preserve the dignity of his parent by showing undiminished respect. Berson feels sympathy for both persons because it's very difficult for a father to be deflated in front of his child and just as difficult for the child to witness it. The advice Berson would give to a boy or girl who sees a parent in a state of humiliation is "to understand the father's position, to remember he's still a father, and to view himself as a compassionate adult and act accordingly."

It's a different problem when a child deliberately sets out to embarrass a parent. Andy found a lower standard of living at home. While he was away, Harvey, his father, used the advantage of an emptied nest to start a music business. To finance it, he sold the house and moved into a one-bedroom apartment. To keep it going, he drew a token salary. When Andy stated his intentions to return to live with his parents, however, Harvey rented a two-bedroom apartment and apologetically explained that Andy would have to contribute his share of the expenses. "But Andy laid a guilt trip on me," Harvey said, "complaining he had always been shortchanged. He even dragged up the time I didn't go to a Little League game. He claimed my work always came ahead of my fatherly duties.

"After a blowup at home because I couldn't send him to graduate school now, he came into the store and made a big scene about it in front of other people. It was goddamn verbal abuse, and I've stopped speaking to him since then. I don't want any more of the *My Father Never Sang for Me* routine."

Harvey doesn't accept the theory of "letting it all hang out" in a parent-child relationship to keep the youngster from burying his frustration. He contends that "just because you scream doesn't mean the problem will be screamed out." Keeping quiet, in his case, will avoid painful confrontations. "It will stop us from inflicting pain upon each other," the aggravated father said. "I may be right or I may be wrong, but I have to find a way to make peace with myself. I often wonder why he came back."

Why does a parent continue to permit a hostile child to live at home? There is no reason for a parent to be put on the defensive for starting a new business or a new anything in the postparenting stage. "He has a legitimate right to pursue his own ambitions," Berson said. "There is a difference in being a mother or father to a small child who is dependent on you and being a parent to an adult who can take care of himself. When a baby has a tantrum, you live with it because the kid doesn't know how else to react. When an adult child goes into a rage, you don't have to put up with it.

"A parent, in all justice, can invite his youngster out of the house on the basis, 'It is not comfortable for us to have you here,' or else, 'If you are our guest, act like it.'

"You don't make a decision of whether a child is welcome or not on the basis of the time he picks to come home. If he is coming home to pick a fight, there is no good time."

There is scattered evidence that some parents believe either the child most like them or least like them would be easiest to live with. From experience, one father relished the presence of Dick, "a prince of a son," who was painstaking where he was impulsive. The homecoming of his other son, "a mirror image," was "worth sour grapes." A hot-tempered father openly favored his milder-tempered daughter who "knew how to cool off an argument." Some mothers made the same contention, insisting that opposites attract because they blend rather than clash.

Just as many parents expressed a preference for the return of a child who shares similar talents, interests, or temperament. "Having Nancy home was fantastic," a sociable mother said. "She's an extension of me." A father who attributed his professional success to tenacity related best to the son "who didn't discourage easily and was hardworking like me." Repeatedly, the ultimate accolade was "He [or she] gets more like me each day."

Pertaining to a relationship with a home-ing pigeon, the clichés "Opposites attract" or "Likes breed liking in one another" are facile observations. Unquestionably, parents who dislike one of their own traits may find it intolerable in their offspring. And presumably it works the other way, too. The good qualities parents see reflected in their children bolster their self-image. "But basically, people get along with other people who meet their needs," Berson said. "A doer and a do-nothing can irritate each other or inspire the other to wind up or wind down. Two sociables may be incompatible because each wants to go at a different time."

A grown child who comes home at an awkward period in his or her parents' life is like the guest who, invited to dinner on Saturday night, arrives a night early. The Friday-night meal is over. The house is a mess. And the host and hostess had planned a cozy evening for two. If the child walks in as a friend willing to defuse the embarrassment, there is no "wrong night" for this arrival. If, however, the child walks in as a complainer ready to put the couple on the defensive by reviving old hostilities, there is no "right night" for this return.

What the parents can keep in mind is that the situation with the grown child, as with the unexpected guest, is temporary. The resumption of living together is not a permanent commitment—like marriage. In the same way hosts can prod a guest to leave when it's "getting late," parents can prod a child to make other plans.

The simplest way to encourage the grown child's independence is to refrain from making home too comfortable to leave. The hardest way is to be held back by guilt. Parents are often appalled to even think they want a child to live elsewhere.

Eventually, the welcome mat will have to be waived to enable a grown child to get on with the business of developing into an adult. It makes sense for the parent to waive it before the rug gets pulled out from under both of them in the slippery course of living together.

12

You're Not Welcome—
But We're Sorry

Mothers and fathers of home-ing pigeons were children, too. But, unlike their offspring, they weren't reared by the book. In depression and postdepression days, they were kept in line with guilt.

A secure childhood in those hard times depended on the answer yes to two questions: "Does daddy have a job?" and "Is mommy well?" The litany was, "Let daddy rest, he's worked hard all day," and "Help mommy, she looks worn out." The response demanded? Obedience. There was no time to worry about the youngster's psyche or falling out of a child's good graces.

Consequences were meted out for transgressions. The severest was withdrawal of approval by daddy, the sole provider, or mommy, the prime nurturer. A fierce glare (and sometimes a swift kick) was provoked by misdeeds as minor as tracking mud into the house or dropping a deposit bottle on the way to the store. Or the misdeed could be as serious as playing hooky from school or chores.

"You're a bad boy" or "a naughty girl" were scarlet words drawn on a child's conscience to keep attention on the primacy of duty to family. Willing hands mattered in households where every penny counted and every minute was accountable. "Working-class families always had a closer kinship system than middle-class families because in the working class people have to provide services for free that in the middle class are bought," said Arlie Hochschild, an asso-

119

ciate professor of sociology at the University of California at Berkeley.

Reared to cooperate (or else), is it any wonder that mom and dad still feel compelled to help anyone they're related to, especially parents and children? Not only are they moved by caring, but guilt is a bitter aftermath for even thinking, "I'm being asked to do too much too long."

"The family has become somewhat more loosely knit than was previously the case, but it's still enormously important, especially in times of crises. In recessions, we see the family absorb the unemployed. In times of divorce, we see people go back to their parents, and grandparents take on some child-rearing functions. I'd venture to say that middle-class families become more like working- or lower-class families in times of crises," Hochschild said.

Where do mom and dad now stand in midlife during another time of economic uncertainty? A few overwrought couples make it sound as if they're caught between a rock and a hard place. Actually, they're torn between obligations to elderly parents, unsettled grown children, and themselves. Each age group is crying, "Take care of me!" The fallout of the me-generation has dropped into the consciousness of the middle-aged couple, in particular mom, who had been promised, "The best is yet to be."

But her conscience finds it hard to accept the tough-minded opinion of, for instance, clinical psychologist Dr. Eugene Southwell, who says, "Society enforced obligations on parents and children through guilt. In reality, they don't owe each other a damned thing. They should give because they want to, not because 'I gave you, so you owe me.' "

Apparently, more people would agree with him if they didn't feel guilty admitting they agreed. At an Adult Children and Adult Parents workshop led by a Chicago social worker, the dominant emotion expressed by more than forty middle-aged women was guilt mixed with bewilderment. The general question was "Why do we feel so guilty when we try so hard to be good?"

Leslie, fifty-two, gave a prototypical answer. She was brought up to please her parents. She took care of a younger brother. She shopped. She cooked. Marriage was like repeating the same chapter in another book. She took care of the kids. She shopped. She cooked. "Now I divide my time worrying about a grown son who came back home and an elderly father in a nursing home." And she feels guilty when one duty conflicts with another.

Dinah, in similar circumstances, expressed empathy. "My career is running to see my mother at a nursing home and caring for my father who lives nearby. I have little time left for my grown daughter who dropped out of college. I've asked her to help out with my responsibilities. I say, 'Give me a break. Go in my place one day.' Her answer is 'I'm no substitute for you.'

"I wasn't raised that way. I was brought up to pitch in at home. Now kids have different priorities."

Fully half the participants felt trapped by guilt. Some admitted compensating for even thinking of putting a parent in a nursing home. Others were ashamed for wanting a grown child to leave home. In only one case did the deed follow the thought. "My twenty-one-year-old son drove me wild," said Katherine, the mother of two younger sons and an adolescent daughter. "His morals were incompatible with the family's. He kept bringing girls home for you know what. I'd hear them tiptoe upstairs at night and heard the noises in the bedroom. After an afternoon out, I'd find a strange girl coming out of the bathroom.

"Besides going against my upbringing, his morals were a bad influence on the younger kids. Finally, I told him to behave or get out. It was only a threat, but he left. Now I feel bad. We hardly hear from him, and I worry if he's all right."

Katherine struck a chord mothers don't like to hear. A mother takes a risk when she tries to enforce her standards on a grown child. But just because there are no world standards doesn't mean she can't set personal ones. A mother has a right to say, "You may not bring girls in overnight," and back it with a consequence for disobedience. The most dire, of course, is "If you don't like it, leave."

It's taken for granted that a parent rarely has the heart to ask a child to move out. It raises the obvious questions: "Will we cut him off from us? Will we lose him forever?" But there is another reason that has a personal connotation.

"Let's face it," the workshop leader said, "we weren't afraid to lay down the law when we were younger, stronger. It was our house. It still is, but now we think, 'In ten years we may be old. We may need his help.' We identify with our elderly parents and are afraid to cross our children."

In essence, a fearful parent is bartering an acquiescent now for a dependent later. The logical answer, by consensus of the workshop participants, is to make every attempt to stay self-reliant as long as possible by maintaining friendships and keeping involved in a job or hobby.

It is an acknowledged difficulty for a generation of women conditioned to the approval of others for self-esteem to be continually assertive. But it's self-defeating to fear a grown child's anger because a woman thinks, "Aha, down the road I may have to depend on a son or a daughter." The workshop leader emphasized, "We have to slip out of the dependency mold."

A different problem can arise if a single parent becomes reliant on a home-ing pigeon. Although some children foster the dependency, particularly in parents who lack self-confidence, children or parents can become uncomfortable in the role reversal. Leaning may seem wonderful at the height of a crisis, but leaning too long defers learning to live together as two adults.

Divorcée Hilda described the terrific support given by her oldest son after the divorce. She "loved" it. He was "marvelous." She let it continue until she realized he had taken over all the decision making in the household. His dominance frightened her. "I was only forty-seven, not senile," she said, "and living together was a temporary situation. It's in the cards for a young person to make a life of his own."

Tactfully, then forcefully, Hilda let him know he wasn't her husband or her father. He was her son, and she was capable of thinking for herself. What she had done was build him up to adult status and then tear him down to the role of child. "I lost him," she admitted. "He left feeling he'd been used."

Hilda avoided this pitfall with another son who came home. They consult each other on major problems, but neither has the last word. She had alienated one son because she had allowed him to set up a condition that led to hostility. She didn't want to lose another son.

Other workshop participants were aware that they walked a thin line dealing with young adults who had been on their own. At least one daughter resented orders to check in by phone at any hour if she was out late. "She claims I can't let go of the apron strings," said her mother who was prone to worry. "I'd like to tell her, 'You can't let go of the purse strings.'" Another mother observed, "My son is communicative when I don't challenge his way-out views. When I do, he stops talking to me." Still another related that since she became outspoken on moral issues, she feels a coldness and a strain in her relationship with her daughters. "It's hard to deal with on a day-to-day basis. Did I do wrong?"

The workshop leader, who has counseled young adults, replied, "I see these young people trying to get their heads together about careers, friendships, impending marriages. Invariably, they bring up the way they get along with their parents. Believe it or not, they're as concerned about relating to us as we are about relating to them.

"But their task is to separate from parents in an emotional and physical sense, and they do it awkwardly. Once they know where they as individuals begin and where their parents' influence ends, they'll be able to resume a close relationship with a mother and father."

Does this mean that a mother should refrain from expressing her feelings? The answer is no. And certainly not out of fear of losing the child or out of guilt for not having been the perfect mother.

Workshop participants were told: "Rid yourself of the pervasive fear of losing a child. Speak up. When we clam up, the relationship withers. But remember, the adult child has a right to disagree. And if there are too many areas of disagreement that can't be worked out with a son or a daughter, you have the right to ask them to live elsewhere."

To the woman who gasped before asking, "Is it normal for a mother to evict a child?" the workshop leader gave this answer: "I've been spending half my life asking what is normal. My conclusion? Normal is what makes you feel comfortable and suits you. Each person develops his own style."

One reason women feel guilty even though they try so hard to be good to their children is public opinion. Parents, as much as kids, are subject to peer pressure. Psychology books may tell them what to do, but people judge their performance. There is always that perfect mother who was able to toilet train her children before they could say "potty." She ascends to the judgeship of who does right or wrong.

Lettie, a conscientious mother, was continually concerned about "What is typical for today's child?" Some grown children, she noticed, lived at home until they married, while others moved on after college. Having determined that staying home was a compliment to devoted mothering, she felt terrible when her home-ing pigeon took a job in another state. "I was sure I had missed the boat as a mother," she said. Her confession of guilt to her hairdresser was overheard by the woman in the next chair who said, "Isn't it great he was capable of going off on his own?" Backed by a contemporary, Lettie began to take the credit for her son's independence.

Another woman was disturbed when her daughter, "a refreshing kind of girl," quit the college where each family member is an alumnus and took a job as a waitress. Jean finds it hard to accept a child who went off the beaten track. "In my day we didn't do things like that," the anxious mother said. "To me, you go to school, you go four years, and you finish school."

Heightening the shame of knowing that she can't stand seeing her daughter at home, was the work the girl chose. "When you say, 'My daughter is a waitress,' it's not too classy," Jean said. "Yet she made nice friends at the restaurant. You could never tell they were waitresses."

When Jean told friends, "I don't understand how she can do this. It doesn't make sense," she got mixed reactions. The general reaction, in effect, was "Don't worry about it. She'll go back to school in six months. But I understand how you feel." Others reacted as Jean had. In effect, "Couldn't you just die? She had all the advantages and didn't take them."

The latter Jean called honest reactions. The others were fake understanding. Jean can't believe it's normal to be casual about a girl leaving college to work at a menial job. The support of others of a like mind eased Jean's guilt for feeling sorry her daughter lived at home.

In reverse, Tess feels uncomfortable about withdrawing her son, an excellent student, from a top university. The young man had been ready to sign up for his junior year when she told him he couldn't go back. A new family business needed his help. "You don't know what we went through," Tess said. "We felt so bad pulling him out of school. Other kids were taking off to go who knows where, and we were treating our son like a small boy.

"The guilt! He had no social life at home, and he's a very social guy. We got in each other's way. He had his habits and we had ours. I didn't sleep nights worrying about what I had done."

A friend's opinion let her resume restful nights: "He may have given up a lot to come back home, but you did, too. You gave up your privacy and the freedom of having no children at home. While he was growing up, he had the best of everything while you did without. It's his turn to give now."

She was using the I-gave-you-such-and-such-so-you-owe-me rationale. Some parents raised by guilt sometimes perpetuate it in their children.

Other mothers go to the opposite extreme. Reared by obedience on demand, they make a conscious effort to place no demands on their children. Then they complain about self-centered offspring and subject themselves to criticism for spoiling their kids. "There were so many theories on child rearing," a puzzled mother said, "that I paid no attention to my common sense."

Nor is a father free from the pressure of abiding by what other people think. But he seems better able to handle adverse criticism. Perhaps it's because the onus of bringing up a child is placed on his wife. George, the father of five, had looked forward to the day of getting back as a twosome in his marriage. He freely admitted, "If I had realized how much time and money children take, we would have had fewer children."

Contrary to the Arizona study showing that fathers suffered the empty-nest blues ("Newsline," *Psychology Today,* October 1979), George was less than happy to have a grown son move back in. He loved his son but would "love him better if he lived someplace else." George expressed this opinion to distant relatives at a wedding. "They were shocked that I could hardly wait for my son to go away again. I could tell they thought something was wrong with me, that I was an unnatural father.

"You know what I think? More people would admit they were tired of caring for grown kids if they weren't worried about looking bad."

Another father displayed altruism upon being criticized for encouraging a grown child to leave. "I think it's a good idea for a kid to go out on his own and learn what life's all about. Something could happen to a parent, and he wouldn't know what to do," he said.

The parent population seems to contain enough people beset by guilt to start a Guiltaholics Anonymous. Part of the therapy should be to realize that guilt, like jealousy and other disturbing feelings, is self-induced. "Guilt is a man-made emotion," states psychotherapist Dr. Sandra Kahn. "It's manifest by what you perceive of your reality. And reality is shaded by the way you look at a situation and how open you are to influence."

For example, an adult child may feel beholden to take in a bereaved parent still able to fend for himself. As a dependent, the parent seems to age overnight. As a caretaker, the adult child has lost privacy and freedom. He knows it's not good for the two generations to live together. Yet the adult child would be a bad son or daughter to discuss separating. Society, the faceless principle-setter, will frown. Friends will think less of him. He'll think less of himself.

"The smart thing to do is urge the parent to go out and start a new life," Dr. Kahn said. "It's the same thing with children. The parent should encourage a child to leave. Childhood is a training ground for self-sufficiency if at all done right.

"Rear your children, then free them. It's the ultimate goal of parenting, and you'll be free, at the same time, to go on to another stage."

So-called big guilts are more difficult to come to terms with than little guilts. Frederick lost a well-paying job the year his son was a sophomore in a highly rated high school district. After months of unemployment, he took a lower-paying job that necessitated moving to an area where the majority of kids could barely speak English. "My boy had a lot more drive at the first school," Frederick said. "Spending two years in the new school ruined him. He lost the motivation to go to college and won't look for a job. He just sits around and waits for me to find him one." The guilt-ridden father blames himself and permits the son to freeload on his time, energy, and money. Someone else might see his initial decision as based on the choice between feeding his son or keeping him in a school system he couldn't afford.

Along these lines, Ella, a victim of Parkinson's disease, feels guilty that the expenses of her long illness deprived her children of material things enjoyed by their contemporaries. "We tried to do our best for our kids," she explained, "but we couldn't give them everything they wanted. I hope they don't hold it against me." Ella tries to make it up to her twenty-six-year-old daughter by stocking the pantry with delicacies the stricken woman can ill afford.

"Parents who want to give their kid everything really want to give it to themselves," said clinical psychologist Dr. Rosalie Kirschner, "and if the kid gets everything, the outside world becomes a culture shock.

"If a kid says, 'You never gave me enough,' ask him, 'What would be enough?' It's a gamble because you could get an answer that shows the kid wanted you. Instead you gave him things. Guilt is sometimes a form of doing penance."

In another situation, Vicki permits a hostile daughter to disrupt her household because of a difficult decision she made on the girl's behalf fifteen years ago. It was either permit a hysterectomy on a twelve-year-old or take the chance that a malignancy wouldn't spread. "When she hadn't menstruated by age sixteen, I had to tell her why and admit I signed the permission slip," Vicki recalled. "She slapped my face and cried—and in a hundred ways has slapped my face since she came home after a divorce."

Vicki would like to say, "This is my house. Show respect or don't let the door hit you in the butt on the way out," but she worries about what would become of her daughter. Vicki was a mother of three at her age, and now her daughter is barren.

Worriers would worry less without the self-expectation of infallibility. "Parents don't readily admit mistakes, real or imagined. They're afraid of losing face," said Bob Keim, an associate professor in the Family Life and Child Studies Department of Northern Illinois University, DeKalb. The refusal to acknowledge a wrong builds up resentment in a kid who knows better. There's nothing wrong with a parent appearing as a human being with hopes and goals and struggles.

Keim's advice is to "fess up to the child. Own up. Admit you have aches and pains—physical, emotional, and mental. If you show him you're a real person, something wonderful can happen. You may learn to love each other more, and the situation of living together again will be less trying."

Little guilts are easier to admit and can serve as the first step on the long journey to a solid relationship. Numerous mothers expressed guilt for dining out while grown children "coped" with leftovers at home. "I still feel I owe my daughter dinner," an overconscientious mother said. "I fix it every weeknight." Others were uneasy taking trips while a child lived at home. "But the longer he stayed on with us, the easier it became to leave him," said a mother who had been accustomed to taking family-style vacations. Still others felt uncomfortable enjoying affluence while a child struggled to establish himself. "Here I was buying expensive furniture, and my kid couldn't afford to buy his own bed," said a woman who had waited twenty-nine years to redecorate her living room.

Along with the little guilts that distort perception are the foolish guilts. Sylvia, whose children were born eleven months apart, believes she has to compensate to the older girl for making her a big sister too soon. Lloyd believes he forced his son to buy a car that was a lemon. "If I had been more generous with the use of my car, he wouldn't have felt forced to buy one," Lloyd said. Another father berates himself for taking naps before dinner. "That was the only time my daughter had to practice piano. Because I complained it disturbed my rest, she lost interest in improving her playing."

If some parents could see situations as their children do, they would shed guilt as birds shed feathers in molting season. Kids feel guilty, too. Cathy knows she keeps her parents from traveling. Dave, a divorced father, knows he has restricted his mother, who cares for his two small sons. Numerous home-ing pigeons know they add extra cooking, cleaning, and expense by their presence. "As far as household chores are concerned, I do some but not as much as I should," admitted a teacher. "But I help my brother and sister with their homework when I'm not working, taking flying lessons, or dating." The majority admitted they pitched in somewhat. Guilt was evident in their manner, but not enough to make them give more help.

"A little guilt can be a good thing," said Dr. Kirschner. "Sometimes it's constructive. Letting a child know he's not carrying his weight isn't laying a guilt trip on him. You're saying to him what you would say to anyone else who used you."

Unrealistic guilt can be a bad thing. Parents have no reason to feel they are in debt to a child, to make up at the end for what they think they didn't give earlier. If the relationship needs improvement, the question to ask is "What do you want now? Let's see if we can work something out."

Kicking the guilt habit can be simple once a parent stops worrying about what society advocates, what friends will think, and what kids will say. Let the kid worry about what a parent does, thinks, and says. For instance, if a kid wants mom to wait around for a package, it may hurt the first time to say, "My time is as important as yours." How can it hurt a grown child? Other arrangements can be made.

Or, if a grown son has been depending upon mom to wake him and he's late because she overslept, should she feel guilty? No! He's over twelve and way past the age of using a parent as an alarm clock.

Testimonies from recovering guiltaholics show that the first time is the hardest time to say no to that inner voice making unreasonable demands. Frances timed a getaway weekend with her husband to the date of her home-ing pigeon's camping trip. Even though her daughter's plans fell through, Frances followed through. "I didn't feel too guilty leaving considering she wasn't expected to be home," Frances said. "She survived. Since then, the coming and going bit has been easier. I see I'm dealing with a young adult, not a child."

Lena had a more difficult form of guilt to overcome: the kind that was thrust upon her. The only female in a male household, she became "the target." Who else was at fault for missing buttons, late meals, or getting behind with the laundry? Lena once found herself apologizing to a table she bumped into. But after her three boys left, she assessed her contribution to the family. "I had raised three kids I'm proud of," she said. "They're independent and hardworking on the outside, if not at home. I helped my husband get ahead. I'm proud of him, too.

"And they can also be proud of me. I've kept my looks and have a good name in the community. I made up my mind I wasn't going to feel guilty about anything beyond my control."

The resolution was tested a week after her middle son moved back in. She had cleaned all three bathrooms and an hour later saw hair clogging a sink. Her son was now in a second bathroom (which had a better light) using scissors to cut his sideburns. Upon telling him, "You're making a mess," the scissors slipped, and he slipped back into the old pattern of blaming her for what he had done. "But I was prepared," Lena said. "I told him, 'You're not going to make me responsible for cutting your sideburns wrong. You're responsible for them. You're a big boy now.' "

A small victory? Not in the realm of living with a child who has lived elsewhere. Congenial living is composed of small victories in sharing bathrooms, closet space, meals, and thoughts. Done with consideration, they build big victories: respect and a renewed sense of family.

Few people expect the interdependence that existed between kin in harder times when family members had to pool salaries to make ends meet or one sibling worked to put another sibling through college. Emotional interdependence is another story. Who would object to being able to count on having a listener, a booster, or an honest critic on hand? Good news is blighted, and bad news seems worse without someone to share it.

To build friendship between family members, each should give the other the respect and understanding usually reserved for people outside the home. To keep anger from building up, they should sit down together and talk as dear friends might about what each expects to give to and receive from one another. Such a move will keep children from asking themselves, "Why did I ever come home?" and parents from saying, "I sent away a nice kid and got back this thing!"

Part Five

Birds of Different Feathers

Everyone's quick to blame the alien.

Aeschylus

13

Carrier Pigeons—
Messages They Bring
Home

A child of any age is a carrier pigeon trained to bring messages home. Some are easy to read: "I'm hungry; I'm thirsty; I need money." These couldn't be more clear.

Other messages need to be read between the lines. These are declarations of independence, and the carrier pigeon is uncertain about declaring them. Telling a parent "I'm my own person" carries risks. The child may be set adrift or more closely supervised, and is unsure about wanting one, the other, or neither.

Yet the carrier pigeon feels compelled to show parents signs of involvement outside the home where a child is perceived differently and does things that make a parent exclaim, "I never know what he'll bring home!"

For a while it was creatures. If a daughter wasn't shooing a stray dog through the doorway, a son was toting an abandoned kitten, not to mention cradling an injured bird or cupping a grounded butterfly. Mom got the message, although turning the ménage into a menagerie was not the way she wanted to receive it. She tipped the messenger. "You've a kind heart," she said while thinking, "What next?"

Later, a son or a daughter showed signs of widening interests. Into the house, in handfuls and pocketfuls, came items for collection: rocks, bits of colored glass picked up on streets, assorted grains of sand discovered who knows where. The carrier pigeon was bringing home the message, "I'm exploring the world, and no one else has found such treasures." He counted them; she guarded them; and they both expounded upon them in detail. But they wouldn't share them with each other.

Message followed message. They indicated the development of pride, compassion, curiosity, possessiveness—and added up to growing up. Each was answered with the level of patience, tolerance, and involvement a parent could muster for mangy pets, clutter, and self-assertion.

Carla, of unusual tolerance, accepted the presence of the pet her son Steven brought home on his sixteenth birthday—a young boa constrictor. "I kept reminding myself 'It's not poisonous,' " she said good-humoredly, "but I never forgot it can love you to death."

In the next two years, Steven and the boa achieved physical maturity. She sent off her six-foot son to the University of California at Berkeley, with a sigh of regret. "He was such a good kid," Carla recalled. "He was a straight-A student, did the heavy chores around the house, and always had a kind word to say."

She sent along the six-foot snake with a sigh of relief. But four years later when the two moved back home, Carla was more charmed with the boa than with her son. "The boa requires minimal cleanup, goes for a week without food, and is even-tempered," she recounted. "I don't know what happened to Steven while he was away."

To gain a fresh perspective on Steven's changed habits, Carla needed to spend a day on the Berkeley campus student watching. She would have marked the differences between the way he had lived at home and the way he lived at school.

Outside Sather Gate, students crowded around vendors selling salty pretzels and spicy ethnic foods. They came through the gate, a taco in one hand, an open book in the other, eating and studying at the same time. Next to the bench Carla might have sat on, brown baggers munched sandwiches and scribbled on legal-size pads. They seemed oblivious to the physical fitness enthusiasts who jogged, ran, or bicycled the distances between class buildings.

Browsers stood before bulletin boards that publicized meetings to fight for gay rights, to stop government harassment, and to increase soul power. At the far end of the promenade, Iranian students argued their case interrupted by spectators who used undeleted expletives. While the debate was going on, a couple laid facing each other on the grass, and a girl with dilated pupils talked seriously to her briefcase.

Trash cans marked Ecology Containers overflowed with garbage. A young man wearing jeans, an open-collared shirt, and sandals shot a food wrapper in the direction of one can, unmindful of where it dropped. Wastepaper baskets in washrooms were just as full, but it was someone else's job to empty them.

An adult was conspicuous in Berkeley where students loitered inside and outside stores that sold books, records, T-shirts, and fast food. These were marketplaces and meeting places for people seeking company. Where once children saw themselves as the center of homes, here students saw themselves as the center of a community. All things were geared to their interests.

With no one to police them, they felt completely on their own. They were individuals moving at a pace set by their own rhythm.

"Then he comes home and has to accept his parents' ways," said associate professor Dr. Joyce Nolen. "He tries to fit in but can't be the way he was when he left. And he isn't rational about living up to his parents' expectations.

"He acts like a guest in the house, expecting laundry done, food ready, and no hassle about his new ideas. He's unrealistic about what he expects of his parents."

Moodiness was the first change Carla saw in Steven. He had always been a little crabby in the morning, but now Carla never knew which Steven she would pick up at the train station in the evening—Dr. Jekyll or Mr. Hyde. When he was up, he was talkative, affectionate, and optimistic about his future. Even so, he blew up easily. The ignition was one wrong word, and Carla never knew which word was wrong. She wished the snake really had all the lines.

Silence signaled a down mood. "He never said he was unhappy as he got into the car," Carla said, "but I could tell by his face that something bothered him." On those nights, the car had the hush of a hearse. "And he would bring the mood into the house. It was very depressing."

A stormy scene would follow the lull, triggered by the food she served or differences in opinion on a subject Steven brought up for discussion. Prior to leaving home, Steven had been easy to feed. If the food on his plate didn't move, it was edible. Now he demanded substantial meals: steak, chops, and roasts, with all the trimmings. He turned down casseroles, a family mainstay from the time he had been given solid food. He insisted upon a specific brand of yogurt and complained that the food served was tasteless—knowing that his parents, for health reasons, were on a salt-restricted diet. "Dinner had always been our social hour," Carla said. "With Steven home, it became our ulcer hour."

Another irritant to digestion was the political views Steven had espoused. As a high school student he had been conservative. Carla described him as being to the right of Goldwater. Now he argued in behalf of a friend who applied for welfare to support the girl he lived with and their two children. He also saw nothing wrong with students getting food stamps they weren't entitled to. Steven wouldn't listen to his father's side of the argument. Carla recalled, "My husband objected to paying for these welfare abuses. He pointed out that Steven was working, and his tax money, too, was going toward his friend's upkeep and the food-stamp program.

"Steven's replies were ugly. He let us know we didn't know our ups from our downs. And every other word was a four-letter one. He goaded us until he left the table. It was awful!"

Carla coped by keeping out of Steven's way, an escape route found by other parents. In Gene's household, whenever his son "popped off" and created a scene, Gene fell back on advice given in a parent-training course he had taken when his son was little: "If you engage in a power struggle with your child, you engage in a struggle you're going to lose. The proper course is to redirect his energy or yours."

With these words in mind, Gene would lock himself into his room, take a shower, or get into his car and drive off. "Anything to break off the discussion," he said. "He couldn't argue with me when I wasn't there." The method had worked with a five-year-old, and it worked again with a twenty-two-year-old.

Still other parents were incredulous about a grown child's behavior. Fred's son began to practice transcendental meditation at college and chose the oddest times to meditate. According to his father, "It was a damn nuisance. We'd be ready to eat. He'd meditate. The phone would ring. He'd meditate. I told him meditation was a way to set himself apart from us, that he'd be better off taking a nap than sitting at the table in a trance."

By comparison Dick's father might have preferred coping with meditation rather than with his son's workout schedule. Dick coincided running laps to family mealtimes. "He either ate after we did or came to the table stinking of sweat," the disgusted man said. "My wife never seemed able to get out of the kitchen."

Nor is a daughter exempt from provoking a din at the dinner

hour. Twenty-three-year-old Marian needed little prompting to come to the dinner table as long as the meal excluded red meat and starches—and was ready to be served. "In the morning, we'd leave together for work as two adults. In the evening one adult and one child came home," complained Julia, her mother. "I made dinner. She waited for it on the couch."

One confrontation stands out in Julia's mind.

Marian (from the living room): When are we going to eat?

Julia (from the kitchen): Soon.

Marian: Can't you hurry up? I'm in a rush.

Julia (seeing red): Just a minute, lady, I'm not your servant.

Marian: You don't have to get huffy about a simple request.

Parents don't have to put up with offensive behavior. They have a right to be bothered by the use of bad language and the right to feel offended when treated like hired help. "Let the kid who comes home know there are boundaries he can't cross. Make it clear that you're not abridging his rights but that others have rights, too," advises reality therapist Phyllis Warren.

With a younger child, parents know their prerogatives, but an offense staged by a grown child can throw them off balance. Many parents are convinced they haven't measured up to the standards of parenting books and are therefore vulnerable to the accusation of being bad parents. In order to gain the respect of their children, they have to start respecting themselves. They have to believe they did the best job they could, and they did this job with lots of competition from outside influences.

Dr. Nolen offered advice on three common problems that can arise from living with a young adult who has lived somewhere else.

MOODS. "Before a young person left home, this was home. He didn't know anything else, other kinds of people or other life-styles. Away, his perceptions change. He meets new people and new life-styles and tries to evaluate them. By the time he comes back, he has met with disappointments in his life—through school, dating, looking for a job. He may still be reeling from them. He feels like a ship at sea without a rudder yet wants to remain his own captain."

FOOD. "If he doesn't like what's being served to the family, he should be told to fix his own meals and that he can either eat with the family or buy his own groceries. Tell the young person, 'You came back to the same address knowing what you'd find on the inside. It hasn't changed that much.' "

DISCUSSIONS. "A young person cannot expect to impose new values on the family—religious, political, or social. He should be told, 'You have a right to expose but not impose values. As long as what you are doing doesn't hurt me or others, we won't interfere with you.' Let him know that you are open to discuss the ideas he brought home, but you don't want to be slammed over the head with them."

In an effort to communicate "I'm my own person" without losing the privileges of a dependent child, the home-ing pigeon sends a mixed message to parents: "I don't need you, but I want you to be there when I do."

Take conversation for instance. Nan, whose husband was gone several nights a week, looked to her daughter for company. "Now I dread the evenings we spend together," she said. "Her moods are bad, and she only talks when she wants to, not when I do." Jess, excited about a business deal, is cut off in midsentence by his son. "He only wants to hear what interests him," the disgruntled father said. And Betty, the mother of twin girls, complained, "We can spend the entire evening in separate rooms, and the minute I'm ready to fall asleep, they come in to share their news."

Meanwhile, other parents consider good conversation the plus of having a grown child home. "Ralph's interests in psychology and mysticism make good table talk," Rhoda said. But it's a reminder of Ralph's membership in a cult whose credo is "Man doesn't need to strive. He'll be rewarded in the Second Coming." To any question of "when"—will you get a job? mow the lawn? make your own life?—Ralph's answer is "When God tells me to."

"That gets pretty boring after a while," Rhoda admitted. "But I try to hide my feelings."

Rather than stating it directly, Rhoda is sending the message that she doesn't approve of Ralph's life-style. Like other mothers, she doesn't know where to draw the line between considering her son's feelings and expressing distaste for his values.

An example of reverse influence was made by a widow whose major four-letter word was *talk* before her son came home. "I'm not the lady I used to be. I can swear with the best of them. He taught me well."

Her son's excuse is "I had to assert my independence to make her accept my hours and need to be left alone. I admit I cussed and used words I wouldn't if my dad was alive. But he wasn't."

What parents object to the loudest and with the least inhibition is their child's using drugs or having sex, out of marriage, at home. Yet, there are exceptions. A man admitted his son was bringing girls home overnight. Asked how he felt about it, he answered, "Envious." A divorcée who didn't want her daughter to go the divorce route said, "The sexual relationship between her and her boyfriend doesn't bother me at all. It's better they get to know each other thoroughly before they commit themselves to marriage."

Generally, the reaction to sex in a childhood bed is negative. "If my sons brought girls home overnight, I'd be envious, but I wouldn't tolerate it," a father said. "And if my daughter did that, I'd be outraged.

"Yes, it's their house too. But there are such things as respect for someone else's values. And they know I was brought up not to do anything, ever, that wasn't on the straight and narrow."

It's a fact of life that a child doesn't always tread a parent's path. Nancy knew her daughter was having sex when she saw birth control pills around the bedroom. "I expressed my disapproval, but there was nothing I could do. I couldn't stand guard at the door twenty-four hours a day. And she was of age." Next, Nancy wondered why the young woman kept oregano in her dresser. It turned out to be marijuana. "I screamed, threatened, ordered her to quit. She didn't. What could I do?" Nancy asked.

Dr. Nolen sees the use of drugs and having sex in the house as an authentic rebellion because young people see nothing wrong with this behavior. (And what do mom and dad know?) She also sees it as a sign of disrespect for a parent's values. Not because the homeing pigeon has been away but because this happens even with a youngster who has never left home.

But very quickly the parent has to put a foot down if these values go against the grain. The young person must be told that everyone in the household has feelings and rights, too, and these should be respected.

"If the young person cannot respect these rights," Dr. Nolen said, "tell him he has to make it on his own. You may continue to support him emotionally or financially or any other way. But you can't allow this young person to mess up the family system. Therefore, you have to tell him to get out."

Is there no other recourse than such drastic action? It would be

painful to parents to have to tell a child "Get out." Couldn't they
try a withdrawal of privileges or other methods that worked when
the offspring was younger? No! A parent no longer has that kind of
control when the kid's a young adult.

One way to handle the kid who lays a guilt trip on the parent by
implying, "You owe me" is to say, "I don't owe you anything except
love and respect. And you also owe those to me."

Carla never faced the sex problem with Steven. He didn't know
any girls in his hometown. They had either married or moved away
or were still at school. She did, however, find marijuana in his room
and handled the problem by flushing it down the toilet. "I never
mentioned finding it. And he never mentioned losing it," she said.
"I didn't take it seriously. If all the marijuana flushed down toilets
reseeded itself, every bathroom in suburbia would look like a lawn."

What she did contend with was Steven's criticism of the way she
was bringing up his younger sisters. He accused her of being too
soft, using the accusation to keep from helping with outside maintenance. When asked to mow the lawn or shovel snow, he said, "I put
in my years helping. Now it's my sisters' turns." Yet, he took an
interest in the way they dressed, how much makeup they wore, and
whom they dated.

Comparing notes with other mothers, Carla discovered it wasn't
unusual for a home-ing pigeon to try to take over the rearing of
younger children. "What he may be saying is the parent didn't do a
good job with him—and he's going to save the younger one from
that fate," Dr. Nolen explained.

"Occasionally, this may be true, because the oldest child is often
a practice child for the parent," Dr. Nolen continued. "Also, the
young adult may resent what he sees as his siblings having an easier
time than he did. This can also be true. Parents may mellow in their
discipline and expectations as other children come along."

Besieged by messages hard to read, Carla heard one that was loud
and clear. Steven was bored in the suburbs. There was nothing to do
in the neighborhood. He voiced it, and she saw it in his daily routine. He worked all day and either watched TV, read, or fought with
the family at night.

Once, he wrote a letter to the local paper complaining about the
lack of facilities for young adults in the suburbs. It wasn't printed.
"That's a shame," Carla said. "There must have been others in the
same boat, and they could have started a young-singles group."

Alternative suggestions were met with disdain. He was encouraged to invite friends, who lived in distant suburbs or the city, down for a weekend. He was urged to take a night class at a local university. "They weren't orders," Carla said. "They were only suggestions. But he acted as if I was invading his privacy. He grew more moody and depressed."

So did Carla. She was turning the frustration of living with him inward. There was a bright moment or two. Steven became less hostile to his father's attitude toward money. At the table one night he gave a surprising answer to a questionnaire that asked how he would vote on a withholding tax to keep the environment clean. It was an emphatic no. He had better things to do with his hard-earned money.

His social life began to improve as former high school acquaintances were coming home as he did. Steven bumped into them on the train or in shopping centers. But as in days of old, new messages followed old messages. He kept finding a dozen new ways to say, "I've grown up. Don't bug me"—then acted like a baby.

Carla was certain she had done all she could to simplify living together. Some authorities would disagree with her.

Conditions have to be set for a young person's return or a parent is asking for trouble. They can't continue, after a separation, where they left off. Each one's rights have to be defined when again sharing time and space.

When the relationship was ongoing, routine evolved in a natural way. But during the interval of separation each began to perceive his or her own needs in new ways. Without a clear understanding of what they are sharing and a reestablishment of priorities, living under one roof can give either parent or child the shingles.

14

I've Regained a Child and Lost Myself

Motherhood is absurd.

It asks a woman to love and care for her children—not to keep them safely close but to help them outgrow their need for her. Is there any other human relationship that demands such selfless devotion? It's like cutting a rough diamond and losing it just as it becomes a gem.

The absurdity began early in the eighteen years during which Charlotte brought Danny from diapers to diploma. When it came time to wean him, her breasts were still full. When it came time to put him on the school bus, she had become accustomed to his presence. Each time he acquired a skill, she lost a jot of feeling needed. He narrowed her horizons while she widened his. And the more he learned, the less he thought she knew. Without the law of compensation, it looked as if a personal defeat followed each maternal victory.

"For everything you have missed, you have gained something else, and for everything you gain, you lose something," Ralph Waldo Emerson wrote in 1841.

To Charlotte, an enlightened mother, the essayist's words rang most true the day Danny, her youngest, left home. She had lost her job but gained time, space, and privacy. She began to understand what seemed like a contradiction in the various parenting manuals

143

she had studied. Simply, she was instructed to make home the most comfortable place to be but not so absolutely perfect that Danny would resist leaving.

It took Charlotte about two weeks to profit from the loss of seeing Danny every day. Out of habit, she continued to set his place at the table. She looked up from whatever she was doing at the hour he regularly returned from school. At night, she awoke to check his room to see if he was safe in bed. Never mind that the room was a reminder he didn't sleep there anymore—the bed was made; the floor showed.

She phoned him every day and began to think she was a compulsive mother. But "a parent is not a 'bad' parent for having an inner child that wants his or her offspring to remain safely close. All of us have such an inner child, and it would be asking too much of anyone to act always on the basis of the more mature goal of launching the child.

"To want to hold on is deeply human, and we can only hope a given parent can more often than not make the hard adult choice of supporting the offspring's growth," wrote Howard Halpern, author of *Cutting Loose* (New York: Simon and Schuster, 1976).

Soothed, and simultaneously encouraged to let go, Charlotte checked the impulse to talk to Danny every day and started a Sunday ritual of keeping in touch. On the first Sunday, she weakened. To Danny's admission, "I'm homesick," Charlotte admitted, "I'm Danny-sick."

There was no one to carry in groceries or take down dishes from a high shelf. During the first week he was gone, the grass grew, and her white car looked dirty. It was nearing time to take in the lawn furniture and give the windows a prewinter washing. "I never realized how much help he'd been until he left," Charlotte said.

She knew why. To obtain his help, she had to become a nag, a self-image verified by her son. Little else had been left of her nurturing role the year Danny was a high school senior. She had been reduced to a listening ear ("Danny, can't I give my opinion?"), a source of information ("The car keys are on the hook."), a cheerleader ("Keep applying. You'll get into college."), and an enforcer ("Turn down the stereo. I can't hear myself think.").

Yet Charlotte wielded some power. Danny depended on the family for wheels, extra money, and a place to hang his hat. She could ground him or withhold the car and money. She became less his mother and more his monitor.

By the fourteenth day of Danny's absence, his contribution to the family, given free (if not freely), was replaced by paid help. Charlotte hired a boy to mow the lawn and wash the car. She bought a step stool to reach high places. And the number of grocery bags she had to carry in was reduced. Danny ate elsewhere, and, very often, so did she and her husband Ted.

As the weeks passed, the pang of lonesomeness she felt when passing Danny's room passed. The room stayed neat. So did the second bathroom, the kitchen, and the family room. (He had rarely used the living room.) She had time on her hands instead of a son.

Charlotte and Ted moved out into the space Danny had vacated. There was more room in the closets, garage, basement, and on the kitchen counter. She used his room as a place to read or sew or as a change of place for lovemaking. "Ted and I became like newlyweds when Danny left," Charlotte said without a blush. "We didn't have to hide in our bedroom or worry whether we had our clothes on."

Motherhood had its compensations. She had raised a fine and independent son. As the Sundays passed, Charlotte detected a new self-confidence in Danny's voice. "I never expected him to live at home again," she said. "Where once the thought of his independence bothered me, I realized it was best for both of us."

Wifehood offered compensations, too. "We had gone full circle," Charlotte said. "Ted and I became the way we were in the beginning of our marriage. We made our own world once our son left the circle."

It was an orderly world based on Ted's need to unwind after an intense day at his chiropractic clinic. One day a week, he played racquetball while Charlotte played bridge. Mondays and Thursdays were television nights. They'd watch their favorite shows, "Lou Grant" and "Knots Landing," sitting close and holding hands as preludes to lovemaking. Other weekday nights, Ted studied professional journals while Charlotte puttered with houseplants or made social arrangements for the weekend by phone. At bedtime, she slipped into a flimsy nightgown and slept with the bedroom door wide open.

The idyll lasted two years. Then Danny reentered the scene.

"When Danny left for an Illinois state college, I figured that was it," Ted recalled. "The kid's packed off. He's going to make his own way. Of course, his major was urban planning, and I wondered, 'What's a nice suburban kid worried about urban planning for?'

"Then, he came home on a spring break and said he'd been accepted in an urban planning program at New York University, and my hopes shot up. Aha, the kid is going to move further away. Charlotte and I would be alone summers, too.

"No such luck. Between spring and summer, someone turned him on to teaching, and he picked a school within commuting distance of home. What could I say? Having him go to school and live at home was better than his being a bum."

The tactful way Charlotte described Danny's reentry was "Sometimes, he's an intrusion. I cherish my evenings with Ted, and Danny doesn't like to live by schedule." Ted was more vehement: "Danny would turn off our television programs and turn on sports. He would cut down what we stood for—whatever it was—and dominate conversation when we had guests. He wouldn't show up for dinner when he was expected, or he'd come home for dinner unexpectedly. He was a disruptive force."

Charlotte tried to accommodate Danny's request to be allowed to come and go as he pleased, but he seemed to arrive and depart, eat and shower, at hours that broke her routine. "And he'd leave a trail of clothes and shoes. I was back to my old image as nag. Believe me, I had bent over backward to avoid it."

Studies of family life show that one reason parents and children get in each other's way when a grown child comes home is a lack of a set routine that takes both age groups into consideration. Neither faces the fact that you need a life plan for every day, even for such ordinary things as mealtimes or doing chores, especially if family members have different priorities.

But most people are resistant to thinking family relationships can be organized in some fashion. "I disagree," said sociology professor Marijean Suelzle. "How else can a person know when his behavior exceeds the tolerance of another if he doesn't talk about his needs?

"By setting a routine, family members don't have to waste a lot of time and energy thinking about mundane matters. They can put this energy into personal relationships."

In other words, if a parent doesn't have to fight with a child to clean up the bathtub and argue about who does what, they can spend the time on a more creative, rewarding level. By organizing and managing a routine, a loving relationship has room to grow.

At Charlotte and Ted's house not only was routine broken, but there were times they worried about their eardrums. Danny had become part of a rock group. Two percussionists and two guitarists using amplifiers rehearsed in their garage. "Once I was three blocks from home when I heard the band," Ted recalled. "It took twenty minutes after I pulled into the driveway for the kids to hear my voice and stop playing.

"I felt guilty telling them our house was off limits. The problem with Danny is, his hobbies and pursuits become obsessive. Since he got into the band, he plays the guitar or blasts the stereo at 3:00 A.M. He argues that he doesn't play them loud. I feel, if they wake me up, they're loud enough."

Who paid for the guitar and the lessons? Ted did. He berated himself, not for bankrolling the musical interest, but because he can't tolerate the noise. He looks at his son as an intruder and asks himself, "Is this the way to feel?" Ted wonders if his father felt the same way when he lived at home. Then he tells himself, "I didn't leave until I got married. He never had a quiet house."

Ted's misery has the company of other parents who object to the reintroduction of noise to a quiet household. Many parents believe that kids offer more noise than company when they return home. A sampling of complaints: "We don't see our son. We hear his stereo. He locks himself into his room as soon as dinner's over"; or "Our daughter doesn't even say hello when she comes home from work. She turns on the record player. She plays it low. At least, her idea of low, not ours"; or "I don't care how softly my son plays his stereo. I'm not used to rock music, and it annoys me."

Few parents, however, voice strenuous objections unless the noise becomes a neighborhood nuisance. Like Ted, they feel guilty about wishing their kids lived elsewhere. For example, Pauline was unhappy with the constant stream of kids walking in and out of her house. Her daughter Kay had come home to get over an unhappy love affair that ended with an abortion. "I didn't want to alienate her and send her out to some other man," Pauline said, "so I put up with her friends who played music loud enough to wake the dead."

She reached the limit of her endurance the night Kay and her friends moved from the rec room to the yard, "running, yelling, and carrying on." Fraught with anger, Pauline took Kay aside and ordered, "No more of this. It's my house, and you'll live by my rules. Find decent friends and start acting in a decent way."

To Pauline's surprise, Kay's reaction wasn't anger. She allowed that the time had come to get her act together. Pauline's edict had jolted her into reality. "She realized I had personal standards," Pauline explained, "and made me wish I had laid down the law sooner in her upbringing."

Pauline belongs to a rueful fellowship of parents who let small children do anything and then complain that they can't control them as teenagers. "We raise our children backwards," reality therapist Phyllis Warren opined. "They should be controlled more as younger children and less as older children."

Who should take control when an adult child returns? The person with the higher standards. If a parent is the standard-bearer, then mom or dad should take the responsibility of setting them. This means spelling out what is considered inappropriate behavior and enforcing the consequences.

Compared to raucous music, the sound of footsteps might seem a minor inconsideration. "Not if you hear them in the middle of the night," Charlotte said. "Danny's a grown man. I couldn't tell him when to come home. So I taught him to tiptoe up instead of clank up."

Other parents who slept soundly during the interval of a child-free house became light sleepers when the children returned. The inference is "I gained a child and lost my sleep." A nurse on a hospital's early shift complained, "We have a small house, and I can hear when a stone moves. My daughter's footsteps awaken me. I know she is trying to be quiet, so I pretend to be asleep. But her late hours disturb my rest. On my job I can't afford to be tired."

In other instances, a parent can't determine whether the child is coming or going in the wee hours. Ethel was frequently jarred awake at 5:00 A.M. Some days, her son was going to bed. Other days, he was leaving the house to jog. "We tell him we can hear him," she said, "but he says it's his schedule and his time. Try fighting that."

An ideal solution would be separate entrances to provide privacy for both generations. The lack of privacy is the basis of most conflicts between parent and child. But only one family, out of more than 250 families interviewed, had the foresight to add a parents' wing when the children were preteens.

Yet, the ultimate issue is that "the child should leave home. If the home is turned into the equivalent of an apartment and simulates apartment living, there may be no reason for him to ever leave. At home, he retains many of the qualities of an adolescent and can't fully develop as an adult," said coordinator of Consultation and Community Services Dr. Robert Mark.

Parents have used less expensive ways than adding a wing to lower noise volume. Ted bought Danny a pair of headphones to be able to listen to the stereo without disturbing anyone else. Another professional man bought earplugs for himself to be able to concentrate on his reading material whenever his daughter had friends in. "Now, I use them at the office, too, if my work requires high-level concentration," he said. In turn, he bought his daughter a pair when she complained that his television habits interfered with her studying. To some, it's a reasonable way to solve that problem.

Cooperation was the operative word in a family with more complicated logistics to work out. A surgeon required an hour or two each evening to study medical journals and to review his cases. One son, a chemistry student, needed the morning hours to do his homework. A second son, a professional drummer, needed time before performances to practice. "We sat down and worked out a schedule," Eleanor, the wife and mother, said. "The student was able to study in the morning. My husband could read after 6:00 P.M., and our musician fit in practicing between noon and six."

Did the drumming bother Eleanor? She was the only one home to hear it. "No," she said. "I feel very close to my son and have empathy for his ambitions. I enjoy listening to his music. And I also believe that a mother can sometimes deal with more inconvenience than other family members."

When the musician took a part-time job in the afternoon, the time schedule had to be realigned. It wasn't easy but was accomplished because the family had learned the habits of cooperation and compromise.

The format was parallel to a college apartment situation where students work out plans deciding who cooks one day, cleans another day, or gets the use of a living room. "Possibly people in a family, if all adults, should treat each other as roommates." Suelzle said. "Since it's rare for people to be attuned to one another all the time, they have to plan to be able to act in concert."

Therefore, the logical procedure is to plan ahead on how time is spent, to decide what demands are reasonable, and what demands are not. Be clear about the times you can be together and the times you should be apart. Living with a grown child can be a positive situation if problems are solved with mutual respect.

One problem, however, cannot be solved with a family conference—sexual intimacy between husband and wife. Charlotte still calls her relationship with Ted "torrid" even though she has resumed wearing pajamas, and he keeps a bathrobe handy "just in case Danny arrives home at an awkward moment." But other wives, after sampling the freedom of being a twosome, find the presence of a grown child inhibiting. Una conceded, "First, I missed my daughter. Now, I miss our spontaneous sex life." Wanda admitted, "My son's presence stops me, but it doesn't bother my husband." Denise felt sensitive about closing the bedroom door and having sex while her son was in the house. She feels sure her son knows what she's doing. Men have regained a dependent and lost a bride. The excuse, "How can we with a grown kid around?" has replaced the headache.

The self-consciousness is difficult to overcome, according to sex therapist Dr. Jessie Potter, the director of the National Institute for Human Relationships in Oak Lawn, Illinois. "Somehow women have difficulty appearing sexual in the eyes of their kids," states Dr. Potter. "We may think we have grown comfortable with our sexuality but as soon as the grown kid comes home, we are brought up short by an awareness he's a sexual creature, too. It makes us uncomfortable to be in there with the door shut and locked."

Is this abnormal? Research shows that it's a natural phenomenon for parents to keep a kid at some distance from their private sex life. "And I agree," Dr. Potter says. "It's not anybody's business including our kid's. The way to handle it is to keep in mind that his stay is temporary."

Generally, kids are unaware that they have invaded their parents' privacy, that the husband-wife relationship may have changed in response to the increased intimacy the two enjoyed while the kids were gone. Rarely is the lack of connubial privacy voiced to children.

On one occasion, however, the unexpected arrival of a father interrupted his son and a girlfriend. The son accused him of "ruining my sex life," and the father couldn't help retorting, "What do you think you're doing to mine?"

Slovenliness is another matter. Approximately 75 percent of parents interviewed implied that a child's middle name was Slob. Charlotte, during a phone interview, said she had been cleaning Danny's room and didn't know if she should use a vacuum or a shovel. To answer the phone, she had to track it down by the cord lying under a pile of laundry on the floor. When she complains about the way he keeps the room, he says, "There's a big difference between us, mom. I have more important things to do."

The big difference, the way another mother sees it, is "I live in a house and my daughter acts like she lives in a sty." The complaint voiced by countless parents of sons and daughters was the inconsideration of leaving a dirty bathtub. Divided by sex, the complaint lodged most often against daughters was their habit of shampooing long hair daily. Often, the result was plumbing bills because the drains got clogged. The major complaint against sons was their habit of dropping wet towels on the bed. One result was extra laundry—blankets plus towels. "Danny took three showers a day and used three towels each time," Charlotte said. "I tried buying bigger towels, thinking he would use only one." She ended up laundering bigger towels.

Pointing out the laundry problem, in most instances, rarely encouraged neatness. Danny invariably replied, "I'll do my own stuff." But Charlotte was afraid the towels would mildew by the time he got around to washing them. Nor did the threat of leaving his room dirty worry Danny. He'd answer, "Just close my door so you won't see it." Danny, like countless home-ing pigeons, spread his possessions over any available surface (except the ceiling) and acted oblivious to the mess.

What does all this sloppiness tell parents? "That the grown child had lived in an environment where no one policed him," Dr. Potter said, "that any neatness he exhibited before he left home was due to parents' policing rather than the kid's need for some kind of neatness.

"It could also mean he was in an environment where neatness wasn't a virtue. Sometimes, people, particularly children, do things a particular way because they haven't seen another way to do them."

Then, they go off to school, see other ways to live, try them, and like them. They see no reason to discontinue the aberrant behavior when they come home. But, if parents are consistent in their demands, they just will not accept sloppiness or inconsideration at home. An adult addition to the family should be a help, not a drain, on its system.

Ted and Charlotte, however, made few demands on Danny. They saw no point in demanding quiet, cleanliness, and help. The demands only resulted in arguments. The couple found it easier to overlook Danny's irritating habits. There are times, however, when Ted feels wrong for not demanding more. He is annoyed to see Charlotte overworked while Danny just sits there. With typical parental ambivalence, Ted defended Danny: "My son's a likable person. My complaints are only irritations, and I have to give him a chance."

15

They're Only Birds
in a Gilded Cage

From a parental view, home-ing pigeons have no reason to complain. Yet, they do.

"I can't understand it," said a perplexed father. "I don't interfere in my son Charles's life because I remember how my dad ran my life.

"He has his own bedroom, keeps all of his money. He goes to work, sees his girl, and goes to the toilet."

Charles's mother was equally perplexed. "I don't know why he's unhappy at home. He takes no responsibility for the mundane details of life—doing his own laundry, picking up his clothes or anything he drops anywhere in the house. He doesn't even bring his laundry down to the hamper."

The results of our questionnaire show that few home-ing pigeons hoot at the amenities found in the nest. They cooed answers to "What's the easiest part of living with parents again?" Uniformly, they no longer had to contend with laundry, phone bills, rent, shopping for groceries, or getting the use of a car.

Their responses sounded like testimonials for Home-ing Pigeon Hilton. Charles, in particular, described accommodations as "a hotel with maid and food service."

Student home-ing pigeons sang the praises of fewer distractions from study at home and more time to earn money than if they lived on their own. Those struggling to get off the ground found home was the natural environment to obtain emotional support and help in making career decisions. Others were drawn by the birdcalls of people around all the time and the certainty of food in the house. In a few instances, parents were the lure to children who had a good relationship at home. "My mom and dad are the greatest people," said Charles's girlfriend Ellen. "They've made their place in heaven handling all my crises when I was in high school."

The strong pull of home has been drawn to the attention of family counselors. "Those who find a loving atmosphere are the ones most likely to come back," commented reality therapist Phyllis Warren. To these home-ing pigeons, home is a place where everyone thinks you're wonderful, where you get emotional nourishment, and where you're made to feel important.

Some counselors are convinced, however, that seeking the security of home is a step backward in maturity. "If a child doesn't break from home," said clinical psychologist Dr. Rosalie Kirschner, "he's always a child. It's like working as a doctor in a place where you have interned. There, despite your qualifications, you're always a student." One of her patients said she would rather die on the streets than return home. "Yet, she did go back because it was more comfortable than taking the responsibility of an apartment," Dr. Kirschner continued.

Ellen moved out twice—once to school and another time to live with a man. She sees no reason to leave unless she and Charles get married. "It's very comfortable here. Too comfortable," she admitted.

"It's nice to come home to a mother's good cooking. It's nice to be able to spill my laundry in the hamper and have someone else do it. It's nice to be able to say, 'Mom, I need these pants shortened.' Even though mom complains, she shortens them."

Yet, maid and food service aren't entirely satisfying. Coming home wasn't part of the average home-ing pigeon's dream, not after having lived away from home. Generally, the home-ing pigeon remarked with nostalgia, "I ate when I felt like it, did nothing when I felt like it, and stayed up all night when I wanted to." Security and stability seem staid alongside a home-ing pigeon's flight of fancy: a singles pad a la Hugh Hefner or a home out of *House and Garden*.

A clear-eyed home-ing pigeon will see a stay at home as an opportunity for a start. Most see it as a form of failure, an inability to take off without help. Like the poor man invited to eat at a rich man's table, he appreciates the good meal but wishes he didn't need it.

"When the kid comes home, he says, 'Let mom do it,' " said associate professor Dr. Joyce Nolen. "He asks for help verbally and nonverbally, but he is ambivalent. When parents do what they as parents are expected to do, he resents the help because he wants to be on his own.

"His self-concept is hurt. He's torn between crawling back into the womb and wanting the experience of being his own person.

"He's uncomfortable about himself. Other kids are on their own. Why can't he make it? Part of the problems he creates is his ambivalence. He's not measuring up, and he resents it.

"Kids in their twenties come to me and say, 'I think my life's over.' They figure they're supposed to be making $20,000 to $25,000 a year just starting out. They feel they have failed if they don't."

Home, like any other image carried near to the heart in a distant place, can be disappointing close up. The first target of a home-ing pigeon's frustrations, according to our questionnaire, is the neighborhood. It's an impersonal place to attack when the company of family members no long suffices.

At school or in a singles' complex, companionship was a door away. Not in the old neighborhood. Eileen, an extreme example, was miserable in Morton, Illinois, after she had trailed adventure to Egypt as a nurse. "All my friends are married," she said. "If I want to talk about diaper rash and the price of tomatoes, I can visit them. Otherwise, there's no one else and nothing to do here."

The suburbs headed the places listed for a drubbing. They were described as isolated, and lacking the cultural advantages of a large city or the slow tempo of a small town. They're depressing because old friends don't live there anymore. The cry "I'm lonely" is beat on eardrums once the honeymoon of family reunion is over. "I love my little brothers," said Charles's girlfriend, "but I won't go so far as to say I'm glad to spend all my time with an eleven-, thirteen-, and fifteen-year-old."

She and Charles are "lucky." They have each other, though they live nearly two hundred miles apart. "Otherwise my social life suffers by being at home," she complained. "There's no one close by to telephone and say, 'Let's do something tonight.' "

Charles echoed her predicament. "But I spend a lot of time going down to see her," he said. "We're thinking of marriage, but with the money situation the way it is, I don't think it will happen right away."

Both are accumulating possessions: a car, sports equipment, a typewriter, a wardrobe, a savings account. Still, their satisfaction is limited by thinking, "We'd never get these things living on our own."

Other young people take trips or visit out-of-town friends looking for other places to live, but the consensus is "There seems no place else to go."

Sweethearts, like Charles and his girl, put off marriage or go through long engagements backing the anticipated results of the 1980 Census Bureau Report that Americans are waiting longer to wed. Nearly 50 percent of all women aged twenty to twenty-four have never been married, a sharp increase from the 29 percent of single women in the same age group twenty years ago.

The irony is that most young people are looking for enduring relationships. But there's little encouragement by our society to place personal relationships such as marriage above personal fulfillment. There's also an increasing fear of entering marriage and putting up with the daily strains of living together.

"Yet, young people want to be someone special, and the place where you seem to count the most and where there are commitments is within the family. So they go home," said Margaret Hellie Huyck, an associate professor of psychology at Illinois Institute of Technology, Chicago, Illinois.

It's not utopia.

As shown in our interviews with home-ing pigeons, the major outside issue is the lack of neighborhood activities—and the major inside issue is the lack of privacy. Physical comforts are soon taken for granted. With few exceptions, they are the same as before the young adults left. But in their emotional turmoil, they have a stronger need than ever to be secluded. This is consistent with their need to be independent. They don't want interference. They don't want to be policed by parents. At best, they expect mothers and fathers to be consultants—and only when they want to consult them.

The home-ing pigeons also get the message that parents really don't approve of the way they live, so the young persons look for ways to say, "Leave me alone. Let me be."

The way young adults use the word *privacy* makes it interchangeable with *freedom*, particularly the freedom to use their time as they please. Charles, whose joy at coming home wore thin, explained,

"My mother's a big stickler on having the three of us sit down for dinner every night, and that just doesn't wash well with me. Once in a while, I get lucky and meet an old friend who wants to go out to eat. It cramps my style to have to inform her ahead of time I won't be home."

In other instances, the demand for privacy is a request for freedom in the space home-ing pigeons occupy. Ellen sleeps in the bedroom an eleven-year-old brother had occupied before she came home. "He sometimes gets in there and locks me out," she said. "It's my turf now. But he can't see that.

"And one of the three boys usually stands outside the bathroom in the morning, yelling, 'You're taking too long.' Being boys, they don't understand that a girl needs time to blow-dry her hair and put on makeup."

Her cousin, Susan, with whom she corresponds, has neither of Ellen's problems. She's the only child home and was reinstated in her old room. But she suspects that her mother invades her privacy when she goes through her room to clean it. "I've stopped leaving my letters or other mail out on my desk," she said. "I've never caught her reading them, but I have this dreadful feeling." Not that Susan has anything shameful to hide. She just doesn't want "to be spied on." For peace of mind, she keeps her correspondence in a locked desk drawer.

A young man she works with in a real estate office insured his privacy by installing a lock that requires a key on his bedroom door. "It distresses my mother, and my father screams, 'I don't want a locked room in my house.' But I got tired of nasty cracks about its condition when mom cleaned my room or dad answered the second telephone line in there. Now, they think I'm wacko or hiding something."

To an impartial witness the measure he took seems extreme, but "each of us needs a different degree of privacy. And it's not for someone else to determine whether our degree is too high or too low. However absurd it may seem to another person, we are entitled to handle it the way we want to in our own space," said therapist Dr. Jessie Potter.

The invasion, real or imagined, was also considered a threat to autonomous action. Grown children who answered to no one while living away from home did not want to be accountable to parents. Charles's girlfriend went up in arms the day her father opened a bill addressed to her. It was for pots and pans (kept hidden under her bed in a hope chest). "He asked what it was all about," she said. "Without definite marriage plans, I didn't want to tell him. He still hasn't gotten over my living with a man.

"But he had no right to open my mail, and I told him so. His defense was 'It's my house, and I can open anything.'

"You know how that made me feel? I may have been raised here, but it's not home. He as much as said so. I've begun to think I'm a boarder, and I feel out of it with my parents."

College friends to whom Ellen writes commiserate about a loss of personal privacy. A consensus is "Things formerly kept private are now becoming public." For example, the way they manage money is under scrutiny. "My folks say I don't handle it well," a friend of Ellen's in Texas said. "They ask where all the money goes—money I earn. I'm asked to account for every penny, and I resent it."

Charles's old friends complain that parents eavesdrop on their telephone conversations and ask questions about what they hear not only after a telephone conversation but during one. "It's like living in a goldfish bowl," said a market consultant who tries to make his personal phone calls during his lunch hour or after work from a booth.

"Policing a kid certainly doesn't help him mature nor add to family harmony," Dr. Potter said. "Whatever parents overhear is none of their business unless the kid calls the conversation to their attention."

In the same vein, coordinator of Consultation and Community Services Dr. Robert Mark stressed the young adult's right to privacy. "Just as an adolescent, growing up at home, needs privacy, so does the adult child, who returns home, need privacy. Parents should avoid intruding into his room and should try to suppress the need to know every movement he makes."

There is no question that adjustments in perception have to be made by young adults and their parents during a reunion. The answer on one questionnaire to "What causes problems at home?" pinpointed the privacy issue for a young adult, who shrouded her identity. "I would say the most difficult part about coming home is having to account to someone after having had absolute freedom," wrote H.F., age twenty-two, female. "Often, parents just don't realize that you have been on your own for four years and have very obviously survived very nicely without them telling you what to do.

"Once you have been a little independent, you are unwilling or unable to revert to precollege days. And it's important that everyone in the family understand this before the tension and misunderstanding set in."

Is there a society other than ours that puts such a high premium on privacy? In some societies, according to sociologists, all aspects of family life are conducted in one room and before the eyes of everyone in the family. One sociologist, Arlie Hochschild, believes privacy is generally a value that arises as a result of privilege

Camille, a young woman who lives down the street from Charles, appreciated her middle-class upbringing. "My mom did a great job of raising me," said the part-time travel agent and student. "Everything she did was always in my best interest. So I wish she would give me enough credit that I now know right from wrong. I'm not a thirteen-year-old girl anymore."

Two habits she'd like her mother to discard are nagging and worrying. Usually, they're part of the same package. When Camille takes a trip, she is expected to call home as soon as she arrives safely. Before she leaves the house in inclement weather, she has to give an inventory of the measures she has taken to protect herself against it. "I can't leave the house without being told, 'Don't forget your key. Lock the door. Put on your galoshes!' And I'm continually asked, 'Do you have enough gas in the car?'

"I try to keep from saying, 'I don't know how I made it this far without you telling me what to do,' but I don't always restrain myself. Then I feel guilty because I know I've hurt them with my rebuff."

It's advisable for parents to give their grown children encouragement and permission to make decisions on their own and to keep from saying "I told you so" if the thinking had been faulty.

Young adults don't stay any one way, and parents have to learn to continually respond to new situations. They have to be flexible. If not, young adults regress to the role of children, and that's not comfortable either for them or their parents.

Camille's older sister understands that their mom, by nature, is a worrier. She tries to appeal to her mother's sense of humor by saying, "I'll call you only if I don't get there." She volunteers information about where she'll be and with whom she's spending the evening. "That isn't enough," she sighed. "I'm bombarded with questions when I come back. And the feeling I get is she doesn't trust me."

Lack of trust seems to be the nub of the privacy problem. Parents, some home-ing pigeons believe, can't let go. It doesn't seem to matter that they've passed their eighteenth birthdays. As soon as they come home, mom feels compelled to resume the role of nurturer and dad resumes the role of advisor. "There'd be nothing wrong with that," Charles said, "if they didn't expect me to act like an obedient son at home and an aggressive man on the job. Sometimes, I think all this mothering and fathering is done with my best interests in mind. Other times, I feel it's done to satisfy their own needs."

Clinical psychologist Dr. Eugene Southwell believes, "If an adult child goes back home to live with his parents, things go right back to where they were when he left. Even when a married child goes home for a short visit, there is a lot of regression. Parent and child fall back into old patterns and habits. The behavior is situation specific. Attitudes have not changed. Parents will treat grown adults as children, and grown adults will revert to childish habits."

Behind the fight for privacy are home-ing pigeons' fears of being taken over by their parents, of falling back into the old role of dependency, a role they believed they shed while they were away. A young lawyer cousin of Charles had come home to wait to pass the bar. "It was a rite of passage I wanted to share with my parents, to sort of repeat other times in our relationship that were exciting and nerve-racking, like waiting to get into college and then law school. I expected it to be a pleasant experience.

"It was terrible. My dad criticized the way I was looking for a job. My mother waited up at night until I got home. When my friends came by, they were treated like kids, too. Can you imagine? My mother served them frozen doughnuts so the chocolate wouldn't be soft and mess their hands and possibly the house."

Other home-ing pigeons complained of feeling uncomfortable about bringing friends home. The chief complaint of young men was the lack of privacy in which to entertain a girlfriend. Young women worried because their dates were assailed with questions. Charles can't have parties at home because his folks don't drink and don't want anyone else to drink. His girlfriend said, "When Charles is over, there's no place for us to talk privately. Either my folks are in the same room or I feel their presence."

Young adults who had the least problems were those whose homes continued to be structured environments. "My mother used the iron fist and my father used the iron foot if I stepped out of line," explained Michael, Charles's best friend. "I always knew the consequences of doing wrong. They'd either make me stay in my room or withdraw my privileges

"I was never disciplined in a wild rage, and once the problem was over, it was never mentioned again. My parents believed that a person is more important than the conflict. Our family is people-people."

Before Michael came home, he and his parents set up guidelines and stipulations. His mother and father clearly communicated, "If you live at home, you have to do your share." His chores were to shovel the snow, put salt in the water softener, change the filters on the furnace, and clean the gutters in spring. "I look at it as a way of paying room and board," said the graduate student whose work load keeps him from taking a job.

The stipulation he gave his parents was not to meddle into private affairs he didn't want to tell them about. In the eleven months since he returned, neither Michael nor his parents have overstepped their boundaries. Both generations know the rules. "I keep my room tidy because I'm a neat person," he said. "As for laundry? Whoever gets to the washer first does it. It's not only mother's job. It's a matter of helping each other out."

Neither his parents nor Michael view his return as a form of failure. They see it as being well-off enough to give him a chance to concentrate on his schoolwork. He sees it as a chance to spend more time together before he goes his own way. He has everything he needs at home except the right to play loud music. "But I won't be unhappy to leave. Leaving will mean I'm independent.

"But don't get me wrong. I'm not dependent on home. When I leave in the morning, my mother is rubbing the sleep out of her eyes. When I come home, she's cooking dinner. And each of us has done enough in between to make good conversation. My friends are envious of our homelife."

A successful relationship generally is based on an exchange situation. Parents who provide sustenance are looked upon as human beings, not as doormats. Grown children who require "the leg up" are given a ladder, not a crutch. They are expected to assume responsibility. And there is a mutual respect for the adult rights of each age group.

Part Six

Relationships

We can be absolutely certain only about the things we do not understand.

Eric Hoffer

16

Sons and Daughters Play Different Tunes—Strains of Coming Home

Ambivalent is the son who returns home to live with his parents. He sees home as a refuge but fears to be seen as a refugee.

He was taught early that manliness was annexed to independence. His sister was permitted to pursue independence in subtle ways. He was asked to declare it.

To be fair to parents, they treat both sons and daughters with few differences. But when the son steps out of his sex role, he doesn't hear "Vive la différence." Disapproval follows his inappropriate behavior.

Author Juanita H. Williams said it succinctly in her book *Psychology of Women* (New York: W. W. Norton & Company, Inc., 1977): "In our society it's more important for a boy to be all boy than for a girl to be all girl."

The nitty-gritty started with choosing a layette. While a mother might have passed down a son's blue bunting to an infant daughter with impunity, she shrank from zipping a baby boy into his sister's pink one.

In the infant's somnolent state, he wouldn't have known the difference. But his mother (and the world) would have known he was wearing a feminine color, and she couldn't bring herself to break this form of sex segregation.

Striving to keep his maleness apparent continued in small ways throughout his development. Parents, relatives, and friends plied him with toys implying male adventure—six-shooters, race cars, airplanes, and rocket ships. By the same token, his sister received dolls, sewing sets, play dishes, and kiddie cosmetics. Brother may not have consciously known the difference until he encountered a double standard.

It was OK for sister to play with boys' toys (if he would share them). She got a lot of smiles from adults when she dressed up in a cowboy outfit or popped a fake cigar between her teeth imitating daddy. But the smiles became frowns when he played with dolls or dabbed perfume behind his ears imitating mommy. And heaven help him if he played dress-up in one of sister's dresses.

The message was clear: What was good for the goose was bad for the gander.

No longer the sleepy infant, the alert male offspring became aware of other expectations. It was OK for sister to cry when she skinned her knees. He was exhorted to be "a little man" and dam his tears. She was kept in the house to be given comfort. He was sent back out to play.

The meaning of that dispatch couldn't be missed. To be a boy was to be tougher than a girl. No wonder when the going got rough in the outside world, the adult-age son was more reluctant than the adult-age daughter to return home for succor.

Throughout his growing-up years, he had to avoid being called a sissy, a tag used at the drop of a hat when he showed a lack of courage. A man, he was taught by parents and peers, entered the fray and emerged a winner. His friends were as intolerant as his relatives when he broke a sex-role precedent.

Within the family, he couldn't help seeing how sex roles were defined. The man was the provider, and the woman was provided for. Even if he was reared in a liberal atmosphere where both parents worked, it seemed more important that daddy go to work than that mommy keep her job. The communication that a man's worth was equated with his work sank into his subconscious.

Yet, a boy learned to enjoy a home where his comforts are provided by females. They cooked his meals, laundered his clothes, cleaned his room, and were responsible for grocery shopping. His responsibilities were mowing the lawn, lugging out the garbage, and other heavy chores reinforcing his prowess as a male. Some young men looked upon these muscle-building jobs as ways to work out.

By the time he reached the age of majority, his parents were no longer financially liable for his welfare according to the law in fifty states. In 75 percent of the states, the age of majority is eighteen, which coincides with the usual year a child graduates from high school.

At eighteen, Jonathan was chronologically qualified to enter college. According to his mother, he had shown no signs that he was emotionally unprepared. She termed him a wholesome kid who brought home good grades, had several close friends, and who, without being asked, took care of the lawn and the maintenance of the family cars.

He was sent off to a college on the opposite coast with a clear-cut career goal to become an accountant.

His cheerful and helpful presence was missed at home, but there was no question that it was in Jonathan's best interests to board at school. His father hoped the experience of being independently dependent would teach him how to be more competitive. One of his disappointments was that his son wouldn't compete in sports even though he was an excellent tennis player.

Jonathan's mother was happy to see her son make the break, believing that staying at home would stunt his growth. His maternal grandmother was also part of the household, and she was afraid he was getting too much mothering.

A year later, Jonathan returned to live at home, the base from which he commuted to a city college. He explained that he was more comfortable at home and made no bones about placing physical comforts high on the list of reasons for returning home.

His parents openly accepted his decision and expected Jonathan to fit into the household the same way as before he left. They had an unpleasant surprise. Jonathan did everything he could to put distance between himself and his family.

"He was friendlier to the cat than he was to his grandmother," his mother said. "I couldn't believe the change."

Always a good eater who enjoyed his mother's cooking, he suddenly decided she didn't know how to prepare food and refused to eat at the dinner table. Instead, he would fix himself a meal from leftovers in the refrigerator, ignoring the fact that his mother had cooked those, too.

Before Jonathan left for college, he would attend family celebrations of milestone birthdays and anniversaries. The longer he stayed home, the more stubborn he became about visiting relatives.

"You wouldn't expect me to go with you if I lived in my own apartment," he told his folks.

At the same time, he fulfilled his obligations of outside work, maintaining the cars and providing his own pocket money. But when he wasn't at night school, at work, or out with his friends, he studied or listened to music in his room—with the door closed.

"Sons and daughters go to their room to escape the family," said clinical psychologist Dr. Rosalie Kirschner. "They're afraid of being engulfed."

His mother accepted his behavior with more forbearance than his father, but she admitted she expected him to go out on his own when he graduated from college. Instead, he found employment in a company located fifteen miles from home and is still living in his parents' house.

Once he was working, Jonathan's parents insisted he contribute sixty dollars a month to the household just to let him know that "when you're an adult, living isn't free." He paid it grudgingly. He could not understand why parents who live in a big house in an affluent suburb should need his money. Obviously, he blocked out the message that they now considered him grown-up.

With enough money to live independently had he chosen to, he moved further away emotionally from his family. Knowing his father's views, he dated a girl outside of his religion and refused to attend church even on Easter or Christmas.

In addition to refusing to eat his mother's food, he showed in other ways that he did not need her. Jonathan would not let her repair or iron his clothes. He did that himself. His behavior bewildered her.

Asked to comment, therapist Dr. Jessie Potter stated, "We raise boys to be OK only if they're independent. So it's far less than OK in their minds to return even to accepting families. This ambivalence causes a lot of friction on the subconscious level. Overly independent behavior is their way of keeping a distance. They have to prove to themselves that coming home doesn't mean they're inadequate."

Although Jonathan's father made it clear it was time for him to leave, Jonathan made no effort to find his own apartment and turned down offers to share a place with his friends. He claimed he'd be ready to move out when he could afford to own a house or condominium and went out of his way to avoid his father. The confused man still feels hurt that Jonathan didn't visit him when he was hospitalized.

Where will the story end? Jonathan's mother believes he won't move out until he gets married. Despite his recent behavior she sees him as the kind of young man who needs to live where he is tied to family.

She tolerated more than her husband who accuses her of babying Jonathan. "I'm very fond of my son," she said. "He's easy to live with in what I consider the important areas. Unlike his sister, he takes care of his health, holds a job, and is going for a master's degree to improve his career chances. I worry less about Jonathan than about my daughter. But he is touchier lately, and I don't know why."

Her attitude corroborates an observation made by numerous psychologists. In general, parents seem to be more tolerant of children of the opposite sex. The boy, for instance, is an ego extension of the father, not the mother. She will have more difficulty when a daughter returns home to live.

Unlike Jonathan, his older sister Rita was unhappy at home before she left for an out-of-state college. Restricted in food and activities by extrinsic asthma, she rebelled against other restraints.

Rita broke curfew, smoked pot, and joined a crowd who made sex a pastime. At each reminder from her mother that she was endangering her health, not to mention her good name, Rita ran out the door or shut herself in her room to play rock music until the house vibrated from the noise.

She saw her mother as an opponent. Whenever the worried woman spoke up, she was reminded that aggravation could bring on an asthmatic attack.

"A daughter may use an illness to be treated like a little girl or use it as blackmail against her mother," Dr. Kirschner explained.

Obviously, asthma was Rita's club against her mother's protectiveness. But her mother couldn't refrain from expressing her feelings, and the din from arguments was often louder than the blare of the rock music.

"I was glad to see her go to college," her mother said. "Not that I worried less. I saw less."

The sense of protection that Rita rebelled against in high school brought her home after college graduation. Having lived four years on campus as just another student, she wanted to return to a caring atmosphere and vowed to handle it this time.

"I see a double standard in the different reasons why a son or a daughter comes home," said social worker Robert Wagner, MSW, whose case load in private practice, at one point, was 25 percent returnees who needed counseling for various reasons. "The son is seen as suffering in his male image, and the daughter is seen as needing protection. Both views are crippling emotionally but less a stigma for the woman."

Rita's mother had also vowed to keep peace between them and promised herself to be more accepting of her daughter's values. Despite both women's good intentions, arguments resumed soon after Rita returned.

Her mother stopped criticizing her daughter's late hours. But she put her foot down about smoking pot in the house. Nor could she sit by and watch Rita chain-smoke without pestering her to stop.

In retaliation, Rita criticized her mother's friends, her clothes, and her role of homemaker. They were all too "conservative," and she spat out the word like an obscenity. Arguments invariably ended with Rita screaming, "I don't have to be like you."

The two women resembled each other in looks and carriage. Their mannerisms were similar enough to attract comments by strangers. Rita, however, was heavier than her mother. When she was dragged to Weight Watchers, her mother, not she, lost weight.

"Problems between mother and daughter are sharper in unpleasantness and strife," said Wagner. "There's an underlying competition between them."

In the classic mode, mothers also tend to be less tolerant of anger directed toward them by a child of their own sex. Fathers show more forbearance to a daughter's hostile attacks.

It worked that way in Rita's household. Dad was an ally who told his wife to stay out of Rita's business.

"Jack would say, 'Leave her alone, you can't change her,' " his wife recalled. "I had stopped nagging Rita about her social life and morals, but I couldn't stop nagging about her health."

Her mother was aware of one reason for the difference in attitudes between her husband and herself. Jack worked late hours and weekends, times when Rita and she were home together. Simply put, he saw less of his daughter.

He didn't hear Rita refuse to help with household chores. He didn't see the dirty ashtrays strewn around the house or the way she sneaked forbidden food from the refrigerator. He pictured Rita as a victim of an overcritical mother.

"Mother and daughter compete for the father," said Dr. Kirschner. "In a household where sex roles are assigned, the daughter becomes manipulative."

Rita's mother finally tried to escape her daughter's second rebellion by getting a part-time job that demanded weekend work. But even in the short times they spent together, Rita's behavior would provoke arguments. In fits of anger, the mother would scream at the daughter, "Why in the hell don't you get out if you don't like it here, love." The "love" was telling, and Rita stayed on.

A year went by before Rita found the job she wanted and the man with whom she wanted to live. It was "Good-bye mama, I have a life of my own."

Her mother still worried about Rita's getting pregnant. Rita could not take birth control pills. She worried about Rita's smoking and drinking, and eating the wrong foods. The mothering habits of a child's lifetime were hard to change—even from a distance.

Six months later the distance looked as if it was going to narrow. Rita phoned asking to come home again. Her live-in lover had left, and she was feeling an asthma attack coming on. With a deep sigh, mother responded, "I'll pick you up."

In the next moment, Jonathan walked through the door announcing he was eating supper out. The mother of two home-ing pigeons said to no one in particular, "I hope to God Rita doesn't make this permanent."

Lila has a son, twenty-five, and a daughter, twenty, perched in the house. Self-doubt plagued her because both flocked home.

"In some way that I don't know, I tied my children to home," she said, setting the dinner table with a cloth and fresh flowers.

Each moved back for the same overt reason. Harold went off to a private college in 1973 looking forward to the fun of campus life. He found it in bars and the girls' dorm. His grades suffered, and he was put on probation. The following year, he was back in the nest.

Lila suggested Harold room with a friend who was attending the same junior college where Harold would make up his credits. The arrangement, she argued, would give Harold two advantages. He would get the chance to become himself, without family interference, and yet be close enough to eat home cooking. Her husband refused to underwrite the cost of separate living quarters for his son.

Harold was pleased by the decision. He admitted missing the tumult of interchanges with his sister and parents while he was away. Instead, he accepted a job in his father's business and lost his ambition to return to school.

"I was against it," Lila said taking a roast from the oven. "There's more to boarding college than education. It gives a young person a chance to be independent."

Not that Lila doesn't love her son. She described him as a wonderful, loving boy who as a kid usually did what she asked. If not, she went after him with a fly swatter.

As Harold grew older, he learned to avoid the swatter with demonstrations of affection and offers to run to the store to bring back Lila's favorite flavor of ice cream. He began to call Lila by her first name, receiving tacit permission by the reward of dimpled smiles. Charming and handsome, he used his looks and personality to wheedle his way into Lila's special favor—and succeeded.

"One of the categories of returnees that I see has overprotective, permissive parents who nurture dependency," Wagner said. "In men, this category of parents is very crippling. It retards the development of responsibility."

Lack of responsibility is Lila's major complaint against Harold. Although Harold starts a project with enthusiasm, he doesn't carry through. He dropped out of junior college. He began a series of tennis lessons and stopped halfway. At last count, he hadn't balanced his checkbook in six months.

"He has no sense of organization, no management of time," Lila said, tossing a salad. "When pressed for time, he gets things done but even then leaves a lot of loose ends."

On the plus side, his personal cleanliness is above reproach. He handles his emotions and becomes volatile only when he is pushed to the wall. Lila found no fault with him as a person. She raised him to be loving, and he has never disappointed her by acting cold.

"I'm glad he considers the house his turf," she said watching the clock. "I only wish Harold would feel he should have his own turf."

The longer he lived at home, the more she enjoyed his presence. Lila disclaimed any selfish reason for wanting him to leave.

"I want him to go for his sake," she said, looking worried because Harold was late. "I want him to know that he has to think and do for himself."

Harold's sister Caryn exhibited the same homing instinct as her brother. She went the identical distance in college that he did. Within a year, she was on probation and back in the home loft.

But Caryn hadn't wanted to go to college in the first place. Never a good student, she had asked for a respite before plunging into more schoolwork.

Her fate was decided at the dinner table. Caryn stated her case. She preferred to work in an office or a store for a year. By living at home, she figured to save enough money to buy her own sports car. Placing her hand over her heart, she promised to give school another try when the car was paid for.

Lila said, "No.

"You haven't any skills to get a decent-paying job," she remembered telling her daughter. "Your goal doesn't seem realistic to me. You can always use my car when you're home."

Caryn appealed to her father. He shrugged his shoulders and said, "Your mother knows best what's good for a girl."

Caryn passed the subjects she liked but flunked rhetoric and economics and had to come home. Lila's disappointment in her performance was one-sided. Caryn seemed content.

She spent the first weeks at home sleeping, phoning college friends, and trying to appease her mother. Once stingy with her time, she began to take over the housework, run errands, and act as Lila's companion when dad worked late.

Lila was unhappy to find Caryn perching in the roost instead of living among young people at college. Boarding college had been denied to Lila when she was Caryn's age. At forty-six, she still felt robbed of the chance to be on her own. Through Caryn she expected to meet the unmet needs of her own adolescence.

"My mom was forty-one when I was born," Lila said. "I was God's gift to her and never lived alone one day. I went from my parents' house directly to my husband's house."

According to Dr. Kirschner, a mother without a strong identity of her own will look for her daughter to accomplish what she has not. It can be exasperating to find out the daughter has different goals, but the wish to accomplish through her won't permit the child to grow.

Finding it unbearable to watch Caryn "waste her days," Lila, through connections, found her a job as a receptionist in a doctor's office. Gleeful to be finally doing what she wanted, Caryn didn't mention her mother's hypocrisy to her face.

"When she wanted me to work, she forgot she had put down my job skills," Caryn said in a separate interview.

In the office, twenty-year-old Caryn met a thirty-five-year-old patient and began to date him. When Lila read in Caryn's diary that he was a recovering alcoholic, she ordered her to stop seeing him. Then she reasoned with her. And then she begged Caryn to break up with him.

Each time Caryn assured Lila that it was nothing serious and that he hadn't had a drink in two years. It didn't matter that he was fifteen years older than her and had been married and was the father of a twelve-year-old.

Another form of control over Caryn had been taken from Lila. Caryn was independently mobile now with the sports car she had bought. In desperation, Lila phoned the man demanding he stop seeing Caryn. His answer was, "I won't do anything to hurt her."

He informed Caryn of the call, and the result was a severe strain on the mother-daughter relationship. Caryn stopped talking to Lila except to say, "Pass the salt" and other trivial comments. She was no longer the child Lila once described as "someone I could always talk to."

The tension in the house didn't seem to affect Caryn. It bothered Lila enough to take a paying job for the first time in her married life. She still cannot understand how the strain between them started and remains a concerned mother.

"I can't say 'Stop seeing him or move out,' " she said. "It's not to Caryn's advantage. Where would she go?"

What do professional counselors say to mothers who cannot untie themselves from children's bib strings? They're sympathetic because it's not easy to unlearn the reflex of picking up crying infants to give them comfort. Professional counselors are also realistic. When infants are adults, they become too heavy to pick up and should bear the weight of their own burdens.

Dr. Potter, wearing the hat of parent, said, "Don't be dependent on your child to define you as a person. A good relationship should be without demand or command."

With characteristic candor she described herself as "the kind of mother you might call a nudge." When she was cold, she put a sweater on her child. If her child said he didn't need more reading light, she turned one on anyway. Not until she became more self-involved did she become less controlled by her children's actions.

"No parent should be bent out of shape by a child's behavior," she said. "Nor should a child be bent out of shape by a parent's expectations.

"In particular, the son who shows ambivalent feelings about his return home should be left alone. The ambivalence is his way of keeping a distance until he is ready, emotionally, to move in."

A quote that pleases Dr. Potter is well loved by young people: "If you love something, let it go free. If it's meant to be, it'll return. When it does, love it forever."

Dr. Kirschner corroborated Dr. Potter's counsel. "It would be great to be a role model to our children," said the mother of three grown children, two sons and a daughter. "We feel safer about kids when they have our values. Still we have to let them go so they come back to us in the first place."

When Dr. Kirschner's daughter came home between terms after living by herself, the mother's first reflex was to impose restrictions to insure her daughter's safety. But she had second thoughts. How could she give a curfew to a young woman who had been living without one?

"I did say, 'Try not to make it too late,' " Dr. Kirschner recalled. "And by treating her as an adult, she responded like one."

She offered additional insight into the situation of a son who acts hostile when he comes home. He may be disturbed by his feelings of closeness to his mother and fights it by being harsher than he means to be. "A parent would be wise to let him keep his distance," she said. "Let him maintain his position. He has a great need for privacy, and it should be respected."

As a psychologist, Dr. Kirschner saw mothers keep adult daughters dependent upon them by refusing to acknowledge they were capable of handling adult responsibilities. These young women were kept under control by the enforcement of arbitrary rules laid down by the domineering parent. At any hint of rebellion, the home-ing pigeons were sent on guilt trips by a recital of "all the things I've done for you."

"The mother is also being put upon," Dr. Kirschner said. "She should remember that a young girl is as strong, if not stronger, than she is and should permit her child to carry a share of the load."

The classic problem facing the home-ing pigeon is trying to maintain a personal identity. Back in the bosom of the family, it becomes easy to nurse old wounds and forget he or she has been weaned.

The classic problem facing a parent is learning to live with an adult who is fighting the reemergence of the child within. Because each parent may perceive opposite sides of the home-ing pigeon's dilemma, parents' split reactions to the home-ing pigeon's behavior can play havoc with a marriage. The young adult can adulterate the new relationship the couple built while living without grown children at home.

17

Fox in the Chicken Coop—Ruffling Mom and Dad's Feathers

Lyrics of the old song "My Blue Heaven" romanticized the little family. When baby made three, left unsung was the harmony or discord the arrival of that first child brings to a duet.

Baby dubbed the soprano "mom" and the tenor "dad," and gave the couple a blood tie. Carrying baby over the threshold was a husband and wife's major step into the world of adult responsibility. Purportedly, parents left their own childhood outside the door.

The lightweight bundle was also a heavyweight contender for mom and dad's time and energy. Ideally, baby was a medley of their love. Really, baby was a purveyor of fatigue. The young mother's travail in the labor room was a prelude to the labor to follow. Written into the score were feeding round-the-clock, changing dirty diapers, and placating yowls—tasks that can take the romance out of parenthood and, sometimes, out of marriage.

"The parents may want babies, but may be dismayed to discover what they are like. Hundreds of couples studied over the years concur that parenthood is a critical experience, and that marital satisfaction drops sharply with the coming of the first baby," wrote Evelyn Millis Duvall in *Marriage and Family Development* (New York: J. B. Lippincott Company, 1977).

By the accident of her anatomy, mom was more directly involved

177

with baby than dad was. Doubtful of her capabilities to be in charge of a helpless human's survival, mom may have allotted baby a disproportionate amount of time. She may have also resented being tied to a little person who offered more work than companionship while the other half of the duet was free to sing his old songs.

Dad, faced with a tired wife, may have regarded baby as a sour note. He had been pushed off-center from his wife's attentions. Baby always seemed to cry at the moment dad wanted to eat, talk, or make love. Home became a "blues" heaven. Mom suffered postpartum blues, and dad sang them. Baby, in all innocence, threw the duet off-key. Mom felt like a second-class citizen and dad like a fifth wheel.

Jill, stunning enough at forty-eight to make heads turn, recalled that "Kenneth, my firstborn, seemed to be a threat to my husband Jim. Jim wanted mothering, too, and felt left out when I was occupied with our son. I had a problem dividing my attention. So I did for one when the other wasn't around or was sleeping.

"As Kenneth grew older, things grew worse. The little kid realized his father was ignoring him. To make up for Jim's slights, I gave Kenneth extra love and added fuel to the fire. My macho husband claimed I was rearing a momma's boy.

"Our major quarrels were over Kenneth. Jim was an excellent provider, a wonderful lover. But he was a dud as a father and put me and our son under a lot of unnecessary pressure."

Jim was an extreme example of a father who has difficulty handling his role. One task of the male parent is to master childish jealousy that might estrange him from his family at the times they need each other the most.

It scaled down the day he and Jill became sole tenants of an empty nest. After eighteen years, Jim got back his bride. They cut a record in harmony until Kenneth graduated from college and came home. After four years of being alone, the old jealousy was replayed. Jim's dissatisfaction gave a new meaning to *second childhood*. The couple resumed the dissonance developed during Kenneth's first childhood.

"I hated having him home," Jim said. "You can call me self-centered, but I wanted Jill's full attention. I didn't want her cooking his meals, washing his clothes, cutting his hair. I was damn unhappy and made no bones about it."

Once more, Jill was torn between preserving her marriage and refusing to alienate her son. She did what she wanted to do for

Kenneth and fought a growing hostility toward her husband. "Jim and Kenneth have such different natures. My son has an artist's temperament, and my husband sees himself as a he-man. Yet they're both so vulnerable. I had to keep them apart to keep peace in the family."

Kenneth was an inadvertent fox in the chicken coop, a role he didn't want to play. "I know I've got to move out. I didn't come home to cause trouble. Some way I'll have to find money to do it," he said.

Other couples with dissonant attitudes toward their children cut hit records when the kids left and reversed to the flip side of the record when they returned.

Jason said he didn't mean to deprecate motherhood, but "Linda still plays mother to our grown daughters. She tells them what to do every chance she gets. And I say what I always said, 'Let them make their own decisions.'

"She also gets involved with the girls' use of time, and it cuts into our time. She goes as far as telling them when to go to bed. They're old enough to make their own plans."

Linda acknowledged Jason's complaints as legitimate. "There'd be less of a strain on our marriage if I learned restraint," she said clasping her hands. "I know the girls are adults and should be allowed reasonable freedom to live their own lives. But I was always more motherly than Jason was fatherly, and it's hard to break that mold."

The daughters, accustomed to a matriarchal family, were surprised to find themselves bones of contention. "My mother and I are quite close," the older girl said. "I'm not as close to my father. He was never terribly involved in my life and isn't now."

The younger girl was equally matter-of-fact. "My dad and I get along. I just don't have the close relationship with him that I have with mom." Speaking for her sister she added, "The last thing we had in mind was to hurt our folks' marriage. As soon as we get decent-paying jobs, we'll move out and share an apartment."

In terms of cunning foxes, neither daughter was a vixen. Their reappearance merely revived old patterns. Mom backslid into her role of survival kit, and dad was trying to do what he was supposed to do but didn't know how. Starting in early fatherhood, "the essential job of the father is to help the mother and child separate from each other," wrote Howard Halpern in *Cutting Loose* (New York: Simon and Schuster, 1976). "The father, then, is the 'other' parent

and is equally important because he offers an alternative relationship that can also be close and powerful but is different because he's
different."

Yet even if both parents take an active part in child rearing, the
reunion after separation from a home-ing pigeon can cause a marital crisis. The severity depends on how each parent related to each
other and the child before the child left. For instance, Bonnie and
her husband had different outside interests. His was primarily business; hers was the arts. But they tried to reconcile them after the
children were gone. "I took shorthand and typing and became his
secretary," she said. "He thought I should know the workings of his
company in case something happened to him. I thought it was a
chance to give us more to talk about. So we worked together for
four years."

It was a comfortable arrangement. With no one to rush home to
at night, Bonnie worked her husband's long hours, and he recipro-
cated by accompanying her to a ballet or concert on a weekend.
Then their daughter, an aspiring dancer, came home. "Laura really
enhanced my life," Bonnie said. "I raced home every night to talk to
her. She was wonderful company after talking business with my
husband all day." Bonnie never suspected that her husband felt
abandoned. "They shut me out like they used to do," he complained.

In a similar situation, Sonja felt excluded the year two sons lived
at home and worked for their father. The three men left for work
together, talked shop at the dinner table, and took off on camping
and fishing trips. "I was lonely and bored," Sonja said. "I didn't
mind being left at home when the boys were little. I needed time by
myself then. But I've counted on my husband's company since
we've been alone.

"I even went tenting in Wisconsin once and backpacked with him
in Colorado. When the boys came back, I didn't seem to matter.
The rapport we built evaporated. I was the little woman who wasn't
there."

The timbre of a marriage can suffer if one member of a duet
changes playing partners when a grown child comes home. A father
may prefer the company of a sports-minded son to watch a baseball
game. A mother may prefer taking along a daughter on a shopping
trip, or one spouse may be more sensitive than the other to what is
sensed as loneliness in the home-ing pigeon.

"It's a delicate situation," said sociology professor Marijean

Suelzle. "Another adult in the house deserves consideration but not special consideration to the extent of altering the husband-wife relationship."

The spouse who feels neglected should communicate these feelings, or else the home-ing pigeon can unintentionally become a disruptive force in the marriage.

Or intentionally. There are times when the home-ing pigeon deliberately introduces discord to drive a wedge between parents.

In cross-sex situations, it's the old story of the unresolved Oedipus or Electra complex. For instance, a child may cater to a parent to the degree of imparting the message, "You don't need each other, you have me," and having an offspring as a rival can be more dangerous to a marriage than competing with someone outside the home. A husband, for example, may not be able to justify to himself leaving his wife alone to spend time with another woman. But, generally, he feels no pangs of conscience spending time alone with his daughter.

Clinical psychologist Dr. Rosalie Kirschner believes that "unless the returning child has a real pathology, like feeling isolated, go on living as a couple when he comes home. Let the child know he's welcome to spend time with you but not welcome to take over your lives."

In the same way that a fox can't get into a chicken coop if the door is tightly locked, a home-ing pigeon can't manipulate parents who communicate. "Jeanie always tried to pit one of us against the other," Barbara, a manipulated mother, said. "She would always ask daddy if mommy said no. He was very liberal, and she got away with murder. He refused to see the power play and wanted to please her."

Jeanie played the same melody in a new key when she came home. Two weeks after she was back, she wheedled $200 from Barbara to settle unpaid bills. "First, I told her I'd have to talk it over with dad when he came back from a business trip. But somehow she convinced me to give her the money.

"The night my husband came home, I confessed what I had done. I had broken a pact we made to act as a unit this second time around. He took the news calmly and smiled like a kid caught with his hand in a cookie jar. The morning before he had left, he had written a $500 check for Jeanie."

Parents also can be manipulated if one spouse gets an ego boost by being treated as an ally. Common refrains from parents of grown children who work the "pigeon drop" are, "He always takes my side against his father," or "He considers me the better parent because I understand him."

Myron Brenton in an article in *Prime Time* magazine ("When Grown Children Won't Leave Home," May 1980) wrote: "You and your spouse have to agree on your goals and your methods; otherwise, you'll fall prey to the child's manipulations. Be on guard against undermining each other, as well."

What does a mother do if a child brings complaints against the father to her? Dr. Kirschner suggested, "Tell your child he has to deal directly with his father, that there are separate relationships in the household such as between you and your husband and between him and each parent." And Dr. Linnus Pecaut, director and founder of the Institute for Motivational Development, believes that "marital problems encountered when young people come home occur in the kinds of families that let them happen. Usually, they're caused by a weakness in the marriage."

Studies show that parents who regularly held family councils to air problems were less vulnerable to children's wiles. "A family council shows the children *both* parents truly care about what is going on and makes it difficult to play one parent against the other, for everything is out in the open," said Barry and Patricia Bricklin in *Strong Family, Strong Child* (New York: Delacorte Press, 1970). They also pointed out that family councils have "a profoundly positive effect on the relationship between husband and wife . . . When a woman sees that she does not stand alone, she will feel more favorably disposed toward her husband."

By the same token, women who stood alone may carry a grudge that grows lighter when the children leave and heavier when the children come back. Ida had been placed in the enemy camp by her husband Lou, who always sided with their children. "I'd get mad at Ida for getting down to the kids' level when they argued," he said referring to their earlier years. "As a mother, she should have made peace not war."

He sang the same tune when Eleanor, a grown daughter, returned. "The two women fought like children," he said. "One had to back off, and I appealed to Ida. She's older and supposedly wiser."

Ida described Eleanor's six-month stay as "ghastly for all of us." The young woman acted as if she was the favored concubine in a harem. "She wanted the privileges of home without any of the responsibilities," Ida said. "I was the maid who had to answer if meals weren't ready on time or if her room wasn't cleaned.

"I got mad at Lou for not putting his foot down. Eleanor was closer to him than to me, and his words carried more weight than mine. She had him wrapped around her fingers. If our son Jerry had come home, Lou would have insisted Jerry mow the lawn, at least."

If Eleanor hadn't left, Ida planned to leave. She tried to be understanding. She knew Eleanor had come home expecting the special treatment she always received from her father. But Ida hadn't expected Eleanor to deliberately provoke disagreements to see if Lou would still intervene in her favor. "I finally insisted Lou tell Eleanor to shape up, or I'd ship out. He surprised me. The two had a 'go at it,' and she left in a huff. She took a room in the home of an elderly couple and tries to make me feel guilty by saying they treat her like a daughter."

In another household where one parent thought the other parent was singing out of range, Martin was delighted to see his twin sons leave. "I didn't miss them a bit," Martin said. "My wife would say yes to buying them anything they wanted. I'd have to countermand her because we couldn't afford everything they wanted. As the naysayer, I was the bad guy. The boys could do no wrong, and I could do no right."

Upon learning the two wanted to come back, Martin asserted himself. He told his wife, "They can't. When kids are gone, they're gone. I don't want them living with us again." The battle raged for weeks. His wife won. The kids came home and she came to a conclusion she had been avoiding. "Martin's attitude convinced me divorce might be the answer," she said. "The kids were my whole life. I'd been unhappy since they left."

The twins came home to a couple at war. Both were partial to their mother as witnesses to their parents' sniping matches. One twin, however, tried to reconcile the pair. "I hated all the tension," he said. "Having matured a bit since I left home, I understood the position my father had been put in all these years. But I only hurt myself by trying to help them. My mother threw my father out. She and my brother keep reminding me I bet on a loser."

In another shaky marriage, children became pawns. One parent tried to use the home-ing pigeons to keep it together; the other tried to use them to make the final break. To Joe, the unhappier half of the pair, his son and daughter had never left home. They had just gone off to college. Because they both flunked out didn't mean he shouldn't take them in.

He's certain that when Ira is ready, he'll cut the apron strings and when Debbie is ready, she'll break the bond and go. Joe says, "Until then, my arms are there to hold them.

"My wife is ticked off by my attitude. She says, 'It's time they left already. I've spent my life raising them.' We fight a lot, but the kids aren't foxes in the chicken coop. There have always been major problems between me and Sylvia.

"In fact if Ira and Debbie hadn't come home, I would have left her sooner than I plan to."

Joe sees himself as the laissez-faire parent. As he put it, "One parent living a kid's life is enough." He called Sylvia an overbearing Jewish mother: "Eat your vegetables," "Don't see that boy," "Take this course," "Don't take that course." He blames Sylvia for Ira's and Debbie's failure in the outside world. "She's part of the reason the kids can't find mates or jobs. They're so used to her direction, they flub when she's not out there with them."

In turn, Sylvia blames Joe for the children's dependency on home. "I asked Joe to subsidize an apartment for Ira. It would have cost the same as college fees. But he said, 'No! Kids belong at home until they can pay for their own place.'

"I want Ira to get away from Joe's influence. He's getting Joe's habit of putting things off. Joe tied him closer to home by taking him into his business instead of giving him the incentive to try his own wings.

"I was also disappointed when Debbie returned. The disappointment was only on my part. She wanted to come back. She's a feeling person and an emotional support for me. But she'd be better off among young people. There's nothing for her here."

Obviously, both children received a subtle message from the parent they felt closer to when they left for school. "If you're an underachiever, you'll have me in your life longer." It's a common message given by parents who are ambivalent about separating from children. After children have been away from home, they become more aware of this conflict in parents. They get the message through phone calls and letters. Often, it's nothing more than a parent's tone of voice or a parent saying, "I'm lonely. I miss you."

Dr. Pecaut believes, "If you could take a child far enough away, Europe, for example, where he couldn't communicate constantly with home, the child would become independent. He wouldn't be getting the message that one parent needs him and wants him home.

"Also, when a kid comes home as a problem for a parent to deal with, a husband and wife can put their own relationship on a back burner. It's a very ginger process to resolve conflicts in a marriage. What parents don't realize is kids need to feel that parents are united and strong, that they are coming home as young adults to older adults."

Ira refused to see his family as it really was. He described them as close-knit, bonded so tightly he was envied by his peers. "Sure, my mother's a nudge," he said. "She made me take night courses and nags me to complete my education. I'm months behind on a paper, but nagging doesn't bother me. It goes in one ear and out the other."

His sister is more perceptive. She'd like to leave but has neither money nor a marketable skill. "My dad takes out his anger at my mother on me. We're both overweight. Who does he nag? Not her. Me.

"Once, after they had a fight, he cracked me across the face because I hadn't finished doing the laundry.

"I'm the scapegoat. He gets no reaction from my mother. My brother stands up to him. So he takes out his moods on me because I cry."

To the outside world, Sylvia makes the kids look like the chief problem in her marriage. "If they'd leave, everything would be all right," she said. "Joe and I need time to ourselves. With the kids back, there's no spontaneous sex, no privacy.

"Both were gone one Saturday night, and it was good to be alone for a change. No one ran in or out. The phone only rang twice. Joe and I looked at each other, smiled at each other. It was a good, quiet evening every couple should be able to enjoy."

Couples who make their children pawns in a marriage are like the farmer who gets disturbed when a fox preys on the chickens yet counts on the animal to rid the farm of rodents. When there is a dearth of foxes in a farm area, some farmers bring them in to kill the mice but forget to lock the chicken coops. Then they blame the foxes for doing what comes naturally—preying on chickens.

If marital satisfaction drops when a young couple brings home a firstborn, it can plummet to zero in a second marriage if grown children barge in on middle-aged newlyweds. Marian, a widow, saw signs of trouble as soon as she became serious with a suitor. Mark, the youngest of three sons, was home the summer Paul came into her life. "He was cold and distant to Paul and kept saying, 'Oh, is he coming again this weekend?' "

Marian, who had deferred remarrying until all her sons were launched, bided her time hoping Mark would adapt to the idea of having a stepfather. With this possibility becoming more remote as the summer drew to a close, she set a wedding date for fall. The month following the wedding, Mark quit school. Using money from a trust fund set up by his father, he took an apartment with a friend a block away from the newlyweds. He kept dropping in for meals, visits, and advice and was openly hostile to his stepfather Paul. "We had no privacy, and I didn't know how to handle the situation," Marian bemoaned.

Paul was unhappy about Mark's impromptu visits but didn't tell Marian. "She had brought up three boys alone. I understood that they were very possessive of their mother, especially the youngest one."

The situation was bearable until Mark lost the lease to his apartment and, without asking, appeared with all his possessions on their doorstep. He set down two amplifiers and two guitars in the front hall and made no effort to put them away. "I was always tripping over them," Paul said, "but I gritted my teeth and kept my temper. I didn't want to come on as a heavy."

But the longer Mark stayed, the less respect Paul felt toward Marian. "She was too lenient with him. I hated to see her overworked while Mark sat around and waited to be catered to. Finally, I blew up. She said it was easier to do something herself than fight to have Mark do it. We made up, but our relationship wasn't the same as when Mark lived elsewhere."

The atmosphere in the house was fairly tolerable until Marian's older sons dropped in for a two-month visit the following summer. "I thought I'd go out of my mind," Marian said. "None of the boys are settled in their careers. Paul didn't criticize them, but he wondered aloud how long it took men in their twenties to do something about their lives.

"His children are settled in professions and are married with young families. Here I was with three sons and not one doing anything. The contrast to his children put me on the defensive. I knew it was my fault. Having raised them without a father, I made life too easy for them. I didn't have the heart to throw them out, and I didn't want to lose Paul.

"Finally, I suggested that the three share an apartment. They had money from a trust fund to finance it. They're not stupid kids and got the message. But they still pop in uninvited, and I don't know what to do. If I were Paul, I'd be at the end of my patience."

A woman in a reverse situation wrote to the "Dear Abby" column for advice. Her husband's grown children used their home without a by-your-leave as a vacation spot, a sanctuary, and a store-house. They went as far as inviting friends to dinner without asking permission.

The husband contended the house was the children's, too, and they could come and go as they pleased. The wife wanted the children to feel at home yet wondered where to draw the line.

Abigail Van Buren's answer (*Chicago Tribune,* April 17, 1980): "The line is (or should be) clearly drawn when a child is grown and leaves home. Should he return for a day, a week, or a month, he returns as a guest. This means he should not come without an invitation. If he's between jobs or marriages and needs a roof over his head, chances are he will not be refused, but he always should ask first. And inviting others to one's parents' home and storing furniture, clothes, etc., without permission is also out of line."

The same advice applies to children coming home to parents in a first or a tenth marriage. Parents who made the best adjustments were those who agreed to agree before handing down decisions. The melody played in childhood lingered on to adulthood.

Yvonne, who is living at home until her wedding date, recalled, "My dad traveled a lot while I was in high school. He was gone two or three days a week but would call every night and ask mom to put each kid on the phone to answer, 'Did you do your homework? How's your health? How are your activities going?'

"He would ask, 'Is there anything you want to discuss before I come home?' That gave us an opening to tell him if there was a big problem going on. We knew mom had already filled him in so we couldn't color the facts.

"Mom and dad always spoke in one voice as far as the kids were concerned. They would discuss discipline between themselves and mete it out together. We had to appeal to both if we thought it was unfair. They're still as together now as they were when we were little. I didn't have to come back home, but I thought I'd learn a lot about being a happily married person if I could spend my last unmarried year with them."

Her mother gave additional insight to the workings of the marriage. She and her husband don't always agree on a particular course to take with the children. "I go off the deep end. My husband is calm. When I complain I'm a screamer, he reassures me that I show I care in different ways. The two of us usually fight out a decision alone. Whether it's right or wrong, the kids hear it in one voice, not two."

She didn't want to imply that they have a perfect marriage. There were times when she wanted to walk away. But, in general, she admires her husband and wants the kids to admire him, too. Yvonne's mother says, "He and Yvonne have sort of a love affair. He adores her, and she can get whatever she wants from him, and I think a daughter should feel she's special to a father. When she was younger, I had him get her a job at his office to see what a great guy he is."

With this attitude, she's able to accept Yvonne's eating habits, the way she handles household responsibilities, and her attitude toward contributing money to the house. Sometimes Yvonne tries to draw them into arguments at the dinner table, but the only ones they enter are about impersonal subjects. If a personal decision has to be made then and there, they withdraw into another room, discuss it, and give an opinion as a unit.

National surveys show that the marital satisfactions of an average couple increase after children have grown and left home. But some couples don't want to wait that long. They practice singing their own song while the children are still with them.

Parents who acted in accord reported that the return of a child didn't disrupt their marriage. The home-ing pigeon may have curtailed privacy, refocused attention, and caused friction with children still living at home, but the couple had long ago learned a good marriage is the bedrock of a family. One wife said, "A kid can be a fox in a chicken coop only if parents let him be. We refused to cooperate."

18

The Pecking Order—
Taking the Bite Out of the
Sibling Relationship

A mother's phantom garment is a referee's shirt thrust upon her the day she brings home a second child, a main event that can turn a house into an arena.

As the size and number of contenders grow, settling fifteen rounds of a boxing match could seem a cinch compared to settling the endless rounds of fighting for power and status between siblings. Although the striped shirt scratches like a hair shirt, a mother is loathe to take it off. Her children will be siblings forever. When friends argue, they can become former friends. But who ever heard of a former brother or sister?

As the parent called upon most often to arbitrate, mediate, judge, and pass sentence on the issues arising from sibling rivalry, mom feels an enormous responsibility. "I wanted to survive. I wanted my marriage to survive. And most of all, I wanted our family to survive," said Kay, the mother of four girls and two boys, born in that order approximately eighteen months apart.

With a ring of annoyance in her voice, she said that her husband found a good way to handle their children's squabbles. "He played a lot of tennis, worked late, and wasn't around much."

As the wife of an organization man on the first rung of the success ladder, Kay had no one to dispel the tension of dealing with six children who fought over toys, taking turns to be dressed and fed, and for her attention. She couldn't afford baby-sitters, nor were grandparents nearby.

To keep her sanity and her family intact, Kay laid down rules: "Share." "Don't fight." "If I'm busy, don't bother me unless you're bleeding." Enforcing them, however, was like stopping raindrops from falling. The demand for a referee continued as long as one child thought he or she was being shortchanged by another.

Kay accepted the situation as troublesome but normal.

"Sibling rivalry has been with us since the human race began," wrote Dr. John F. McDermott, Jr., in *Raising Cain (and Abel Too)* (New York: Wyden Books, 1980), a parent's guide to dealing with relationships between young children. "You can't instantly 'teach' your children to love each other, and you can't simply stamp out rivalry between them. But you *can* influence it, especially if you view it as a universal part of development, not as a threat of total chaos. We know that it gradually decreases with age, given informed guidance."

The chaos in Kay's house didn't subside. By the time the three older girls were high school students, they were still clamoring for a referee: "It's my turn to take the car." "My sister has more clothes than me." "My little brothers are brats."

Nor could she remove the referee shirt as, one by one, the older four went off to college. Having two bickering children at home was deliverance compared to six, but the girls complained about each other long distance, and she wondered when the competition would end.

In 1974, it was dissipated by a tragedy. Lois, the second oldest, came home in her sophomore year fatally ill, a sobering experience to Kay's healthy offspring.

The two boys spelled Kay's vigil, taking turns at Lois's bedside to offer their comatose sister a familiar face should she open her eyes. The three college girls coordinated weekend visits to lend helping hands. The fatal illness of someone so young shook them. "They became very close before and after Lois died," Kay said. "They didn't fight anymore. They talked over problems. Sibling rivalry was out the window. They were just glad to have each other."

Kay's referee shirt was left in storage even when the girls resumed living together after each graduated. "The entire family has become more cooperative since we lost a member," Kay said. "Of course, I'd rather have Lois and less cooperation. But I had no choice in the matter."

Under ordinary circumstances, the referee shirt comes out the day a sibling's possessions are unloaded in the front hall. Along with the guitar, amplifying system, waterbed, and two weeks of dirty laundry, the home-ing pigeon also brings tension into the house. A sibling's reappearance, expected or not, changes the family composition, and the companion of change is stress.

"There were strains when he left, and there are strains when he comes back," said Audrey Begun, MSW, an affiliate of the developmental psychology department of the University of Michigan, Ann Arbor. "He comes home expecting to take his place. But he's not the same, and neither is the child he left at home.

"He's outgrown his old role and sees no clear new role at first. The returning child has a real hard time fitting back into the family."

For example, Jeffrey, fresh out of college and engaged to be married, looked forward to resuming the hero-worship relationship with his younger sister. But he had left behind a twelve-year-old child and came back to a sixteen-year-old adolescent undergoing some of his former experiences. The hardest one to accept was her preoccupation with the opposite sex. He felt a twist of jealousy each time she "drooled" over a young man and tried to keep himself the focus of her admiration.

In turn, his sister was bewildered by his erratic behavior—calling her boy crazy one moment and offering advice to the lovelorn the next—and tried to ignore his presence. Jeffrey couldn't accept being second-best. "She'd promise to spend time with me and break it if she got a date," Jeffrey said. "Sure, I had my own girl, but it hurts when a sister who adored you doesn't want your company."

The younger sibling could have said, "Look at me. I'm not a baby anymore," but Jeffrey, in the throes of sorting out changes he found at home, might not be receptive. He may also wish he was back in the same stage as his younger sister.

Generally, parents are advised to refrain from butting in to solve problems between children who are close to or of adult age. But it can be helpful if a parent explained to the younger child what a home-ing pigeon is going through at this point in life. "For instance," Begun said, "he gave up several safe relationships to come home, and here he's no longer momma's baby boy or younger sister's idol. Soon, he'll be married and become someone's husband. Shedding old roles and taking a new one puts him under a lot of pressure."

The younger child given this understanding will be better able to cope with strains of having an older sibling home. The rest is up to them. They should be encouraged to discuss the issues that stop them from getting along.

But, and psychologists stress this point, ensuing talks should be held between the children. Mom's job was to provide insight. The kids have to work out a new relationship on their own terms. The well-meant umpiring of a parent may revive sibling rivalry—"You're taking her side again"—and aggravate the shaky situation.

Another disappointment felt by the older siblings may be the felled expectation of resuming the perks of seniority, namely, to be shown that their needs take priority.

In Pearl's home, the conflict between Helen, a law student, and Jim, a high school senior, gave her a sense of déjà vu. Bickering little kids who had tugged at her skirt to settle disagreements had grown into bickering big kids who complained about each other.

Helen accused Jim of disturbing her sleep and her study habits when friends rang the doorbell to pick him up on the way to school and hung out at the house at night blasting the stereo. "I told mom I was the older sister, and he had to listen to me," Helen said. "She sided with the brat, saying it was Jim's turn to be a high school student."

Jim accused Helen of hogging the telephone and getting off easier on chores than he. "Mom took Helen's side saying that law school was tough," he complained, "and she needed more time to rest and study. But I was going to school, too."

Assailed from both sides, Pearl removed her referee shirt and put on boxing gloves. She gave her side. "I told Helen that if I could live with Jim's noise, so could she. And I told Jim that if I could live without a telephone, so could he.

"I refused to hear any more complaints from one child about another. I insisted they work out their gripes between themselves. They both exploded. But, in time, they not only became good friends, they became allies."

Each had a curfew they occasionally broke. One time, Jim was "dumb enough" to bring in the morning papers, and his parents knew how late he'd stayed out. "I told Helen, 'If you come in late, leave the paper on the porch.' Now, she vouches for me if I'm accused of something I didn't do," he said.

Fathers also discover that children form stronger ties when a parent steps out of the ring. "My boys work hard to get along," a single dad said. "They may have words, but if they do, I don't hear them. They gripe between themselves, and it makes for more peace in the household."

Still other parents reported that a new relationship doesn't happen overnight. They corroborated at home what psychologists see in their office: It takes time for brothers and sisters who have lived apart to outgrow old patterns and adjust to new roles. Returning children try different ways to get back into the family. They go about it by trial and error, shuffling back and forth. It can become a family issue and strain everyone's patience.

"A way for parents to bear this period is to recall other changes in the family composition they survived, like a prolonged visit from grandma or bringing home a new baby," Begun said. "Like everything else, this too shall pass."

Different tactics are called for, however, if the trouble is not between children close in age but between those born years apart.

In Millie's house Jennie, the home-ing pigeon, was eight years older than the oldest of three boys who lived at home. "She wouldn't lay off the older boy," Millie said. "She kept laying into him about his study habits, the amount of time he spent watching TV, and the language he used.

"I tried not to exert my authority on matters that pertained to Jennie—like when she came home, where she went. After all, you can't tell a twenty-five-year-old to do such and such. But when her behavior affected the younger kids, I had to set the record straight.

"I let her know they were my domain. I told her to befriend them, not boss them. Jennie's reaction? She said I was judgmental. I didn't deny it. I had to be."

Handling an issue between children of disparate ages can be tricky. Parents (generally) don't want the returning child to feel unwelcome, nor do they want the younger child to be responsible to a third parent. But parents should not step into an adult-child relationship any more at this time than they did when their offspring were younger. Professional advice is "Play it by ear. Speak to the younger child first to find out if he or she can handle the situation. Give the younger one a chance to cope."

If the younger one can't, ask the older one to stop playing parent. Let a brother, for instance, know he can be a good influence on a younger sibling by providing an example.

Only a handful of parents complained that the home-ing pigeon was a bad influence. Most mothers described the home-ing pigeon as a cheerleader who encouraged a sibling to "Try. I passed chemistry." Or, "Don't give up. You'll make the football team."

With mutual respect between children spaced widely apart, the younger child can benefit from this friendly parent, this older playmate who isn't authoritarian. The older child can also become the younger one's confidant. "My adolescent daughter confides in my son," said a mother whose children were born ten years apart. "He's someone she can trust to talk to about boyfriends. And she seems to be gaining confidence as a female from his approval."

Other parents reported that older children tutored younger ones and helped them improve school grades. They, too, donned referee shirts and intervened if they thought the treatment of a younger sibling was unjust. "The kids who come home can be mediators, middle managers who help things work, or a spoke in the family wheels to make things go around," said sociology professor Marijean Suelzle.

Or a bad influence, too.

A father, who realized his son thrived on tension, said, "Carl sets our teenage girls against each other. And for no reason I can see except perverseness." Another claimed his son set a poor example for his daughters by staying out all night with a girl and walking in when his sisters were leaving for school. A third discovered the older boy had introduced the younger boy to marijuana.

In situations where the health, welfare, or safety of a family member is threatened, parents are advised to send the policy of nonintervention flying out the window. But it's not necessary to send the offending child flying, too. The way children are influenced at home can be an indication of the way they can be influenced outside the home. Professional opinion is to hold a family conference. Clarify the dynamics of what's happening. This will allow both children to gain an understanding of their actions—how they're being hurt and hurting the family.

The older child might feel displaced and be looking for a way to reinstate a senior position. The younger child might be placing less importance than a parent on the older sibling's morals or be unaware of being manipulated.

It takes time to gather the information on exactly what is happening in the sibling relationship. Parents should step back and review the strengths that kept the family a unit this far. By focusing on strengths and shoring up weaknesses, the situation can be solved without the pain of the ultimate solution—telling the adult-age child to leave.

Psychologists point out that each time a family member comes or goes, new ways have to be found to interact. Dependencies change. Privileges are reallotted. There are new family norms when a child comes back. Therefore, new limits have to be set and the old rules have to be reestablished. The consensus was that this will take time in the sense that problems will not get worked out as soon as the kid comes through the door lugging suitcase in hand.

Phantom baggage carried in the other hand may be a Pandora's box filled with childhood resentments ready to fly in the face of the family as soon as the lid is triggered open by real or imagined slights. Gerry, twenty-four, always worried about being displaced in her mother's affections by Jane, a younger sister. In high school she was disgruntled that Jane ate steak at home with mom while she brown-bagged lunch in the school cafeteria. In college she "knew" that Jane was being spoiled at home and getting tighter with mom than she was. "I tried to make things equal," their mother said. "But Gerry didn't perceive my actions that way. If we were having steak, I sent along a steak sandwich with Gerry."

A week after Gerry came home, Jane, who had never left home, brought the news she was getting married. "Jane was canonized," Gerry said. "All I heard for the next couple of months were wedding plans. No one considered the way I felt. It was a shock to see a younger sister marry first."

The girls' mother was aware of Gerry's feelings and appalled at her behavior. "She started to smoke and let us know she became sexually active. She kept saying life was passing her by. I felt for her," the mother said. "I also felt she was spoiling a beautiful time in Jane's life and in our family's.

"She refused to be Jane's maid of honor. I didn't know what to do. We had to talk about the wedding whether or not Gerry stalked out of the room."

There's no simple solution when an older child feels surpassed by a younger child whether in marriage, a career, or school. In parallel situations, Anthony, a mediocre student, came home to a sister named valedictorian of her high school graduating class; Steve, a government lawyer, saw his young brothers get high-paying jobs with large law firms. What can a parent do? The issue isn't between parent and child. It's between child and child, or to be more specific, it's the problem of the child who feels surpassed.

It's not the parent's place to interfere. If he or she does, the tension between the two combatants can spread through the entire family instead of remaining the problem of the jealous person.

It would help if a parent tries to understand how the second-best child feels. For instance, if an older sister gets promiscuous when a younger sister is getting married, she may be saying, "My sister is doing something respectable and getting the approval of my parents. So I will do the opposite."

"The older sister feels rejected and is asking herself, 'Aren't I attractive?' " Begun commented. "She's also ambivalent. She's pleased that her sister is happy, but she's hurt that she's not getting married, too."

A sensitive parent will avoid adding pain by refusing to compare the status of both children. In fact, "Don't compare" is a good rule to follow in any situation that may arise between siblings, especially if one is in the naked stage of having just come home.

Richard, for instance, was openly judged by the standards his brothers set when they lived at home. He continually heard: "How neat they kept their rooms." "How they loved classical music, not the junk you play." "How aggressive they were looking for jobs. Not like you." The comparison, to Richard's discredit, didn't help his self-esteem. "Especially since I had to live at home because I wasn't making it," Richard said.

Insensitive parents fall back into old styles of interacting even though these ways are no longer appropriate. A parent shouldn't have compared in the first place, and definitely shouldn't compare when the kid comes home. A home-ing pigeon doesn't need it. He or she is under enough strains.

Unwittingly, a chauvinistic preference for the company of a child of a parent's own sex might make the other children feel left out. "When my sons were home, they were companions," said Sam, a hard-hitting businessman. "We played tennis, racquetball, and golf and talked business. I didn't ask my daughter to come along. She would have been out of place." It never occurred to Sam that his daughter was an able competitor on the courts and on the course.

Sam's wife eschewed the company of her sons. "Boys who spend time with their mother would be considered 'femmy' and I brought them up to be masculine. If they wanted to play tennis with me, I'd think there was something wrong, that they were acting girlish." Instead, she relied on her daughter for company and did "girl" things like lunching and attending theater. Although she took it for granted that male adults and female adults go their separate ways, she complained, "We're rarely together as a family. My sons and my daughter might as well be strangers."

Young people reared in a sexist household generally find it difficult for a family to operate as a unit. Sam's sons relished their father's company but were jealous of the open affection he lavished on their sister. At the same time, they were the subjects of their sister's resentment. She got her father's hugs and kisses, but she also got the major share of housework. "I would have traded all the bear hugs for help with the dishes or an invitation to play tennis," she said.

The sexist condition of the household can become a cause of dissension after a child has been away and encountered more liberated attitudes. Unless parents are willing to let go of stereotyped ideas of "proper" male and female behavior, the household is in danger of being divided like public bathrooms—one place for him and another place for her.

Traditionally, the child who benefits from the designated sex roles is considered the favorite by the others, an honor that rarely fosters good will between siblings. For example, Verna could never successfully vie with her brother for her divorced mother's attention. The divorcée was wrapped up ministering to the needs of "the man in the family." When Verna came home, he was in charge of the household and supervised the way she did her chores.

Although Verna told her brother, "You're not my father, and you can't make me do them," her mother invariably ordered, "Listen to him. He knows more than you do."

Old wounds reopened. "The way I'm treated goes way back," Verna said. "He was considered old enough to go outside by himself at eight. I was ten. I always got girl treatment and still do. I hated it because it was unfair. I still hate it.

"In our house, being a girl means cleaning up the mess a man makes. My mom says a man has to concentrate on making money, and I have to be supportive. Well, I have a career, too."

It's not unusual for home-ing pigeons to complain that the children still at home are given privileges at an earlier age even in a nonsexist setting. In Betty's household, almost every other sentence spoken by her oldest daughter began, "At their age, you never allowed me to . . ." Betty admitted she's easier with the younger girls. She let them stay over at a friend's house or go downtown without a chaperone along. For reasons she didn't remember, she kept Sharon, her firstborn, closer to home.

She tried to explain the change: "I've mellowed. Besides, things are different from when Sharon was a child. Her sisters are growing up in different times and seem more mature than she did at their age."

Accused of a past injustice, a parent might say, "I never claimed to be fair. I made a mistake. But what I learned from rearing you, I passed down to the younger children."

The worst thing you can say is "I'm sorry and I'll make it up to you." Then it will put a parent over a barrel and provide fuel for jealousy.

The home-ing pigeon has to accept that times have changed, parents have changed, and the norms of society have changed. Discuss the privilege issue on that level.

If a child makes a parent feel guilty, the relationship is really finished, and it will hurt the interaction with the other kids.

What are the covert reasons home-ing pigeons hurl petty accusations against parents? Favoritism. If they were the favorite, they suspect they have been unseated while they were gone. If they weren't the favorite, they suspect another child is. Sometimes, they voice their suspicions openly. If these suspicions are valid, home-ing pigeons wouldn't be able to escape old patterns. To be important in Michelle's family, a child had to be male. "My father had little to do with my upbringing," she said, "and he showed the same lack of interest while I lived at home the second time.

"I hated the brother he loved more than me until mom told me all the good things my brother said about me while I was gone. I didn't know he was aware of my father's preference or that he was proud and happy to have me as a sister."

Sometimes, the charge of favoritism is made on circumstantial evidence. Jonathan, looking from the inside outward, felt his parents showed more warmth to his brother who lived on his own. His brother Wally, from his vantage point, envied Jonathan who was getting a break on food, shelter, and being the only child at home. Their feelings were picked up by their parents. "It was a bum rap," the father said, "and my wife and I took each aside to let them know where they stood."

The gist of their explanation to Jonathan was "It's sometimes easier for parents and a child who live apart to get along on a more adult basis. We don't rub each other the wrong way as often. What we don't see, we can't complain about. But that has nothing to do with the affection we feel toward you."

The gist of their conversation with Wally was "It might seem that Jonathan is getting VIP treatment. He isn't. We'd do the same for you if you lived at home. Ours is a practical arrangement, a convenience for your brother. It's no sign that we love him more than we love you."

While there's no question that change in the makeup of a family induces tension, some families adjust better than others as they wait for siblings to settle into new roles. In Elaine's family, for instance, her daughters were never able to share a room: Andrea was neat; Debbie was sloppy. They also had different interests: Andrea was a good student; Debbie was a good athlete. As soon as these traits became obvious, they were given separate rooms, and each was praised for her particular accomplishment. "The girls learned to accept their differences in personality," their mother said.

The old pattern was a comfortable one to fall back into when the girls resumed living together as adults. Not that they didn't fly off the handle with each other. What made it easier on the parents were the standing rules since childhood.

"No bad language," their mother said. "They may yell at each other but not use four-letter words." Their father, however, was less tolerant of noise. As soon as a pattern of arguing emerged over borrowing clothes, he laid down the law. "I told them they didn't dare borrow from each other as long as they lived in this house. Unless they continually fight over one thing, I don't let the girls' fights concern me. My wife and I stay out of it and let them work it out."

In another household, two brothers were prototypes of the major characters in Neil Simon's play *The Odd Couple.* One was neat, the other a slob. The fur flew between them until the neat one surrendered his habits. "In self-defense, I became less concerned about tidiness," he said. "We began to joke about our differences. I called him Oscar, and he called me Felix."

A new source of conflict arose over television watching. Each had a different taste in entertainment. Their mother, tired of refereeing a TV match each evening, solved the problem—or so she thought—by buying an additional television set. Now the odd couple argues about who gets to watch the old set in their room or the new set in the basement.

The real solution is obvious, although it may be hard on parents' ears. Unless parents cause the argument between siblings, they shouldn't step in to settle matters between grown children.

Parents should ask themselves, "What was the pattern when the kids were younger? Did they survive? Did we survive?" The kids should be given a chance to establish new patterns if the old ones don't work. Have faith that they'll work the new ones through.

The sibling relationship should be seen as an issue, not a problem. "If you look at it as a problem, you begin to think of it as one," Begun said. "Even when talking between themselves about situations that arise, parents should view them as issues.

"What is really at stake when children live together again after a separation? Taking turns with the car? Television time? Borrowing? A neat room? Not really. Family solidarity is at stake. The other issues are unimportant next to the ideal that has been turned into a cliché. Blood is thicker than water. Remind the kids that they have each other for companions, trusted friends. Chances are that a brother will support you over a stranger. They have a closeness that can't be duplicated outside the house because they have lived together as children and shared things people can't share with new friends."

It helps to capitalize on the positive aspects. Close relationships between siblings, hopefully, will continue. Friends may come and friends may go, but being a brother or a sister is forever.

A referee's shirt might not be a mother's favorite garment. She may need a referee in her own dealings with a child or a mate. But the phantom garment is as important as the apron. It's a matter of learning when to cut the strings of one and when to take off the other.

Part Seven

The Currency Exchange

Father's a banker provided by nature.

French Proverb

19

Bills That Go Jingle, Jangle, Jingle

Some young adults remain steeped in nursery lore. They no longer need the tooth fairy, but they find it hard to give up a belief in Santa Claus, who, as the years went by, began to resemble dad.

Once upon a time, they asked the legendary old man for a Betsy-Wetsy doll, a gun and holster set, a Ping-Pong table, and a Schwinn bike. Later, they upgraded their requests to a stereo, cash for the junior prom, and a car. Santa, a Christmas figure, became a gift-giver in all seasons.

But they had an identity crisis about their benefactor. He was so busy in his workshop, they had more of his presents than his presence. And they found it hard to tell where dad began and Santa ended.

Mrs. Santa Claus was easier to identify. She either doled out their allowances or acted as a bondsman. When they ran short of money, she bailed them out. Rarely did mister or missus prepare Virginia for the inevitable reality—there is no Santa Claus.

"Everybody asks a kid, 'What do you want to be when you grow up?' But nobody asks, 'What are you going to do with the paycheck you'll earn as a fireman?'" said Jean Bischmann, a counseling supervisor for Family Financial Planning, a division of United Charities, in Chicago. "The kid goes to college or out into the world.

He has money at his disposal but no idea of what to do with it, so he spends it. Without a background in money management, he usually finds too much month left at the end of the dollar."

Students, in such circumstances, sign letters asking their fathers to sign checks. Working young adults look for financial shelters. Bischmann sees clients from their late teens through their late twenties in debt just short of bankruptcy. Their last resort is to go back home, but there is no reason for children to assume parents will support them past adult age.

Few parents can say no to children who need help, especially if, like Humpty-Dumpty, they had a great fall. But sometimes, parents are as powerless as all the king's horses and all the king's men. For example, it will take a long time for Will to put himself together again. He dropped out of a Colorado university almost $10,000 in debt. He came home owing repayments of a student loan, nonpayment to a health club, late payments to a finance company, and specified payments to an auto accident victim. Will was without insurance when he crashed into another car.

From a salary of $240 a month as an orderly in a nursing home, he has monthly payments of $160 to be disbursed to the man he hit and to the finance company that has a lien on his car. Installments of $107 a month on the school loans have been deferred for a year, and he has no intention of paying the health club. "They didn't cancel my membership, and I asked them to," he said. "Besides, it's going to be like getting blood out of a turnip to get the money now."

Will was offered another job by a family friend at double his present pay. He turned it down. "I don't want any favors," he said. "And I like working with old people." Since he gets through with his job as an orderly at 3:00 P.M., his parents suggested he take a second job. "I've looked," he said, "but I'm picky. I don't want to sling hamburgers."

Yet Will has a goal. He intends to go back to school to become a social worker. Despite zero savings, he is optimistic about resuming his education before his school loan payments begin. "I won't have any trouble getting another loan because I'm more destitute now than I was the first time I got one. And also, even though I'm living at home, I'm considered an independent. My parents don't take me off their tax return."

His mother was less optimistic about Will's chances of returning to school. She had to prod him to send for a loan application, and he didn't fill it out. "Also, he's the kind of kid who spends twenty dollars if he has fifteen. Not on himself. He's content with torn jeans and a battered car. But he likes to impress others. He'll borrow to give to someone else."

She didn't know he was accumulating debts while in school until he called collect to ask for $100. He had laid out the amount to paint the apartment he shared with two other students. "But he was too embarrassed to ask them for their share. He didn't want them to know he needed the money," she said. "My husband sent it to him against my wishes. We didn't have to be ripped off just because he was."

Will's father sees a lot of himself in his son. He's as picky as Will about where he works and at one time went into personal bankruptcy. "I'm a generous guy and hate to see my family do without anything," the salesman said. "But I've learned my lesson. I'm working two jobs. So's my wife. My other two boys are working their way through school. I give Will a couple of extra bucks because I know what he's going through. But he seems to have no idea of the financial shape we're in. He thinks we're loaded. I can't tell him different. He'll think I'm a flunky."

Both of Will's parents are disgusted as well as disheartened about their son's financial troubles. On one hand, they push him to work harder. "Then I tell myself, 'It's his life,' " his mother said. On the other hand, they like him as a person. "When Will does something, no one does it harder or better," his father said. "I haven't exactly been the best example and, because of it, can't talk to him about money."

Young adults who get into debt aren't stupid. They're ignorant of the financial facts of life and generally have an unrealistic attitude toward earning and spending money. They place more emphasis on the legend of Santa Claus than the nursery rhyme about Old Mother Hubbard's cupboard. Possibly, they expect the jolly old man to give her dog the bone.

Also, parents are generally more comfortable telling children about the birds and bees than about the amounts they keep in bank accounts and how interest is computed on a loan.

"Money matters are kept more secretive than sex," said money-management workshop leader Dee Dee Ahern. "A kid, while growing up, never realized that a father who was earning $20,000 a year wasn't taking $20,000 home, and he got an inflated idea of what a parent earned."

Parents who refuse to discuss the actual amount of their cash flow and how they budget give kids no reality to budget from and no realistic goal for their own money. These children grow up thinking money is an extension of themselves and develop money roles that they change depending on their audience.

To friends at a state university, Sheila showed the better side of the little girl with the curl in the middle of her forehead. She was very, very good in schoolwork and earned pocket money from part-time jobs. She let it be known she was responsible for her tuition and had worked since she was fourteen. "I had subtle pressure from my mother," she said, looking for sympathy from subsidized friends. "Mom always told me, 'So-and-so's working,' and I got the message."

Despite her financial straits, Sheila faithfully paid her portion of expenses for the apartment she shared, and she managed money well enough to accompany her roommates to Florida during spring breaks. On special occasions, she bought tasteful gifts and was respected for the way she handled money. "I always had an extra dollar in my pocket," Sheila said, "until I came home."

There, she was horrid. She threw barbed remarks about having wasted her carefree youth earning tuition while her parents had a houseful of furniture and two cars. "I came out of school penniless," Sheila said, "or I wouldn't have come home."

Her parents were taken aback hearing Sheila deny receiving help with college expenses. "Not the first two years," her mother said. "We were coming out of the tailspin of enormous medical bills and nursing home expenses for my mother-in-law incurred over an eight-year period. We never told the kids. We didn't want grandma to look like a charity case.

"As soon as we had freer dollars, we sent Sheila money to take trips to Florida and enclosed a check with our weekly letter. I'm tempted to show her the canceled checks. But that would be petty."

Sheila's father feels guilty for sending his daughter to work so early. He had made a difficult choice: helping a helpless woman or providing for a daughter's education. "But I tried to make it up to Sheila when she came home."

Sheila accepts her father's atonement (in cash) as coming to her. Once boastful of her solvency, she's now in debt. Although her job as a restaurant manager trainee is six miles from home, she bought a "muscle" car costly in insurance, gas, and upkeep. (A bill for an oil change and tune-up ran close to $100.) She opened and uses a charge account at a high-fashion clothing boutique and ran up a bill of $1,800 in two months. She also bought an expensive stereo on time payments. "Why not?" she asked. "I started my job a week after graduation and had to work on my birthday."

Originally, she intended to move out within a year of moving in. But, deep in debt despite frequent bail-outs from her parents, she can't afford even a tent on camping grounds. With a trace of the good-girl image she projected to her peers, the twenty-three-year-old asked, "When you're out on a limb, how do you get back to safety?"

Bischmann would like to spank parents who let kids grow up with the attitude that the world or the family owes them something. "The seeds are sown early," she said, "and when they come home, it's hard to undo twenty-some-odd years of bad work."

She doesn't believe parents should compensate adult children for earlier financial difficulties nor give them money without expecting repayment. "It should take a kid who lives at home about eight weeks after he gets a job to get on his feet," Bischmann said. "Based on a net salary of $200 a week, $1,600 should be enough to outfit himself and put a down payment on a used car. A kid's first car doesn't have to be the latest model.

"Once he has wheels and clothes, a parent should find out a child's overall goal. If it's to live independently, the young adult should start saving to put security deposits on rent, telephone, and utilities. If the goal is grad school, he should earmark his savings for tuition. Without a clear-cut reason for saving, a young adult will be more prone to get into debt."

The cases of gross money mismanagement Bischmann has seen include young adults who, deep in debt, allot themselves $250 a month for clothes and $100 for entertainment. "People in that shape shouldn't be spending that kind of money," she said. "It's a matter of values, orientation, and goals. Many of them are living at home expense-free but have the attitude of the free ride. Folks are not meal tickets, and kids shouldn't come home expecting to sponge."

Not all young adults who come home are in debt. Broke? Yes. Michael, a college dropout, left home the first time without a plan and without sufficient money to get started. "I jumped out of the house because I was mad," he said. "My folks were always on my back to do something with my life. I couldn't be my own man. So I took off."

His salary as a truck driver barely covered the expense of setting up an apartment and left him short of paying for car insurance. "I could only afford liability," he said. "When I wrecked my car three months later, I wasn't covered."

The financial setback sent him back to mom and dad. Fortunately, he was tied to a month-to-month lease and didn't incur the additional expense of breaking it. After six months of clearing debts, he's become philosophical about trading financial security for fiscal inexperience. "Well," he said, "you make a lot of mistakes when you're on your own. You spend money on the wrong things and when you shouldn't. It hits you all of a sudden. This time when I go, I'll know better. I'll be ready with some cash."

Other young adults come home without bills, without cash, and without jobs. They also come home with a laid-back attitude about finding work. What was the rush? They were given food, shelter, and credit cards. For instance, Cathy came out of school wanting to teach art therapy. "But it's impossible to get into this field," she said. "I need another degree, but I don't want to mortgage my future by taking a student loan." Temporary jobs Cathy took seemed boring compared to the one she wants. Rather than be bored she paints at home to relieve the depression caused by her money problem.

There was no ready market for the studies Hal took in American culture except in France, where he sojourned the summer of his junior year. But, as an American citizen, he couldn't get a French work permit. "I'm living on my parents," he said, "until the market opens up. They don't seem to mind."

Cliff's another Simple Simon type. He wants to catch a whale but, like the nursery-rhyme character, the water he fishes in is in his mother's pail. To qualify for a car loan, the aspiring writer took a job as a proofreader. Then he quit because it paid too little. "I'd rather earn nothing than less than what I'm worth," he said. "My folks have enough to keep me going."

Some parents are stronger though their children interpret their actions as a lack of generosity. When a twenty-four-year-old musician couldn't afford to pay his car insurance or buy a village sticker, he knew better than to turn to his parents as a financial resort. "They bought me the car at the end of my sophomore year," he said, "but I was made responsible for its expenses. I had to sell it. I wasn't going to take a mainstream job just for a car."

The tenor of the times often contributes to a young adult's attitude toward earning and spending money. In the sixties, a student's way of life made few economic demands. It was OK to wear jeans, eat vegetables, and put a barber out of business. What did a student know about taxes or Social Security payments? They weren't taken out of the checks dad sent. Nor did the young adult have to contribute to the "us" of the family. "In the depression, money was traded for a warm coat, but in the sixties, it was traded for a fake fur," said Ahern. "In other words, money was used for luxuries, not necessities."

In the early seventies, young people caught the inflation mentality of "no value in saving." There was also no reality between earnings and disposable income. More bought less. Faced with the inflationary spiral, many young people lost their motivation.

In the present economy, young adults claim they can live better at home than they can on their own. Reared in comfort, they want to know what more they can aspire to.

The answer may lie in a conversation overheard between two graduate students. The first criticized the second for living at home. He said, "It's part of my survival to live on my own. I took a job outside my field and beneath my abilities to make the money I need." The second student shook his head. "I'm willing," he told his friend, "to make the sacrifice of living at home to live better for less."

The difference between the young adult who relies on Santa Claus and the one willing to start a workshop is value judgments. Those eager to become independent pared their living standard. Tammy, who wanted her own apartment, did without get-away weekends and high-style clothes. She banked the sum she would have paid a landlord to save toward moving out. Jim sold his car and used public transportation. Prospective brides and grooms put the brakes on spending now to accumulate money they would need later. In a sample survey, home-ing pigeons with a long-range goal were noticeably more solvent than young adults whose immediate goal was a nice wardrobe, a new Honda, or a trip to Europe.

With few exceptions, the savers had been taught early some of the basics of money management, had been made aware of the family finances, and had participated in the family budgeting process. These children had been given an allowance and told what the allowance covered—clothes, entertainment, and so on. These children were also informed if money was short at the moment.

On a money-manager's scale of one to ten, those deepest in debt were "ones" given the least guidance in money matters during their early years. Bernice, who now earns $10,000 a year and contributes nothing to the household, said that the sum "isn't a great deal to play around with." She spends most of her money visiting friends out of state to scout places where she'd like to live. "I was never taught money management," she said. "When I got my allowance, all I was taught was one-tenth goes to the church and do what you want with the rest." Helene was never given an allowance. "Whenever I needed money, I asked my folks. They were very generous, and I never lacked for anything." Don depended on cash gifts for extras, and when he began earning money in high school was told, "It's your money. Spend it the way you want to."

Moneywise, they had a more carefree childhood than Bill and his sister Amy, whose parents taught them how to use money at an early age. "I got an allowance as soon as I was in first grade, and the amount had to cover my school lunches," Bill recalled. "It was given every Friday, and if I spent it over the weekend, my mom would say on Monday, 'There's peanut butter in the cupboard.'

"By fifth grade, it was big enough to cover bus money, and if I blew it, I walked. It didn't take me long to know I had choices to make: resist buying the latest in toys or walk a couple of miles in the rain clutching a soggy brown bag that held a peanut-butter sandwich.

"Any money left over from the expenses I was supposed to meet was mine. I learned to save up for a record album or game or whatever I wanted. Immediate gratification wasn't the name of the game in our house."

Amy recalled finding it easier to manage her allowance when it was smaller and covered fewer personal needs. The temptation to spend a large sum of money at one time grew stronger as she grew older.

"By the time I was in high school, my allowance was expected to cover school supplies, clothes, activity tickets, and cosmetics. Almost everything except my medical and dental bills. I got it in a lump sum each month.

"One month I blew most of it on makeup and dress-up clothes for a turnabout dance after the guy I had a crush on said yes. The turnabout wasn't fair play. I didn't have enough money to take him. He offered to pay for the tickets and dinner, but my mother wouldn't let me accept his offer.

"I thought she was an ogre. She could have advanced my next month's allowance. She wasn't hurting for cash. But, no, I had made my choice and had to pay the consequences. That incident sticks in my mind. To this day, I separate what I call my bill money and my play money."

The mother of these high scorers said that teaching her children the financial facts of life was time-consuming and aggravating. And although they stopped believing in Santa Claus, they began to believe in Scrooge. "I just didn't hand over their allowances and forget it," she said. "I guided their decisions, took them comparison shopping, and taught them consumers' rights.

"They didn't always listen and sometimes fell flat on their faces. I never picked them up. They'd be out on their own one day, and I tried to prepare them ahead of time."

She didn't expect them back after they left for college. But both children learned money management, it may seem, too well. Each chose a graduate school close by to spare themselves living expenses. Bill, who worked for two years and lived on his own, used his savings for personal needs and took out a student loan. Amy, just out of undergraduate school, is on a scholarship and gets an allowance she supplements by supervising a morning newspaper route. "At least," she said, "it keeps my dad from asking, 'What am I—a money machine?' "

Her dad doesn't mind feeding and sheltering his adult-age children or continuing Amy's allowance. "Money's a tool, not a possession," he said. "I'm investing in their future. It's not like I'm paying to get them out of hock or for a mistake they made."

In another situation, family circumstances dictated a single parent's attitude toward supporting two sons. Alarmed at having to rear them alone, a widow told the boys when they were ten and twelve, "You're going to college, and the day you graduate or turn twenty-one, whichever comes first, the free ride is over. We'll be the best of friends, but hell or high water, you're on your own."

The younger one recalled being really scared. "But mom didn't make us feel like poor orphans," he said. "She gave us an allowance to use for snacks and movies. Every dollar we saved, she matched with another dollar. If we didn't save at least one dollar a month, she cut our allowance in half the next month. We began to look upon saving as a reward and overspending as a vice."

The older son added, "Mom pushed us to get jobs, and if we couldn't find one, she found one for us, like a paper route. I passed it down to my brother and later got him into the supermarket where I worked throughout high school. We knew we had to pull together."

Their mother, now remarried, is proud of her children. "A year ago I went to my older boy's law school graduation and felt like I did after I gave birth to him. I was thrilled. My boy's hard work had paid off. He was a lawyer.

"My younger boy got a good engineering job in Alaska. I cried when he left. We'd all gone through a lot together."

Both sons lived at home for a time—one while waiting to pass the bar and the other while looking for a job—and would like to repay mom for motivating, encouraging, and teaching them how to get along in the world. "But she refuses any help," the older son said. "She claimed she had to let us know in advance what was coming, and everything she taught us was to give us a good start in life."

Financial managers agree that no parent can afford to be like the old woman who lived in a shoe. A parent has to know what to do with children. Some contend it's never too late to teach a child who's not knowledgeable about money. "First, you can't baby him anymore," said Gene Mackevich, a vice-president of E.F. Hutton and Company. "Second, stop being a shelter. The key is to anticipate the costs of having a kid come home. Find out what he wants. Tell him what you want. Give him the rules of *your* game.

"If you can't teach him about money yourself, send him to financial seminars, give him books to read, buy journals. For instance, if you couldn't teach him about sex, you'd send him to someone else."

Bischmann believes it may be too late to start teaching a twenty-five-year-old how to manage money. "And a parent may not be organized enough to show him how to keep records or balance a checkbook," she said. "That's where organizations like ours can help. We usually see people who are already in trouble. But we would like to prevent rather than put out fires."

Does asking young adults for room and board teach them the fine points of money management? The consensus of financial advisors is no. But paying their share of household expenses can dissolve the belief in a free lunch, impart a sense of financial responsibility, and keep parents from footing all the bills. In the same way that young adults outgrew their need for the tooth fairy, they can outgrow their need for Santa Claus and start to believe in themselves.

20

Splitting the Bills, Not the Relationship

Ralph claimed that his dry sense of humor kept him from swigging a liquid antacid. What sours him? The way he and his twenty-two-year-old son Steve related at home.

"We had a money connection," the internist said. "Before I left the house in the morning, I left money for Steve propped in a napkin holder on the kitchen table. When I came home at night, the money was gone."

Not that Ralph begrudged the ten dollars or more he bequeathed his son each day. Steve's upkeep at home was no more costly than when he had lived in a dorm. Ralph paid Steve's tuition at a commuter school plus dental and clothing bills and his car insurance premiums. But he was less comfortable leaving cash for an adult son than mailing a check. It was like setting out a bowl of milk for a stray kitten. "Supposedly, Steve earned pocket money on weekends as a waiter," Ralph said. "But every night, my wife would say, 'Leave money for Steve.' So I left money for Steve."

How did the marketing student lap up the cash he found upon waking? Ralph didn't ask. He assumed it paid for a train ticket, parking fees at the railroad station, and lunches. "We don't talk much about how we spend our money except when my wife asks, 'Did you leave money for Steve?' "

In the home of fifty or so other families, money talk was a Tower of Babel on the verge of collapse and ready to cause chaos. Joanne, in charge of family accounts, was boiling mad. The object of her disaffection? For one, Nancy, a twenty-year-old college dropout working at a job "leading nowhere."

The disappointed mother immediately cut off financial support when Nancy dropped out of college and returned home. "If she was a student, I'd pay for everything," Joanne said. "But she's not. So I won't pay for anything. That's my way of forcing her to give up making doughnuts and get an education.

"I didn't understand why Nancy wasn't fazed a bit. To my face she said, 'There's nothing I want you to pay for. I don't want your money.'"

Joanne's anger came to a second boil when her stand was undermined by her husband. He slipped cash for extras to their daughter. It spilled over when she confronted him. "He was always more open-handed than me to the kids," she said. "And we can't talk about the situation rationally."

In a dozen or more households, the disbursement of money was a measure of momentary temperament. Phillip, a twenty-four-year-old special education teacher, had never been held accountable for a specific household expense. "It depended on my mother's mood," he said. "Sometimes, she asked me to pay back money she laid out for dry cleaning, stamps, or shaving cream. Other times, she pooh-poohed taking money from a son."

His father refused Phillip's offer of room and board. But annoyed by a light left turned on, a thermostat set too high, or long-distance telephone calls made by Phillip, he would lash out, "If you paid for living here, you'd know what it cost to run a house."

Phillip made no second attempt to pay his own way. Based on prior experience, he said, "They'd only get embarrassed and change the subject. Money was always a touchy issue in our house. No one liked to talk about it. Mom and dad just blew up when you least expected them to."

What's needed between parents and adult children is open communication about who pays for what. A parent who takes in a grown child is tacitly offering economic help. But to what extent? A home-ing pigeon is tacitly expecting economic help. But how much?

Although a lack of money makes strange bedfellows, both generations reported they would like to live together in peace and eventually part as friends. Featherbedding was an artificial solution. Yet, the two sets of adults seem to prefer sleeping on a cactus to discussing financial arrangements. They were unable to divorce monetary decisions from family feelings.

"Emotional attitudes toward money began way before the youngster left," said money-management workshop leader Dee Dee Ahern. "But problems can be avoided when he comes home if parents clarify to each other how much they expect the kid to contribute financially. It can be a flat sum, a portion of his salary, or nothing.

"If financial problems brought him back, he may be unhappy about making any contribution. But if parents decide beforehand how much they are willing and able to give, they should be able to discuss the situation with him and work it out."

But, just as there are Ph.D.s in economics who can't balance a checkbook, there are husbands and wives who can't be intimate about money. The bundling board between them is a difference in attitude, personality, or experiences encountered before they ever met. Tess, for example, came from a fatherless family that worried about its next meal. Reared under these circumstances, she was forced to be frugal. Al, her husband, grew up in a well-to-do family and was accustomed to only the best. "Buying me things was his way of showing affection," Tess said. "It was great until we got married."

Whereas she would spend $5 only if there was $10 in her purse, Al would charge $100 without a penny in his pocket. To her objections, he invariably answered, "Don't worry," and he would use his charm to steer the conversation elsewhere. "We've had ups and downs moneywise in our twenty-seven years together," Tess said, "but it hasn't changed our attitudes."

The rift became a chasm the day their jobless daughter Valerie came home. Tess decided she would ask Valerie for fifteen or twenty dollars a week as soon as the aspiring buyer found employment. Verbally, Al offered Valerie twenty-five dollars a week until she found work. He also gave her the use of his credit cards. "Why not?" Al asked. "I'm still a parent. It's my pleasure to give."

Tess could have given Al fifteen thousand reasons for being less indulgent, namely a debt in that amount for a failed business deal. She didn't. Instead she lay awake nights worrying. "Valerie came home completely dependent on us," Tess said. "Not like my son who just needed room and board. Besides, I know what Al's answer would be. 'Don't worry.' "

To avoid money quarrels, parents should discuss the state of their own finances before a child returns—openly and without tension. They should try to anticipate a child's needs and whether or not they can provide clothing, free use of credit cards, and pocket money. "This is a different situation than just feeding him and giving him a place to sleep and has to be worked out ahead of time," Ahern said. "But if the parents' relationship concerning money has always been a closed subject, it will be hard to open."

Under such circumstances, "Know thyself" is an important exhortation. Psychologists believe that a person who understands his or her own attitude toward money will be more comfortable broaching the subject than a person who feels guilty or uncertain about the use of money. They suggest taking time alone or with a spouse to answer questions such as: What does money mean to me? How do I feel when I spend money? When do I hoard or spend the most? Is money to be used or to be saved?

Answering questions of this nature can open a crack in the door of money communication. It can help modify behavior that interferes with the real goal of money talk within a family—to negotiate financial matters in a way that makes it the root of good relationships instead of the root of arguments and tension.

Couples with a similar background may differ in money habits, too, depending on the role each was asked to play early in the marriage. "I bargain hunt, comparison shop, and save coupons," Sharon said. "They're habits left over from our lean years. Our thrust was to further Howard's career."

Her husband, now a successful attorney, buys without looking at price. "Kiddingly, I used to call him Diamond Jim and he'd call me Secondhand Rose," she said. "But we never made a big issue over our wants until our son Jay came home."

Over coffee one night, the couple agreed to ask for $150 a month once the novice account executive got on his feet or had been home six months, whichever came first. "I thought Jay would be happy to pitch in," his mother said. "He's a very independent person. But he resented our request. He said it was still his home and he had never paid before." Howard, when faced with presenting the decision, did an about-face. "He gave a fair argument," Howard rationalized. "And we didn't need his money."

It was as if two dry sticks had been rubbed together. The involvement of a third person in Howard and Sharon's money relationship started fiery arguments. Friendly teasing turned into flagrant insults. "I don't know who I'm madder at most," Sharon said. "My husband who made me look like a secondhand mother, my son who refused to assume the responsibility of the man he claims to be, or me. I should have gotten our agreement in writing."

Not according to Ahern. She feels written contracts are unnecessary in a family situation. "Your word should be sufficient," she said. "Nobody should be intimidated, and everybody should be cooperative dealing with these matters."

Another round of negotiations is in order if financial affairs become an issue between parents when a grown child comes home. Pauline, for instance, was reluctant to ask her daughter Ellen to pay for room and board. "I grew up in the depression when sharing was a matter of fact," she said. "I thought, 'Why not help her? It isn't a hardship on us.' "

Her husband Jim thought otherwise. "Ellen needs to learn life isn't a free ride," he said. "I learned that in the depression, and it was a good, although a hard, lesson."

The pair reached a compromise after several discussions. Once Ellen found a full-time teaching job, they asked for a modest amount, sixty dollars a month, as her share. They arrived at the sum with Ellen's help by considering her salary, her expenses, and her habits. "She eats little at home," Pauline said. "She also pays for her long-distance calls and buys her own shampoo, toothpaste, deodorant, and other personal items. The only things she really uses are her room and water. She's an unselfish girl. Even as a substitute teacher, she'd stop at a bakery or cheese shop to bring us something special."

Ellen's pleased with the arrangement. "It makes me feel better paying something," she said. "I know that by living at home, I'm able to do things I couldn't do living on my own."

In still another household, Dan and Mary bickered on and off for two years—should they or shouldn't they ask their son for room and board? "Money was no problem in our house," Mary said. "My husband was the problem. To me, anyway. He wanted my son to pay room and board so he'd learn how to budget. I wanted him to save enough to move out." Finally, they came to a mutual conclusion: charge him $100 a month and bank the money in his name. "He was very good about it," Mary said, wishing she had compromised sooner. "We never had to ask. On the first of the month, the money was in an envelope on the table."

How did their son react after he lost his financial deferment? "I wondered when they'd ask," he said. "But I wasn't going to."

A small percentage of parents had no trouble decreeing, at the start, how much financial responsibility they expected a home-ing pigeon to assume. But in some instances one or the other couldn't present the joint decision to their offspring. "I want my son Kevin to get his act together," Alice said. "He doesn't need creature comforts and is happy to use a sleeping bag to bed down.

"He has no materialistic goals. He wants to live in the north woods, find a mate, and write the great American novel. How could I bring up the subject of money with a kid like that? He made the word sound profane."

Alice's husband Jack was less squeamish. "The kid lived from hand to mouth doing odd jobs and running home each time there was nothing to move from hand to mouth. Alice and I agreed to ask for token board, to give him the message he won't be able to sponge forever.

"It was hard for me to ask him for money. But I did it for his own good. It's my fault he's this much away from being a bum," Jack said holding his thumb and index finger parallel. "I made it too easy for him."

Despite the growing tendency of parents to offer refuge to grown children, Susan was tired of the whole thing. She wished that her children who were chronically broke would fend for themselves, and she let her husband take care of the financial arrangements as the children came and went. "I don't know exactly what they give us," she said, "except trials and disappointments. Somehow, they always had money to buy pot and contraceptives."

Well-fixed parents may have found supporting a child past adult age an emotional burden. But parents of more modest means or parents saving toward retirement have found additional demands on the pocketbook a financial hardship as well. Mike, a fifty-eight-year-old factory foreman, planned to take early retirement. A long-time widower, he also tried to compensate his daughter for being reared as a motherless child. He paid the legacy of her divorce—legal fees and personal debts—and didn't ask her to share household expenses when he took her in. But when she began taking luxurious vacations from her job as a computer operator, he had second thoughts. "In a way, they were coming out of my pocket," he complained.

The day Mike found out she had brought home a stereo was the day he lost his patience. "It wasn't an ordinary stereo," Mike said. "It cost more than $800. I blew my top. Here I was paying all her living expenses while she used her savings to buy a big item. In a confrontation, her answer was that no matter how little I had, it was more than she did."

Mike, however, insisted she pay twenty-five dollars a week for room and board, and his daughter grudgingly complied. "I feel guilty taking it," he said. "She's been through a lot. But I worry about getting old and not having enough to live on."

In another situation, Laura feels used. After putting her fourth child through school, she and her husband took second jobs to clear up education debts and to accumulate funds to retire to the warm climate they'd talked about for years. But the twenty-four-year-old son who came home put a crimp in their plans. He was inveterately short of money for car insurance or a car payment. "These are the elephants," she said. "The gnats were lunches he took from home, special items on the grocery list, and entertaining his friends at our expense. He borrowed my car when his was at the service station and always returned it with the tank empty.

"If we asked him to pay us back, he became abusive. He'd remind us of the things he did without as a child because we couldn't afford them. He ran with kids from wealthy families, and we just didn't have the money."

There's no need for parents to justify asking grown children to pay their share of expenses. If the home-ing pigeons are financially able but unwilling to pitch in, there are two ways to deal with the blatant freeloader. Each is a strong measure and requires strength on the parents' part to enforce it.

First point out: "If you're acting like a dependent, you'll be treated like one." The essence of a parent's argument can be, "OK, for all intents and purposes we're supporting you—housing, food, extras. As long as you won't contribute, you'll be treated as a minor. You'll have a curfew and will account to us for your actions."

If the home-ing pigeon asks, "Why should I pay for board, the room's empty anyway?" a parent might state the obvious: "If you were out of the house, you'd have to pay rent plus utilities and all your own expenses."

The second measure is usually done in desperation: pull out the plug. If push comes to shove, say, "Pay up or find your own place."

Neither measure is palatable to parent or child. "But you can't keep bailing out a kid," counseling supervisor Jean Bischmann said. "And don't worry about losing him. Once he's out on his own, the initial resentment will fade. He'll see what it costs to live."

Sitting down with grown children beforehand and hammering out who pays for what is the simplest way to avoid problems once they are ensconced at home.

Children should come home to a partnership agreement. As in any deal, this calls for a lot of negotiations, but the maxim to remember is "An ounce of prevention is worth a pound of cure."

Critics of a businesslike manner between parents and children don't take into consideration the emotional impact of a financial arrangement (or lack of one) that favors one party more than the other. Over a period of time, resentment can turn into a force of anger that can tear families apart more surely than frank talk about what each party expects the other to pay. Family members should provide a support system for one another. They should contribute to each other's growth. At the same time, they shouldn't allow themselves to be used.

Katie, for instance, came home with school loans, a car loan, and a modest-paying job to a mother in the throes of a divorce. She had anticipated financial help in addition to free room and board. "But there just wasn't any extra money," her mother said. "I had to let her know she was expected to pay all her own expenses and eventually a portion of the mortgage.

"I was able to manage the slight increase in the grocery bill. But if the phone bill was higher than usual, she had to pay her share. Once she got over her disappointment, we had no financial problems between us."

As time passed, Katie cleared her debts and began to contribute forty dollars a week toward board. She also picked up the tab when she shopped for groceries. "I know I'm a help, not a drain, on my mother's resources. She tells me so," she said. "And it's nice to know my contribution is appreciated."

Families who were always interdependent had the least financial adjustment to make upon reunion. In Myrna's home, the house rule was once a child went to high school, he paid a share of household expenses. Each teenager's share was ten dollars a week. "We didn't want them to feel they could always lean on parents," Myrna said, and her husband believed "contributing gave them a feeling of independence and a taste of responsibility."

The year a twenty-seven-year-old son came back after losing a business, they were willing to defer any contribution. "But with his tremendous sense of failure, we had to accept his wishes to pay board as soon as he came home," Myrna said. "Financially, he would have been better off if he had kept all the money he made on his new job."

The parents and grown child settled on twenty dollars a week, and the son insisted they take the money he made selling the inventory from his former business. "My folks paid in dollars, and mentally, too, for my failure. They literally came down to Louisiana to bring me back. I wanted them to keep the money as appreciation for everything they did for me."

In good conscience the parents couldn't accept his generosity. Like many couples who could afford to, they put the money in trust and made it available at a time he could accept it without losing face. "Our kids are careful about taking money from us," Myrna said. "They had each put hours into my husband's restaurant and knew how hard he worked for a living."

Other parents were hesitant about building capital for a child using money earmarked for the household. "That's game playing," one father said. "It's taking money out of his left pocket to put into his right pocket. He'd never learn how to manage money that way."

But such a move, toughened with a stipulation, had Bischmann's approval. "If a parent doesn't have to use the money a kid contributes, he can save it for him," she said. "But he shouldn't be silly enough to open his mouth and tell him what he's doing.

"To repeat a strong point, asking for room and board doesn't teach children money management. They know they won't be evicted if they skip a month. It will teach responsibility, but only if parents insist that grown children keep their word."

Communicating beforehand the expenses grown children are expected to carry can prevent the petty situations that arise without guidelines. Guidelines can be reset if the overall financial picture changes or if one party becomes unhappy with the arrangement. Open communication is the best policy. Parents should be honest, loving, and tough. If they're professional in what they say, children will respect it.

Most parents, however, tend to lead with their hearts, not their heads, when children in need walk through the door. For example, Larry and Beth based their decision on their own experience in the late forties and asked nothing from their accountant son, Vic. When they were newly married, they had lived with Beth's parents until Larry found a job. "We were penniless except for my mustering-out pay," Larry said, "and my in-laws asked for room and board. I was horrified. If you have a child starting out, you don't charge for helping him unless you need it."

Larry felt that way until Vic had been home three months. Despite a well-paying job, he ran up cleaning bills, and telephone bills, used their car, and charged gasoline to their account. "The upshot was his reason for charging the gas," Larry said. "He couldn't figure out how much of it each of us used. So we began to charge him ten cents a mile."

In another household composed of two home-ing pigeons and a divorcée, Lisa's room and board bill started at $50 a month and climbed by tens and twenties until by the end of the first year, it was up to $150. Concurrently, she was paying off school loans and a car she needed for work as an ad salesperson. In addition, she was eventually asked to split the phone bill, the heating bill, and the cost of the salt for the water softener. "Those weren't in our original deal," she said, "but I didn't want to hassle about money."

Realizing that she rarely ate at home, she logged the cost of the food she ate and proved to her mother and sister that she was eating less than they. "I stopped chipping in for food and would buy my own," Lisa said. "But when we made holiday dinners, we kept receipts of what we spent and split the bill."

In a similar situation, a mother and daughter had incompatible eating habits. One liked dairy products; the other preferred vegetables. Each shopped and paid for her own food. "Sometimes, we'll switch," the home-ing pigeon said. "I'll use my mother's milk and give her some of my vegetables. If we both like something and one of us buys it, the purchaser puts her name on the wrapping. This way neither of us feels gypped."

What may seem a unique financial arrangement to one family may be an ordinary situation to another. Parents have asked home-ing pigeons for contributions ranging from $40 to $200 a month after ninety days to two years from their return. Some parents continued to pay children's car insurance, dental bills, and clothing costs. Others who had never allowed their children to drive the car until they could afford the gas and insurance enforced the same rule when they came home. Some families cut off clothing allowances as soon as the children turned twenty-one.

This would seem liberal to the home-ing pigeon who was expected to sew her own clothes by age sixteen. "Without being told, I knew I'd have to carry my own weight if I lived at home," she said. "But they told me anyway."

Other families who stressed the value of savings refused compensation but insisted children bank a prescribed amount of their salary each month. Few parents expected students to contribute any money to the household and gave them an allowance to keep them from being diverted from their studies. "A student is a consumer, not a producer," a father said. "I wanted mine to consume knowledge so he could make a living."

The proof of any method's validity is based on the answers to these questions: Does it smooth out financial wrinkles and keep a home free of tensions in the money-managing sector? Does the arrangement satisfy family members, or does one feel put at a disadvantage by the others? Often, the only destructive money talk is the conversation parents or children have with themselves. Inner resentment becomes open hostility if they hear only their own voices.

Economist G. S. Becker in the *Swedish Journal of Economics* ("A Theory of the Allocation of Time," 1973) likened the running of a household to the running of a business. Each needs inputs such as time, money, and rational decision making to produce the quality of life valued by the people involved. Decisions, according to Becker, should be based on whether or not they allow a household to enjoy a higher level of satisfaction if they are enforced.

Applying this theory to the refilled nest, few parents derive satisfaction from children who feel happiest freeloading. Nor do children derive satisfaction from parents who begrudge providing economic support. Circumstances, personalities, financial needs, and goals should be considered at the time parents and children strike a deal. Once parents jump the hurdle of approaching the subject, it's advisable to let the children help with the decision of who pays for what. Parents should let children know about any money problems and give them room to express their own values. Everyone's standard is slightly different, even within a family.

21

Taking Stock of the Money Bond

Parents and grown children who live together have a task in common with a stock market investor. Periodically, they must review their objectives and make new investments if they're falling short of a goal.

Since the job of parents is to foster independence in offspring, any stock they add to their portfolios must be chosen in this light. "It's destructive to go back to the parent-child dependency relationship in money matters," said mental-health director Lawrence Berson. "To avoid it, the terms of financial help should be made very clear even if a parent has to do something that looks cold."

Parents knew that merging with children was risky. Young adults' financial contributions were marginal, their assistance negligible, and their reaction to company policy volatile. But few parents sold children short. Children were promising growth stocks, and parents underwrote them hoping they'd take off.

The merger had a down side for the children, too. Cheap living can arrest their motivation. Daily interest can compound dependency on the parent organization. Supported as a subsidiary, they can lose the ambition that drove them home—to build enough assets to make their stock go up and then split.

When children lost sight of their target—to become self-suffi-

225

cient—parents rightfully worried. The stock was flat, going nowhere. Why? In an attempt to rally the kid, parents became promoters. "Study harder." "Save more." "Work smarter." The kids' book values dropped. Each kid was certain "Something's wrong with me. They're pushing me out." Such negative indicators lowered the yield of satisfaction on the family bond.

What may be needed at this time is a technical correction to help the child-independence ratio edge upward. Inventory has to be taken of assets equipping children to start their own "companies." They might need the infusion of additional education, a job, a car, savings, a housing start, or other amenities. To keep children from staying put, parents may get a call for capital outlays.

Opinions are divided on how much financial aid parents should provide, especially if children see themselves as glamour stock. "One reason a grown kid avoids responsibilities is his unrealistic expectation of the outside world," said sociology professor Marijean Suelzle. "He refuses to settle for anything less than a high salary and an expensive home.

"In a restricted economy, these are difficult ambitions to realize immediately, and although these kids are materialistic, they don't want to make sacrifices to reach their goals."

For example, Jordan was a perennial student. From 1966 until 1979 he earned two bachelor of science degrees and a master's degree, and he intended to pursue a doctorate. Eight of the thirteen years, he lived at home supported by parents and part-time jobs taken in the fields of psychology, sociology, and education. All during this time, he studied with a guru who planned to build a new society based on the barter system. "There was no point taking a job," said Jordan, a Mensa member. "I had my needs taken care of at home. I could take all the time I wanted to find myself."

After eight years of housing a scholarly goldbrick, Jordan's father gave up. Asked to bank-roll a doctorate, he told his son, "Let the guru support you." The thirty-one-year-old was given three weeks to find an apartment and a job. He found both. Now living in a furnished room and working full-time in a mental-health center, Jordan blamed his parents for his former dependency. "Their years of total support lowered my self-esteem. Without their help, I'm more into making my own way in the world."

Less patient parents tired more quickly of children with a wide disparity between "wanting to" and "willing to" make their own ways, especially if the offspring vented their frustration on doors, walls, or fences and in verbal abuse. Faced daily, weekly, or monthly with their high volatility, parents stepped in to literally help children out.

Greta, for example, decided she could no longer cope with Don, who changed majors as often as bank tellers change twenties. During the sixth year of his fruitless education—spent at home—he smashed walls, broke doors, and knocked down a fence. "He couldn't settle on a career and got a fit each time we asked him to make a decision," she said. "He'd always been hotheaded. Our saying was 'As Don goes, so goes the house.'

"My husband and I asked him to take a job to defray our cost of his education. But we had to watch our words. He accused us of valuing money more than him. He lied to us, saying he was working when he wasn't. And he threatened to retaliate if we stopped paying tuition. He'd have us at his mercy when we were old and would put us in a nursing home.

"After a horrible scene, I decided I didn't want to be a parent anymore. I told him, 'Get out. Manage your own life. Stand on your own two feet.' "

Greta was uncomfortable forcing her son to leave, but she was more uncomfortable living with him. Through friends, she learned that he found an apartment 200 miles from home and a job in a feed store. Now, a department head and about to be married, Don said, "At first I hated my folks for kicking me out. But it was the best thing that could have happened. I'm doing a million times better than I did at home."

Asked to comment on kids who come out of a slump when forced to depend on themselves, therapist Dr. Jessie Potter said, "In a highly industrialized country, kids come out of childhood conditioned to think they need adults (such as teachers and parents) to lean upon. But anyone with enough sense to go out and seek experience gets a new view of life and can grow into adulthood."

On the ground that some offspring need "a boot" to get on their feet, bearish advice can make sense and save dollars. But even bears were bullish about helping children obtain additional education if these parents were convinced that the children really had goals, that they weren't choosing to continue school to escape the real world.

"After college is no time for a kid to begin finding himself, and I wouldn't subsidize a child on that basis. Nor would I finance additional degrees just because the kid doesn't have a job," Berson said.

Those bullish on education took it for granted that parents would negotiate the cost of the education with the student—how much the parent would contribute, whether repayment was expected, and, if so, how much and when. "I see nothing wrong with parents helping a child further his education," said counseling supervisor Jean Bischmann. "But any kid who wants to go on to graduate school should be providing part of the help himself."

Everyone knows which road is paved with good intentions. A deal today may not be ideal tomorrow while working toward a long-range goal. For example, Arnold's son, Murray, came back to parents in better financial shape than when he had left. They had no children in college, and Arnold's most recent promotion had considerably boosted his salary. "I was a lot freer with money to Murray than to my three older children," said Arnold, a vice-president of a household products company. His wife Maggie, too, had fewer money worries. "And I was more generous," she said. "In fact, it was nice to lose the role of nay-sayer."

Conditions were ripe for Murray to make his bid. Newly graduated as an accountant, he wanted an M.B.A. from a top school as a passport into management consulting, a career with salaries starting from $28,000 to $40,000 a year depending on work experience. Murray promised to work days in an accounting firm and enroll in an evening program if his parents would become stockholders in his career investment. "I was sold," Arnold said. "I liked to see a kid who knew where he was heading, especially my own."

Arnold made a firm agreement to pay half the tuition (three courses a semester at $385 a course) and to provide free room and board. Murray was responsible for his car, insurance, books, and clothes. He expected to manage well on a gross salary of $250 a week—a fortune to a kid who had never worked full-time before.

To get started, Murray needed an advance for his half of the tuition, a car down-payment, and a business wardrobe. He was given $1,600 toward school and a car and an outright gift of $350 for clothes. By the second semester, Murray was still in debt. He had begun car payments, paid the insurance rate of a twenty-two-year-old single male, and bought two suits and a winter jacket. "And I was faced with tuition again," he said.

This time Arnold paid for books, and Maggie stopped asking reimbursement for dry-cleaning expenses and other incidentals. By the time the third semester rolled around, Murray was tense about his job and behind in his schoolwork. "One was draining the energy of the other," Maggie said.

At year's end, the former A student was downhearted about getting Cs and a poor review of his job performance. "The load at school was incredible," Murray said. "I could understand why the university doesn't want a student to work."

What does a nervous investor do in a down market? Murray wanted to pull out. "I could have had a fat savings account or paid for my own pad if I wasn't going to school," he said. "I'd also have my self-respect. I like to pull my own weight, not have mommy buy me shaving cream."

Arnold and Maggie had faith in their stock. It just needed the right conditions to rise in value. They made a tender offer to support Murray in graduate school. Except for pocket money and car payments, they would pay all expenses. In turn, Murray sold his car and took a night job as a waiter. The thirty-hour-a-week job requirement, however, cut into his study time. So he took a weekend job in a shoe store instead but was uncomfortable working alongside high school students. Finally, he joined the ranks of the unemployed and accepted thirty dollars a week as an allowance from his parents. "Once you start to take, it gets easier," Murray said. "Even so, I can't consider myself an adult under these circumstances. An adult takes responsibility for himself and anyone who may depend on him. I depend on everyone else."

Arnold and Maggie see their capital outlay from a different perspective. "Giving my son a break is more important to me than how many bucks I have in the bank," Arnold said. Maggie considered her son a preferred stock. "He's in the top one percent of a top school," she said. "That's a lot more satisfying than a quarterly dividend."

The response of other parents to children who asked to be subsidized for additional education was mixed. Few refused to provide free room and board. Those who did had clashed with their children and didn't want to prolong live-in relationships. One set of parents went to the opposite extreme. They not only paid a daughter's tuition at a nearby college, but also provided the law student with an apartment so she could study and they could live in peace.

Some parents couldn't afford peace at any price. They worried about depleting their savings. "I was afraid I might later need the money my son was asking for now," said a woman whose husband was nearing retirement age. When he didn't want to start out in debt by taking student loans, she encouraged him to find employment in a firm offering higher education as a fringe benefit. "The bank he works for is paying for an evening program," she said. Others who worked for companies with such a policy recommended an offspring for a position. "My English degree didn't exactly make me marketable," Ellis said. "So my dad got me a job in his insurance company, and it's paying for my M.B.A." Ellis had no say in the salary because his father set up the job. Knowing nothing about insurance, he had to go through a training program. "But it was worth it to get an education that prepared me for something," he said, "and that kept my father from shelling out more dough."

Children seeking second careers sometimes ask parents to become personnel offices rather than student-loan offices. Asking help to find employment is a reasonable request. But parents shouldn't use their agency unless the offspring have knocked on doors themselves. As one parent commented, "There's a difference between leaving the striving to us and the inability to find a job."

Again, merging with a child is risky, especially if a parent is an employee not an owner. "My son grumbled about the hard work from the minute I got him a job in the company where I work," an embarrassed father said. "He quit without notice and made me look like a fool." Another son gave a company a false reference. "And it put me on the spot," his father said. "How could I vouch for a skill the kid didn't have? I told personnel to take it up with him."

With a child of more integrity, becoming coworkers can strengthen the family tie. Helen, a tax consultant, helped her daughter get a foot in the door of an accounting firm. "I made it clear that the rest was up to her," Helen said. "And she did fine. My employer thinks she has a lot of potential."

Counselors saw nothing wrong with parents helping a child get a job—even in a family business. "To give a broad example, the Rockefellers did it," Bischmann said. "But I would fuss if a father immediately made a son a vice-president."

And money-management workshop leader Dee Dee Ahern pointed out, "It's no longer a stigma to go into a father's business. It doesn't imply a kid can't make it on his own. Now the attitude is 'My father does well; so will I.'"

A sign comparable to Seidman and Son can delight parent and child. It's a glorious bond if they get along. Today's economic needs may make the family pull together again.

A recommendation high on the buy list is to bring children into the family business only after they have worked for a similar operation. Restaurateurs, clothiers, and other small business owners discovered that a successful outside work experience raised children's self-confidence and their appreciation of the parents' accomplishment. Lorna, for example, never realized the knowledge her mother needed to head an interior-decorating firm. Nor did she believe in her own talents until she worked elsewhere. "I needed to try my own wings," Lorna said. "Mom thought I was great, but she was mom. I needed a stranger to verify my ability before I went into her company."

Regarding jobs in general, counselors believed young adults should actively seek employment. And, if necessary, take a part-time job while waiting for the big one to come along. There's no reason for grown children to depend on parents for pocket money.

The current outlook for buying children their first car was mixed. In some families, purchase of the first car as a graduation gift was a tradition. The maternal grandmother in Miriam's family, for instance, started the custom ten years ago with her oldest grandson. Since then, Miriam and her husband chip in to allow the retired widow to uphold the tradition with their younger children. "It's a way of saying congratulations on a major milestone," Miriam said, "and it's more useful than a piece of jewelry and more lasting than a trip."

Her sister refused to allow the same grandmother to buy a car for her graduates. She contended that American children have few rites of adulthood and considered the purchase of a first automobile one of them. "The kid should have the satisfaction of accomplishing this on his own," she declared, "just like I wouldn't want to find him his first woman." She compromised her principles by permitting her daughter to borrow the purchase price of a car from her grandmother and repay it without interest.

Offspring were sometimes recipients of old family cars which were to be used as trade-ins when they were ready to support car payments. But this plan could backfire. "The old clunker has more than 70,000 miles and continually needs repair," Kim said. "I drive it thirty miles to work each day and it burns so much gas I can't save for a new one."

Counselors generally agreed that putting children on the road with a car was no detour from independence, but they had stronger views about supplying housing starts and other amenities. "Although I don't see it often, I think it's appalling to buy a child a house or condominium," Bischmann said. "Compared to financing an education, it's the difference between giving someone a fish and teaching someone how to fish."

She didn't rule out financial assistance as opposed to a handout.

"I can see advancing the security deposit, the down payment, or the first month's rent. But not buying," she said. "And the advance should be repaid. Whether interest is charged on the loan should be a matter for negotiation."

Berson left a door open to buying a young adult a house or condominium. "I don't completely rule it out," he said, "particularly if it makes the difference between 'go' and 'no go' on the child's part. I can see it as a wedding gift or in the form of a no-interest loan."

Some parents provide children with separate dwellings by buying houses for themselves and renting them to offspring. Parents may see a double advantage: giving the kids a housing start and making a financial gain. But, according to Bischmann, this method is a cop-out. "What do you do if the kid doesn't pay the rent?" she asked.

For example, Florence and Tom looked for a way to relieve the tension building between themselves, their son, and his family while the four adults and three children lived together for six months. "We were overcrowded," Florence said. "They never contributed toward the groceries or paid rent. My daughter-in-law thought I was taking over the children. We wanted to help, stay solvent, and get back on good terms. So we invested in a two-bedroom house down the street and let them move into it."

The older couple had exchanged one problem for another. The younger couple regarded the house as an extension of the parents' home and ignored the responsibility of paying rent. Irked at reminders, they moved out one night leaving Tom and Florence bereft of the family they wanted close by and saddled with an investment they couldn't afford. Both lacked the temperament to be landlords and eventually sold the house at a loss due to rising mortgage rates and tight credit.

Another couple bought a trailer for a son because he was indecisive about leaving home to marry the young woman who was the mother of his child. "When I saw the baby, I fell in love with her," the grandfather said, "and would do anything to keep her in our family."

Still a third couple bought an extra home to be used as a halfway house for their grown children. Each lived there rent-free until financially able to move into an apartment. "It turned out to be a good investment. We made a huge profit selling it after the last child passed through," the mother said.

Each of these homes bought specifically for the children's use was a small tax shelter and the object of capital gains for the parents. But the children may be more sheltered than their parents. The IRS is beginning to look askance at deductions given on homes rented by relatives.

Parents first consideration, however, was to help make the children independent. The financial advantage was secondary. "To some parents the tax shelter might be more important," Berson said. "I have no argument if that's their perception. But fulfilling what I see as a parental responsibility—to help the child make it on his own—is more important."

The impetus to enter the housing market frequently occurs when children come home because they have had bad experiences with roommates. Warren, for instance, roomed with a closet homosexual. "I accepted his sexual preference intellectually but found out that I couldn't handle it emotionally." His father provided a down payment for a forty-five-year-old house and deferred repayment of the loan until the house was sold. "I don't expect to get it back," he said. "But this kid was ready to live alone, and that's the best way I knew of handling it."

Sarah, another home-ing pigeon purportedly ready for her own place, was taken condominium hunting by her parents. "I thought it might be some kind of tax shelter for me," her father said. They found a one-bedroom condominium near Lincoln Park in Chicago with a $385 carrying charge the first year and $495 from then on based on the graduated mortgage plan. They asked Sarah how much of this amount she could afford to pay. Her answer was dead silence.

The carrying charge was more than double the sum Sarah was paying at home. "I decided I already had a good deal," the young woman explained. "My friends who have their own places have very little food in the refrigerator. They can't seem to afford a high living standard and an apartment."

Until faced with paying for her own place, Sarah had complained about paying her folks $150 a month room and board, which is one percent of her annual salary without counting a $2,000 yearly bonus. "You can't beat that," she said.

An estimate of an affordable shelter cost was once 25 percent of an annual income. By 1980, it rose to 33.33 percent.

Roommates, for the most part, are unreliable sources for sharing expenses. They are often in transit to marriage or out-of-state jobs. In such a climate of expanded housing shortages, unemployment, and job mobility, more and more young people will be returning home, a reversal of the trend of the past twenty to twenty-five years. Parents will be called upon more and more to give financial aid.

In some instances, working mothers are sending their kids home to grandma because they can't afford baby-sitters. One way or another home-ing pigeons are turning the family home into a rookery.

Billie has been caring for her grandson since he was born. She minded him Monday through Friday, and his teacher parents kept him on the weekend. As soon as he started school, he slept at home each evening except when he was sick. Ten years later, Billie, at fifty-eight, is involved in car pools, den meetings, and school plays. "I'm gaining weight out of frustration," she said. "But my daughter and son-in-law couldn't own their own home or build up equity on one teacher's salary. Besides, I'm used to having my grandson around and miss him when he's gone."

She refused to talk about the situation from a financial point of view. Initially, her daughter supplied baby food, formula, and diapers. Since he passed this stage, Billie receives "big gifts" on Christmas, Mother's Day, and her birthday. But the idea of being paid back is repugnant to her, and she wished they had set up a different type of arrangement—one that didn't smack of a business deal yet stipulated what each family would be giving or getting.

Several counselors suggested a written contract. "It isn't legal or binding but serves its purposes not only in financial matters but in helping a parent and child live comfortably with one another," said clinical psychologist Dr. Rosalie Kirschner. "There is great value in a written contract if both sides help write it. It forces people to spell out exact expectations."

Too often expectations can be unrealistic or assumed rather than verbalized. How can one person live up to another person's expectations without knowing what they are?

Items to be negotiated in a contract are those a parent or child must have, those a parent or child cannot tolerate, and compromises between wanting and getting. Advocates of a written checklist spelling out living and financial arrangements stressed the importance of reevaluating the contents periodically. "A parent shouldn't wait until she's ready to explode," Dr. Kirschner said. "And neither should a child."

Reviewing rules and expectations will prevent the problems of miscommunication. Parents and children have to continually recheck the rules. Situations may change, and therefore rules may have to be changed, too.

The basis of any contract between parent and child, verbal or written, financial or temporal, should be a sharing of rights and responsibilities. "Children shouldn't live vicariously through the financial means of their parents. Each generation should share what they want to share," said Suelzle.

In an exchange situation, for instance, young people might acquiesce to parents' requests to let them know their whereabouts. "If he calls and says, 'I'm not coming home tonight,' the trade-off answer is, 'Thanks for calling.' No recriminations, no who, what, why, and where. Put the relationship on an adult basis," Suelzle advises.

If conditions for living together are tailored to promote an adult-to-adult relationship, financial matters will be easier to arrange. Reviewed in a calm and reasonable manner, the give and take will be more equitable with neither parents feeling rooked nor the homeing pigeons pushed out.

Generally, parent and young adult need nothing more than a verbal agreement to clarify sharing ordinary expenses. But in a borrowing situation where large sums of money change hands, counselors advise something more tangible like an informal written contract spelling out the terms of repayment and the interest rate if any is charged. A written document is not only useful for tax purposes or settling a parent's estate, but it can also prevent hard feelings on both sides.

In a faltering economy, it is becoming more common for family members to turn to each other for support not only if they're jobless but also to acquire productive assets such as an education, a house, a car, or a business. But in dealing with young adults, the bucks should stop there.

Helping a young person buy a major asset shouldn't be the first in a long series of support ties where the parent becomes the kid's private welfare system. Paying for groceries, utilities, insurance, and so forth should be a young adult's responsibility.

Ideally, money given to an offspring should be a means to end untoward reliance on parents and presented as a means to encourage self-reliance. It should be used neither as a tool of control or a security deposit to be refunded in a parent's old age. As long as parents and children treat each other with respect, the dividend of concern won't be withdrawn. It will be compounded.

As members of society, parents and children are rightfully concerned about having enough money to live a decent life. But money shouldn't be used to create a financial deficit for parents or an emotional deficit for children. As surely as death and taxes, separation from each other is inevitable. Parents shouldn't be left flat broke and children so indulged that they'd fall flat on their faces without support.

Part Eight

Emptying the Nest

Going away: I can generally bear the separation, but I don't like the leave-taking.

Samuel Butler

22

You're OK and They'll Do Fine

Although the sign Out to Launch was tacked to the front door as soon as the home-ing pigeons returned, mom was assailed by self-doubt the day they showed signs of leave-taking. Their imminent departure raised a mother's eternal question, "Did I do my best for them?"

Certainly, their homecoming was a storm, a disturbance in the atmosphere marked by flashes of resentment, claps of anger, or, most deadly to a relationship, withdrawal into silence. They precipitated quarrels, reigned like royalty, and in the wake of their return, mom was snowed under by responsibilities she was ready to relinquish.

But in the eye of the storm—the calm center of the turbulence—she saw the baby she had carried, the child she had reared, and her link to posterity. It had always been a struggle to "do right by him." Child rearing wasn't taught in school. She didn't have to pass a test or qualify for a license to procreate. She brought them up by instinct, hit-or-miss, and guidelines set by experts who went in and out of vogue. She may have recalled hearing, "It isn't easy to be a mother," but she was a young adult then, and what did an older person know?

By comparison grandma's motherhood was easier. *Oedipus complex, regression,* and *enuresis* weren't part of the matriarch's vocabulary. It seemed easier to deal with possessiveness, inappropriate behavior, or a kid who wet the bed. No wonder, as mom prepared a youngster to stand alone, she worried her child might fall. There was a good chance, to her way of thinking, she had perpetrated psychological damage. In other words, she might have reared her progeny wrong.

Self-doubt became a habit. If a child was intense, "Perhaps I pushed too hard." If a child was lax, "Perhaps I should have pushed harder." Although the misgivings were sincere, they smacked of hubris. A mother certainly influenced her children, but it was wanton arrogance to discount the possibility that they were separate persons, each with a mind, a will, and the right to choose a destiny.

Dad was less dubious about his children's outcome. Unlike mom, his self-confidence was fastened to success outside the home. His major contribution was to be ready, willing, and able to finance the youngsters' futures. The rest was up to mom. By giving her the freedom to stay tied down, he took himself off the hook.

Mom's self-doubt subsided the first time the kids left home. She must have done something right if they found something "out there" to strive for. At least they were more motivated than a neighbor's daughter who never considered moving out. The twenty-three-year-old cosmetician told why: "My mother, stepfather, and I have an ideal situation. We clean up our own messes and take care of a different part of the house. My job is cleaning the bathrooms.

"I have my own room and privacy and no curfew. My mom and I have the same social morals. She had men friends stay over before she remarried and lets my boyfriend sleep in my room. The only thing she told me was 'Get on the pill.'

"I pay ten dollars a week for board and know I'm getting off easy. There's no reason to move out. I have all the advantages of an apartment, no bills, plus the warmth of home."

To mom, this meant her neighbor had shackled the young woman to home. Not her. She had done her best to help her children stand alone. But mom's smug facade cracked the day her own grown children returned. They still needed the underpinnings of family. Without them, they wobbled. Having once before laid down the burden of self-doubt, she detached her self-image from her performance as a parent. The uncertainty she had felt about herself she transferred to her children.

Consider the dichotomy of Thelma, a gregarious real estate agent, who spoke in hyperbole about her son Lawrence. He was the sweetest, the dearest, the most gentle kid in the world. But by her standards he was the shyest person she had ever known. Her proof? Because severe burns in infancy had disfigured his neck, he referred to himself as "the ugly duckling."

While he lived in a college dormitory, Thelma didn't witness his social disappointments, and she admitted, "What I didn't see didn't bother me." At home, however, Thelma felt every bump on Lawrence's road to adulthood. One incident of rejection stuck in her mind.

"This fantastic kid of mine, this great wit, bought play tickets and found a girl to go with him. He was really looking forward to the evening. Usually he went out in a crowd of guys and girls.

"Then his date canceled at the last minute with a lame excuse. She had forgotten she had class that night. He called four other girls, and not one of them could go.

"I hurt for him, but I couldn't help him. And it's very hard to watch a child hurt."

The day Lawrence secured a two-bedroom suburban apartment, she became extremely fearful for him. Despite his wit and grace, she described him as a kid who was "twenty-four going on seventeen" and who had "made few decisions" in his life. "I wasn't the perfect mother," Thelma said. "I nagged. I gave advice when I probably shouldn't have. I didn't treat him as an adult until he finished high school. When he came home, I still talked to him as though he was a child. But that was in retribution for something childish he had done."

Until he moved his belongings to the apartment, Thelma was filled with misgivings. "I knew, to have any kind of a life, he had to make it himself. But I was frightened for him. I was afraid he'd get lonely. I was afraid he'd meet rejection by new people."

Or consider the case of Jeanie's mom, who checked on her daughter even after she moved into her own place. Each morning (the time she could catch Jeanie home) she phoned and asked, "What did you do? Where did you go? Who did you go with?" Jeanie's mom felt asking was within her rights. "I was the one who drove Jeanie to an abortion clinic the day her boyfriend said he hated children. I overheard their horrendous fight. He comes from bad stock. I met his mother. She's a loud-mouthed hypochondriac. I'll never give up trying to keep Jeanie away from him," her mother explained.

Or Maxine, a practicing Catholic, who doubted that her sons would choose the right mate if they got out from under her influence. "They're good kids," she said. "I can't wait for them to marry, but I raised them to be choosy about the people they go with. I want them to pick someone of their own color and religion. Not only to keep the faith. Even with your own kind, marriage is no bed of roses."

Or a situation of particular concern to mothers who sheltered their daughters in the suburbs. "I hated the idea that Terry was moving to Chicago," her mother said. "I read somewhere that sixteen rapes a week are reported, which means there are double that many. I taught her the usual. No rides from strangers. Lock the house door. Lock the car door. But I never gave her karate lessons or forbade her to go out at night alone. How can she defend herself against a rapist? I wouldn't know how. I'd faint."

Other mothers were anxious about a son's or daughter's ability to stay out of debt. "I didn't think Ellen had enough brains to budget," her mother said. "She worked fourteen months out of the sixteen months she was home, and all she saved was a couple of hundred dollars. She didn't have a car and never paid room or board. Sure she was old enough to leave. That didn't mean she was going to make it."

Or consider the dilemma of Mark's mother, who knew that the twenty-three-year-old artist couldn't rely on her if he ran into money troubles. She had no money of her own, and her husband was indifferent to their son's insolvency. "He thinks Mark screwed up every opportunity we gave him and deserves the bind he's in. I told him we produced a fine young man and only we could have produced him. His answer was, 'You didn't teach him the outside world is a hard place. Let him learn it on his own.' "

Why does all this anxiety emerge at the milestone a mother awaited? "When a child leaves the second time around, there's a kind of finality about the act," commented clinical psychologist Dr. Rosalie Kirschner. "Unlike the first time he left, chances are greater that he won't come back. He's finally giving up his childhood, and a parent feels she's giving up a child who may not be ready to leave. She has to remember he may have the same doubts for different reasons and should give him the heart to go."

In *Leavetaking* (New York: Simon and Schuster, 1978) by Dr. Mortimer R. Feinberg, Gloria Feinberg, and John J. Tarrant, the authors analyzed this "most predictable of leavetakings. There is ample time to prepare for it. But some parents are not prepared when the moment comes. They try in various ways to keep their children from leaving. They become angry at children when they do leave. In extreme cases a parent will attempt to forestall the parting by reverting toward childhood and undertaking a futile effort to become comtemporary with the children.

"It's called the 'empty nest' syndrome. We might more accurately term it the 'empty heart.' "

Mothers claimed they had their child's interest, not their own, at heart when they expressed doubt in their child's ability to stand alone. Parents had lived through a homecoming fraught with disappointments. They may have magnified a kid's pimple into a case of acne, but they also bore witness to a lack of motivation; a disregard of family values; a prodigal waste of time, money, and energy; and the attitude "You didn't do right by me."

One summer, for example, Lola's son Fred was embittered. He had done all the right things—graduated from a top school and kept in physical shape—yet he couldn't find a high-paying job nor a beautiful girl. Mom became his target. If he had the memory, he would have brought up her injustices against him from the time he was a sperm cell. Instead, he started from the time he was six. Succinctly, she had reared him in a suburban wasteland, sent him to the wrong school, and encouraged the wrong choice of profession. Fred also claimed she had paid his college tuition out of an embarrassment of wealth and bought him a car to show off to the neighbors and two business suits for the pleasure of seeing him dressed up.

Lola recalled, "I felt something inside of me snap with his clincher 'You shouldn't have been a mother. You never showed you cared.' With that accusation he discounted more than half my life. I told him to get out of my sight. To go. I never wanted to see him again."

Her temper cooled in the inordinate time Fred took to leave. As he ran from the bedroom to the kitchen stuffing clothes into grocery bags, she rationalized, "He didn't mean it. It's hot today. The humidity's high. He's tired." Then, realizing the way he was packing, she said, "Don't you have a suitcase?" His answer: "No, you never bought me one."

If parting on friendly terms raises doubts about a child's future, parting estranged makes a parent worry about their future relationship. A kid may leave a mother's house, but rarely leaves her mind.

Consider Ruth, who literally prayed for her daughter's departure. "We were continually at odds about her sloppiness, the way she cluttered the house, and her refusal to pitch in to clean up," Ruth said. "She knew exactly how to get my goat. It was as if she wanted to provoke fights with me. Finally, we came to a dustoff, and she left in a huff. I wondered what would become of her."

Or Bunny, who kept finding strange men in the bathroom each morning and finally told her daughter to get out. "She was doing too many things I wouldn't do," Bunny said. "I knew she'd been sleeping around before she came home, but it was hard seeing it in your own house. I kept asking myself, 'Did I put her on the streets?' "

Or a case described by Bernice, who had reared three soaring eagles and one lame duck. "I felt that Kenneth, who didn't finish college, should get out of the house and be on his own. Life was too easy for him at home. He wasn't going to school and just seemed too comfortable, too content. I pushed him out. He left, taking what he could put into a car, and left behind his dirty clothes and unpaid bills. I hoped he'd come back for clean underwear."

How can a mother reconcile throwing out a child? Eviction wasn't written in her lease on motherhood as it is for her avian counterpart. "But sometimes it's a matter of your own survival," Dr. Kirschner said. "It takes precedence over other considerations especially if you've used up all the alternatives and gotten nowhere. There's no question that it's difficult. No mother wants to push a bird out of the nest thinking it's going to die."

A feathered hen, however, seems more confident of a fledgling's survival outside the nest than does her human counterpart. Mom is less sure of a grown child's competence. How could her fledgling endure without her? Perhaps mom should take up bird watching. Nestlings forced to try their wings have one recourse. They have to learn to fly.

Remember Thelma's ugly duckling? He didn't become a swan. But he learned how to fish in his own pond. As a hedge against loneliness and the high monthly rent on his apartment, he took a roommate. Living among singles, he waded into the complex's social life and found friends on his level—males and females. Nor did he mind spending time alone. "I had looked forward to having privacy," Lawrence said. "The only private place in my mother's house was the bathroom. And I think she timed me. If I took a minute longer than usual, she knocked on the door and asked, 'Are you all right?' "

Or Jeanie's mom, who was an accessory to an abortion. Jeanie saw her hit-and-run lover once or twice after she moved out and speaks to him occasionally. "But the thought of having sex with him is putrid," she said. "Compared to men I've met since I've been out in the world, he's a zero. Too bad I can't get that through mom's head so she'd stop checking up on me."

What happened to Maxine's sons, who were strict Catholics before they left home? Two married "their own kind," and the eldest fulfilled Maxine's foreboding. He married a Jewish girl without a by-your-leave. "I had a hard choice to make," he said. "To live my life or my mother's. I made it."

The marriage caused a rift in the family until her daughter-in-law became pregnant. Now Maxine stays in close touch. "I want to convince them to bring up the child Catholic," she said.

Terry's mother was the second parent to see proof of her forbodings. Terry was assaulted in the laundry room of her city apartment despite its security. She broke the lease, lost her security deposit, and came home to mom. "I thought my mother worried too much," Terry said. "So I was careless about safety measures and almost got raped."

Her mother's reaction? "If Terry had taken a suburban apartment, she wouldn't be having nightmares now! And," she added wistfully, "my husband and I would be alone. It was nice."

The money worriers were happy to be proven wrong. Ellen, who once used money as if it was water, turned off the faucets. She borrowed a van to move and furnished her apartment with relatives' castoffs. She practiced her mother's shopping tricks, watching for sales and shopping for clothes out of season. She learned to like liver because it was cheap. In her year of independence, she even managed to save a down payment for a car. "I ask for a doggie bag when I eat at mom's," she said. "It blows her mind. I used to hate leftovers."

Pecunious Mark shared the house of his employer, a gallery owner, and paid $100 a month rent. "It sounds like a little," said the once carefree nonmaterialist, "but it was really a lot on my meager earnings as a beginner in the art world. Neither I nor my boss cooked. I subsisted on fast food and for a while looked like death warmed over. But I never took a penny from my folks."

Whoever said that adversity is a tough teacher didn't have a mother willing to soften the blows. The kids who left on friendly terms were offered some form of help—as much as the wherewithal to set up an apartment or as little as a standing dinner invitation. Most accepted the help. A few rejected it. "Whether a kid moves a block away or across the country doesn't matter," said Dr. Kirschner. "The separation is in his mind, not physical. In effect he's saying, 'I'm no longer dependent on you,' or 'God forbid, I should ever be dependent on you again.'

"If a mother helps with the move, it should be done to help—not because she wants to tie the child to her. The relationship, up front, has to be adult to adult. She can give him the sheets, recipes, whatever, but not go over and cook meals when he's not home. This isn't separating. A kid senses the difference.

"If the kid doesn't want help, it could be he wants to prove to the parent he's now an adult. It also could be getting even a little bit because the parents formerly controlled him."

Surprisingly, kids who left on bad terms with their parents did as well as kids who parted on friendly terms. Ruth's slovenly daughter wasn't badgered by the Board of Health. She kept the same immaculate home she'd been reared in. "I guess I had to provoke arguments in order to be able to leave," she said. "If not, I'd have found a hundred excuses to stay."

As soon as she was settled, she asked her mother to dinner. "And you know what?" Ruth said. "She made me take my shoes off before coming into the apartment."

What happened to Bunny's bed-hopper? She went back to Yellow Springs, Ohio, where she had gone to Antioch College and moved into the house of an old boyfriend. When he took a job in Oregon, she refused to go along unless he married her. He went alone, and she married a widower who had two grown children and his mother living with him. "He has money, and they take nice vacations and own a summer home," Bunny said. "I went to Ohio once, but the visit wasn't successful. Her husband's my contemporary, and with me there, the difference in their ages was more apparent.

"She used to write often. Now, I get about three letters a year, and she no longer calls on special occasions. I know it's better for her to be there, settled and married, than here. I just wonder if we'd be better friends if I hadn't thrown her out."

Only one mother was without misgivings, or didn't admit any, for having cut the apron strings with a hatchet. Bernice's lame duck showed the family propensity to become a soaring eagle when forced to leave the aerie. He found an apartment, a job, and a wife. Bernice didn't recommend a fall from grace for every home-ing pigeon who was unmotivated to leave. "It worked for him," she said. "I felt I was responding to that particular child's needs by shoving him out. He was past due to grow up."

When grown children leave of their own volition, they have come to the same conclusion. They found something outside the family to compel them to do what was necessary to becoming adults. A career, a person, an ideal gave meaning to the difficulties and sacrifices they had to make to become grown-ups.

Moreover, even if the kids came home bringing the double message "Take care of me but remember I'm independent," the care can become oppressive. "My mother wouldn't let me grow up," a twenty-nine-year-old female wrote on our questionnaire. "She treated me like a helpless child and didn't let me do anything for myself.

"At first, she was terribly upset over my leaving. It took about a year for her to accept the situation. Dad helped me move and came to see me. He and I are closer than ever before."

Her mother admitted she couldn't separate moving from moving apart. She was afraid of losing her daughter. "I needed to feel needed, and my daughter let me do so much for her," she said. "I instigated my husband's help and his visits. If I helped, it would have been admitting she made the break. Finally, I faced the fact she wasn't a baby, but I lost a whole year of her companionship and love." Like Miles Standish who sent John Alden to court Priscilla Mullens because he couldn't face her, the mother put herself out in the cold.

A sense of humor can help a mother who has a hard time separating. "I kept thinking I'll be able to stop writing notes when the kids leave," Ina said. "I'd leave reminders all over the house before I left for work." Another mother imagined his room looking neat as a pin. It took a lot of conjuring, but she did it. Other mothers can look to the past. Marcie recalled the first summer she sent her son to sleep-away camp. "I worried he'd get poison ivy, starve on camp food, or drown. He came home healthy, eight pounds heavier, and holding a lifesaver card. He even compared my meals to camp meals, and guess whose came out the loser?"

Actually, Marcie deserves some credit for his survival. Hadn't she always told him, "Eat whatever's on your plate"? The little bit of jealousy she felt because he managed to survive without her was in keeping with the paradox of motherhood. Mom's job is to make a child self-sufficient, and when she hears "Look, ma, no hands," it's time to take off the training wheels.

Every mother was a teacher, and the family was an educator. At adolescence, a child may have become a recalcitrant pupil fighting the lessons given by mom, dad, siblings, and close relatives. But even in those rebellious days, a child often applied lessons absorbed by osmosis to the extent of making the same mistakes parents did.

A similar process was at work when parents and a grown child lived together except that the relationship started on a collision course. As the child came through the door, mom was going out the door. Despite coming home in need, the child wanted to feel independent. Although willing to accommodate a home-ing pigeon's needs, mom wanted to feel free. Just the way the meeting of hot air and cold air can cause a storm, their conflicting goals caused atmospheric pressure.

But the value of the struggle to get along under one roof was seen at launchtime. Time and money spent to give a young adult a psychosocial moratorium came back in psychic income. Parents may give lip service to the martyrdom of "not looking for thanks," but a grown child's appreciation was as heartwarming as the first time baby said, "Mama." It was feedback for loving care. Or, at the least, baby recognized the hands that fed him.

In fairness, it must be noted that young adults may have shown signs of prizing their parents before they left, but the murmurings of respect went unheard in the din of the turbulence. They were indelibly etched, however, on parents' minds given in the calm of leavetaking. "Our son thanked us for being understanding and apologized for giving us a hard time," Barbara recalled. "And once he got his apartment settled, he had us up for dinner—bought the groceries and cooked the meal. I was very proud of him."

Vivian's son, in the wake of a divorce, took her aside and said, "I'm glad I had family to see me through a hard time." And Kris's daughter gave her the tribute "You're a remarkable woman. You took me and my son in and helped bring him up while I went to work. It wasn't until I wondered how I could have done it alone that I appreciated what you've done."

Most touching was the letter left by Shirley's daughter on moving day.

> Dear Mom and Dad,
>
> We've had our troubles living together. At times, I didn't act like a daughter or a friend. But I know I have always had my family to help me. I want my family.
>
> You taught me enough to let me go on my own. You gave me structure, faith, hope. You gave me religion and taught me there was always someone who cared about me.
>
> I saw how other friends felt without a supportive family.

Independence doesn't mean I'm giving you up. When I first started to learn speech therapy, I needed guidance. Now, I'm far enough along not to have to ask for help. It's the same thing with growing up.

You created me. You told me to become independent. I'm not backfiring by leaving. I'm just showing you the good job you've done.

Love,
Lynn-Anne

Her note was left in lieu of facing her parents. "Even though I looked forward to having a place of my own," she said, "I was afraid I'd start to cry if I left when they were around."

If a mother had a strong say in the way a child left home, it would be to enter marriage. Such a departure allays the doubt in a child's ability to stand alone. It also wrests from mother the major responsibilities toward a child and places them in the hands of someone else. But, as the seventies and eighties have shown, welding two immature adults isn't a final answer. One or the other or both, plus a third, can refill the empty nest. And a parent has little recourse except to take them in.

Why? Because they and theirs are family, a category different from any other category in the world. Remember, it was parents who made them memorize their names, addresses, and telephone numbers in case they got lost. In a way, that's the reason children come home. Somewhere out there they feel lost in the shuffle and remember what parents told them when they were little kids, "This is where you belong."

But parents are not dealing with little kids when young adults come home seeking shelter. A kiss, a hug, and a cup of hot soup won't ease the anguish they come home to weather. Even though the short-range forecast shows gusts of anger and intermittent outbursts, grown children have to learn to batten their own hatches and parents must give them the chance to fight the elements alone.

There are some umbrellas open to parents who have heard or expect to hear the knock on the door. Professionals, parents, and home-ing pigeons offer these suggestions:

Be aware of the circumstances that drive grown children home.

Realize home-ing pigeons sometimes need a respite from adult tasks to become adults.

Admit you enjoyed your respite from child-rearing tasks.

Clear the air. Talk to your children and let them talk even if it means saying or hearing things you'd rather not.

Tell young adults what you expect of a grown-up child, and be prepared to wince when they tell you what they expect of a grown-up parent. Fair is fair.

Accommodate their needs, and, if need be, they'll accommodate yours.

Establish a bill of rights and be willing to pay the costs.

Handle your money matters as if your money matters. Give children a hand—but not your right arm. Even government aid to dependent children has its limits.

Don't let grown children adulterate your marriage.

Don't let them displace your spouse. Remember, grown children's stays are temporary.

If it becomes apparent they're playing parent to the younger children at home, set the record straight. Home is still your domain. But don't referee sibling rivalry between grown children.

Taking in grown children can be an opportunity to strengthen the family bond. Treat them as you would beloved friends.

Tolerate their faults, especially the ones they inherited from you. Any stranger will appreciate their virtues. If all else fails, tell them to turn in their house keys. That's what they may need to hear to overcome their reluctance to leave. Home should be where the heart, not the hearth, is.

Throughout the child-rearing years parents didn't mince words when the time came for children to do for themselves. Parents reveled whenever their children took another step toward independence. Each skill children learned set parents free. *This* time parents should reinforce the lessons of survival and set grown children free for their own sakes. The best is yet to be: a friendship between adults.